CALVIN
and
COMMERCE

The Calvin 500 Series

CALVIN *and* COMMERCE

THE TRANSFORMING POWER OF CALVINISM IN MARKET ECONOMIES

DAVID W. HALL *and* MATTHEW D. BURTON

P U B L I S H I N G
P.O. BOX 817 • PHILLIPSBURG • NEW JERSEY 08865-0817

Printed in the United States of America

Library of Congress Cataloging-in-Publication Data

Hall, David W., 1955–
Calvin and commerce : the transforming power of Calvinism in market economies / David W. Hall, Matthew D. Burton.
p. cm. — (The Calvin 500 series)
Includes bibliographical references and index.
ISBN 978-1-59638-095-0 (pbk.)
1. Calvin, Jean, 1509-1564. 2. Work—Religious aspects—Christianity—History of doctrines—16th century. 3. Economics—Religious aspects—Christianity. 4. Business—Religious aspects—Christianity. I. Burton, Matthew D., 1967– II. Title.
BX9418.H265 2009
261.8'501—dc22

2009033272

Contents

Preface

This short treatise should be viewed as a dialogue, except lacking the artistry of distinct voices from various characters. Although our feeble efforts below will never rank with classic dialogues like Plato's *Republic,* Buchanan's *The Crown Rights of Scotland,* Hume's *Dialogues Concerning Natural Religion,* or Lewis's *Screwtape Letters,* multiple voices may still serve to hold a reader's attention while instructing. While this book, at times, reveals the distinct voices of its authors—one a financial expert, the other a theologian—the voices also unite to form a chorus more often than not.

We believe that the reading public and business professionals can benefit from a nontechnical summary of the Calvinistic business ethic in the format below. Under the heading of the Calvinistic business ethic, this primer seeks to extract the major financial, business, and economic aspects of Calvin's teaching and then to apply them to modern markets and decisions. If the resulting dialogue sounds at times like a sixteenth-century theological voice conversing with a twenty-first-century market voice—and then back and forth—that is, in part, our goal. The voices of other advocates and adversaries are also represented in this discussion. Our hope is that this primer will provide an informed discussion of the spirit of Calvinism and how it has impacted business sectors.

Of course, this is not intended to be an economics textbook per se; nor is it exhaustive of all that Calvin wrote on subjects related to business and finance. Yet, in offering this work as part of the quincentennial celebration of John Calvin's birth, the authors believe that both a tribute and an elaboration of his thought on these subjects are worthwhile. We hope that under one cover a sufficient summary and representation of Calvin's views can be accessed. If, under the same cover, the reader also finds discussions about how Calvin's views unfolded, what consequences followed from them, and how his theories can be helpfully applied in modern societies, that is all the better. We believe that business leaders will appreciate Calvin's insights above most other audiences.

We invite the reader to sit in on our discussions. We are certain that the sum is greater than our individual voices. Doubtless, many others will add more to these discussions in the days ahead, but this update on the value of Calvinism, both for markets and for understanding business and economics, is intended for any who wish to understand our history.

We have no illusion either that this is an exhaustive treatment or that it answers all questions. A considerably humbler approach is adopted in which we wish simply to tell others what we have learned from Calvin and to apply aspects of his theology to the marketplaces that we encounter.

We wish to thank the following individuals for their help: Dr. Scott Cunningham and Dr. Jon Payne for reading the entire manuscript and providing extremely thoughtful suggestions and critiques, as a result of which this book has been immeasurably improved; Andrew Hall, an intern at Narwhal Capital Management, for his research and assistance; Michael Brock for many years of insight and friendship; David Westall for his clarifications and suggestions; Mac Plumart and Sean Dunehew, both of Narwhal Capital Management, for reading and tracking down stray references; and the Invisible Hand Foundation for its educational grant to assist in the final stages of this work.

This book is affectionately dedicated to our wives and children, without whom we freely confess we would be losers and slackers. It is also dedicated with our thanks to our fathers: to Jack Burton for modeling leadership and teaching me more than I can unpack in a lifetime; to Bob Matthews, who not only came to love Calvin's ideals but also is hands down the best businessman either of us hope to know; to Richard Hall, who taught me to live within means, to avoid excessive debt, and to work; and to Pat Fleming, who has given and continues to give us love, encouragement, leadership, and discernment.

Introduction

John Calvin (1509–1564), whose birth was celebrated in quincentennial fashion in 2009,[1] made one of his most enduring contributions as he paved the way for modern, market-based business practices. Standing at the juncture between the Middle Ages and early modernity, Calvin both witnessed and contributed to a sea change in the world's economy, and he did so upon an unapologetically faith-based platform.

One mid-twentieth-century summary of Calvin's teachings shows how advanced his ideas were over medieval teachings: "Few theologians related economic facts with the cosmic drama of redemption as clearly as Calvin did. For this reformer, wealth is only an agent in this drama, never neutral but always an instrument of grace or evil. This refusal to objectivize material goods stands out clearly in contrast to medieval thought."[2] Of course, Calvin did not glamorize poverty and sought to "rehabilitate material life"[3] as a part of human vocation and Christian obedience. Moreover, he was able—as many of his predecessors were not—to see that

1. Several biographies of Calvin are available at http://www.calvin500.org. A short one is also contained in the author's companion volume in the Calvin 500 series, *The Legacy of John Calvin: His Influence on the Modern World* (Phillipsburg, NJ: P&R Publishing, 2008), 43–81.

2. André Biéler, *Calvin's Economic and Social Thought* (1959; repr., Geneva: World Alliance of Reformed Churches, 2005), 302.

3. Ibid.

saving and profit could enhance future productivity, something that was different from selfish hoarding.

André Biéler has summarized Calvin's contributions this way: "By giving the faith the whole sphere of human activity, which Christians have to submit to the Lordship of Christ, Calvin undoubtedly bestowed on work, economic labor and money a place they had not previously had, and one that enabled Calvinists to draw from them all their human and social potentialities."[4]

From a slightly adversarial perspective, Calvin's role in business history has been assessed in these terms: "One who attempts tracing capitalistic development in whatever country of Europe... would always encounter one and the same fact: Calvinist *Diaspora* is at the same time a seedbed of capitalist economy. The Spaniards had expressed this in the following formula of bitter reflection: heretics facilitate trade spirit."[5] While some economists may assert that "the most noteworthy feature of the Protestant Ethic thesis is its absence of empirical support,"[6] others report:

> The Protestant Reformation triggered a mental revolution which made possible the advent of modern capitalism. The worldview propagated by Protestantism broke with traditional psychological orientations through its emphasis on personal diligence, frugality, and thrift, on individual responsibility, and through the moral approval it granted to risk-taking and to financial self-improvement.[7]

4. Ibid., 453.

5. Cited in Sergey N. Bulgakov, "The National Economy and the Religious Personality," *Journal of Markets and Morality* 11, no. 1 (Spring 2008): 167. (Orig. pub. 1909.)

6. Laurence R. Iannaccone, "Introduction to the Economics of Religion," *Journal of Economic Literature* 36 (September 1998): 1474.

7. Jacques Delacroix, "A Critical Empirical Test of the Common Interpretation of the Protestant Ethic and the Spirit of Capitalism" (paper presented at meetings of the International Association of Business and Society, Leuven, Belgium, 1972), 4. Cited in ibid., 1474.

Social theorist Rodney Stark has found liberty to be an essential ingredient for capitalism's growth. Like Max Weber a century earlier, Stark's recent work *The Victory of Reason: How Christianity Led to Freedom, Capitalism, and Western Success* seeks to answer why some European societies cultured capitalism whereas others did not. He suggests that many factors—such as the support of the clergy for capital markets, the belief that technological progress was a blessing and not a curse, education, manufacturing innovation, the rise of science, and expectations for rational management solutions—contributed to what is often spoken of as a Protestant ethic, which appeared simultaneously with the eruption of capitalism.[8] At least on the point of collecting interest, if not on business in general, Calvin's position is "absolutely decisive in the economic history of the West."[9]

While many have misread Calvin or think of him as equating material prosperity with eternal election, this study will show how inaccurate that caricature is. However, Calvin's contributions to the area of asset development are relatively stunning achievements, especially when one considers that his personal wealth was always modest and that he managed no financial business. He was a pastor, a churchman, who taught his people from the Scriptures, so recently rediscovered by the Protestant Reformation.

Before launching into the waters of Calvin's thought, honest readers will have to overcome the residual prejudice that stems from the criticisms and caricatures offered by the likes of Max Weber.[10] Although this prejudice often colors our perception of

8. Rodney Stark, *The Victory of Reason: How Christianity Led to Freedom, Capitalism, and Western Success* (New York: Random House, 2005), xiii, 38, 48, passim.

9. Biéler, *Calvin's Economic and Social Thought*, 400. Biéler also adds that "Calvin was the first theologian who removed the veto the Christian Church had from its origins laid on trade in money" (ibid., 402).

10. Max Weber (1864–1920) was a German sociologist who published numerous wide-ranging sociological studies, including one of the most thorough attempts to analyze the impact of Calvinism in economic sectors, *The Protestant Ethic and*

Calvin's beliefs, it is important that we commit ourselves to understanding what he actually taught.

To that end the modern reader must ask the following questions:

- What did Calvin teach or not teach that led to such massive change in business?
- Were his teachings quickly adopted and if so, by whom and where?
- What were his views of wealth, money, greed, and finance?
- Where can we find specific comments by Calvin on the subjects of wealth and commerce?
- What cultures either have benefited or might potentially benefit from Calvin's economic teachings?

This brief work attempts to answer those questions.

Accordingly, this also is an unabashedly theological work; to make it otherwise would be to distort the original sources. Thus, each chapter below centers on one mega-theological value: creation, the fall, redemption, philanthropy, stewardship, and eschatology. As we seek to understand Calvin's views on these topics, we will also measure the stalwart Protestant Reformer by the Scriptures themselves and analyze which business practices most concur with the biblical truths that fueled so much of Calvin's thinking.

---

the Spirit of Capitalism (1905). Weber wrote that the obtaining of as much capital as possible with as little enjoyment as possible was the *summum bonum* of Calvinistic thinking. This work, which should be congratulated for seeking to explain the seismic shift in business that occurred after Calvin, surveyed various sects, contrasting the effectiveness of capital accrual among various Protestant groups. Weber sought to explicate Calvin's doctrine of calling, providence, thrift, and the use of creation and to explain why Calvinists seemed to blossom into communities of wealth. For a modern Roman Catholic response to Weber's thesis, see Michael Novak, *The Catholic Ethic and the Spirit of Capitalism* (New York: The Free Press, 1993). For an Orthodox response, see Sergey N. Bulgakov's pre-Bolshevik "The National Economy and the Religious Personality," 157–79.

Throughout we will discuss the paradigms presented by various business philosophies. Each school of thought has its own faults and weaknesses that support behavior or decisions that are contrary to certain economic realities. We will compare these various schools of thought to the business concepts contained in John Calvin's works. A secondary goal of this book is to point out the incompatibilities of various systems when compared to a transcultural standard, the Bible.

For the sake of clarity, let us take a brief moment to distinguish this book from other economic commentaries with a biblical approach. After all, there are many books that present various economic systems or business practices and attempt to overlay them with Christianity as a way of illustrating similarities and/or differences. As a result, many of these books reach the conclusion (either explicitly or implicitly) that Christianity and economics are two completely independent arenas of thought. In other words, the two linear schools of thought are examined for possible relationships at various points, but do not necessarily share an equation or even a single value. As a result, the two separate identities are used to evaluate or test each other.[11]

Our approach differs from that which regards Christianity and economics as two separate arenas. In contrast, we find that views about wealth flow from theology or ultimate values. The thesis of our claim is that financial and business concerns are not separate from but rather an extension of theological (in this case Christian) beliefs. Therefore, we will examine financial behavior under the biblical lens crafted by John Calvin. We will observe business and economic behavior in the same manner that one would observe the behavior of an individual on the Sabbath or the behavior of an individual under the influence of alcohol, thus determining which business decisions and actions are consistent

11. See, for example, Paul Heyne, *Are Economists Basically Immoral?* (Indianapolis: Liberty Fund, 2008).

with Scripture and which may be aptly characterized as sinful. For philosophical minds the logical hierarchy would radiate as follows: from religious beliefs flows theology; from theology flows political thought; political thought then flows to institutional thought; institutional thought flows to cultural thought; cultural thought flows to macroeconomic views; macroeconomic views flow to microeconomic views; and microeconomic views lead to personal economic decisions and actions.

Furthermore, this treatise will review business and financial concepts articulated by Calvin in an attempt to have the voice of this great Reformed thinker reintroduced to the marketplace of ideas. Embracing his belief that business practices are derived, in part, from theological thought, we will seek to mine his writings for useful lodestone, while also seeking to avoid naively collecting proof texts to demonstrate that Jesus was a tightfisted capitalist.

Values, Faith, and Truth

Not only do we believe that underlying values or idea-habits affect marginal economic decisions, but also this book accepts the reality that certain seed ideas—or presuppositions—can have immense effects on broader actions or systemic concerns. Accordingly, such presuppositions should be identified as a matter of intellectual honesty and understood for clarity. All economic systems and business cultures have core assumptions that are necessary in order to support the system's peripheral economic variables. The range of such presuppositions is so extensive that every economic system becomes attractive for certain constituent ideas. That partially explains why various economic theories and practices are appealing.

Just as historical epochs and literary time periods often commence as a reaction to an aspect of the past or present, so also economic actions develop as reactions to discontent, shortages, or excesses. Therefore, it would be naive to approach such a study without first recognizing the interconnectivity of the various economic systems and models. The common thread of the systems can often be identified accurately by each system's presuppositions. As John E. Stapleford states, "Economics is obviously about value—the relative worth of this coin to that loaf of bread—but it's also about *values,* and it always has been."[12]

Consider, for example, the underlying presuppositions of Karl Marx's socialist economy. While unpopular among conservatives and evangelicals, merit can be found—even if only at surface levels—in many of its assumptions and accompanying values. In fact, the general idea of equality for all is appealing in and of itself. Furthermore, the reduction of interclass struggle seems desirable at times. Similarly, the underlying presuppositions of the capitalist school of thought endorse the value of hard work through incentives. In both cases the economic theories have definite assumptions.

In reference to these two particular schools of thought, most scholars agree that Calvin's economic viewpoints are much closer to free-market capitalism than to centralized socialism. However, our intent is to avoid caricaturing Calvin as a proto-libertarian. Rather, we would argue simply that economic actions are both value-driven and based on foundational premises. Furthermore, this work asserts that Calvin's theological beliefs transcended religion and overflowed into the realm of business theory and behavior—not only in his explicit writing on these subjects, which influenced the modern development of economic theory, but also through his influence on the private business decisions of governments, families, and individuals.

12. John E. Stapleford, *Bulls, Bears & Golden Calves: Applying Christian Ethics in Economics* (Downers Grove, IL: InterVarsity Press, 2002), 35.

Moreover, awareness of such presuppositions is necessary when examining any economic or philosophic system. With that consideration in mind, it must be recognized that presuppositions and assumptions can greatly affect what is researched and how—ultimately even shaping ideology itself. Therefore, a competent study of any economic policy, business system, or financial theory requires extensive examination into the foundations of its worldview and some assessment of how those pillars affect the system's practices. Business theory is seldom a neutral proposition. Deconstruct any business theory, and its foundational presuppositions about the nature of man, the purpose of profit, poverty, providence, etc. will become clear. John Calvin spoke volumes on these subjects, and to ignore his voice is to overlook or minimize a key participant in the development of modern business theory. Furthermore, Calvin was quick to admit that all human thought flows from sound theology. To properly analyze a system of business or commerce, students need to ask the following: (1) What are the presuppositions that make a given business theory appealing? (2) What theological perspective supports those presuppositions? (3) Do the actual results of business practices stemming from a theory fit with its best presuppositions? Before we advance much further, a few examples will reinforce this initial point.

Karl Marx,[13] of course, was skeptical of capital accrual, criticizing capitalists as those who callously accumulate and profit. While we do not wish to be overly simplistic, it is hard not to think of Marx under the elementary rubric that economist Paul Samuelson provides. According to Samuelson, all economic systems seek to solve three problems: (1) What should be made? (2) Who should make it? (3) How much should be made? Samuelson then notes that historically there are two major solutions to this trilemma: centralized solutions or decentralized solutions.

13. A German philosopher and writer, Karl Marx (1818–1883) is referred to as the father of Marxism, upon which various strands of socialism and Communism have been constructed.

Karl Marx provided one of the strongest arguments for a centralized solution, while simultaneously offering one of the boldest countermovements to capitalism. His centralized economic model held that private property was more of a curse than a blessing. Many economic systems today have taken that to heart and although we wish we could confidently affirm that the world is a better place for it, conclusive proof is lacking. Marx contended that "the pursuit of self-interest would lead to anarchy, crisis, and the dissolution of the private property-based system itself . . . for Marxism the simile is the iron fist of competition, pulverizing the workers and making them worse off than they would be in another feasible system, namely one based on social or public ownership of property."[14]

His ideas were not shrouded in mystery. *The Communist Manifesto* included a ten-point program, advocating the following:

1. The abolition of property in land and the application of all rents of land to public purposes.
2. A heavy progressive, graduated income tax.
3. The abolition of all right of inheritance.
4. The confiscation of the property of all emigrants and rebels.
5. The centralization of credit in the hands of the state by means of a national bank with state capital and an exclusive monopoly.
6. The centralization of the means of communication and transport in the hands of the state.
7. The extension of factories and instruments of production owned by the state; the bringing into cultivation of waste

14. John E. Roemer, *Free to Lose: An Introduction to Marxist Economic Philosophy* (Cambridge, MA: Harvard University Press, 1988), 2–3, cited in Mark Skousen, *The Big Three in Economics: Adam Smith, Karl Marx, and John Maynard Keynes* (Armonk, NY: M. E. Sharpe, 2007), 64–65.

lands, and the improvement of the soil generally in accordance with a common plan.

8. The equal obligation of all to work and the establishment of industrial armies, especially for agriculture.
9. The combination of agriculture and manufacturing industries and the gradual abolition of the distinction between town and country, by means of a more equitable distribution of the population.
10. The free education of all children in public schools; the abolition of existing forms of child factory labor; and the linking of education with industrial production.[15]

Each of these individual concepts—not to mention the sum of them in a greater degree—is far from value-free. In fact, if a society implemented all of these measures, it would look dramatically different from one that protected private property, encouraged free enterprise, lowered taxes, and did not advocate centralization of agriculture, education, transportation, and the like. With his presupposition that private property was actually a *cause* of class warfare and slavery, Marx advocated centralized solutions. Attracting more disciples than many realize, such notions have seeped into many societies. The values that underlie these notions have consequences—primarily, we think, adverse.

Values also have consequences in another modern business sector. The burgeoning school of ecological economics, with its ultimate principle to mitigate any perceived sins against the environment, also brings assumptions, values, and consequences to the economic table. Ecological economics, according to one writer, "is built upon three fundamental tenets: (1) nothing is more valuable than the natural environment, both at the local and global level, *as it exists today*; (2) the dual pressure of population growth and increasing consumption demands are squeezing the

15. Karl Marx and Friedrich Engels, *The Communist Manifesto*, trans. Paul M. Sweezy (New York: Monthly Review Press, 1964), 40.

planet toward resource exhaustion; and (3) the earth is fragile in unknowable ways."[16]

Those premises, if implemented in the business world, would incite massive measures that consistently levy additional surcharges on production. The elevation of the interests of the environment—personified almost to the level of a living being—over the social benefit of producing affordable goods and services often hurts those with the lowest income. Accordingly, one of the implications of such unadorned environmental ethics is that greening can become more important than the poor, if push comes to shove. Ideas have consequences, and the present authors join with John Calvin in seeking to call attention to that from the outset and throughout.

Yet another illustration may be found in the reflexive resorting to government bailouts for many crises. As we are finishing this book, there is much pressure in the United States to have the government bail out several large mortgage lenders. On the surface, the argument is made that failure to do so will spawn even more severe economic problems. Thus, the assumptions supporting such a rescue policy are that: (1) the central government's charter includes a responsibility to bail out private entities, whose collapse might lead to further economic deterioration; (2) all slumps are catastrophic; (3) users who have borrowed too much, or lenders who have overextended themselves, must not bear all the consequences for their behavior; and (4) further taxation to fund such bailouts may be assumed by the government without prior approval. Certainly folks with interest in this issue may claim an unparalleled state of events to justify government intervention, but reasoned analysts might also measure the magnitude of any perceived crisis differently if a longer stretch of history is used

16. Victor V. Claar and Robin J. Klay, *Economics in Christian Perspective: Theory, Policy, and Life Choices* (Downers Grove, IL: InterVarsity Press, 2007), 100. While some ecological economists would dispute these presuppositions, systems that do adopt these presuppositions are founded on unattainable platforms.

as a basis for comparison. This kind of interventionism shares "the mistaken belief that governmental intervention in economic matters can successfully achieve desired results while still falling short of the total controls that characterize a socialist system."[17] Economic programs, thus, are not as value-free as some imagine, and many modern proposals are more reminiscent of Marx's manifesto than of free-market principles that allow economies to self-correct by eliminating those who unjustly overextend themselves, which in turn creates an opportunity for new businesses to operate efficiently.

One's view of man and society also crops up in certain economic applications. Following the pioneering theory of Nobel economist Mohammed Yunus, many wonderful advances have been funded over the past twenty years by privately held microfinance groups. Among these successful programs, one clearly indicates not only that private capital is needed and appreciated in developing countries, but also that loans function best if they are tied to several types of accountability. Customarily microcredit organizations loan small amounts of capital as seed money for a productive business to those who do not have adequate resources. Such loans are then to be repaid after profitability and recycled again in the local economy. Those loans are then issued again to others, and the original recipients have learned much about responsibility and entrepreneurship. To fail to require repayment would be to instill economic expectations that are wrong.

Moreover, after several decades of this lending, another key component of responsibility has been developed as some lenders now treat a group of borrowers as a family or a community. Lenders have found that if eight or ten small-loan recipients in developing contexts are bonded together as a unit, a discernible social pressure develops to decrease default rates. In other words,

17. James P. Gills and Ronald H. Nash, *A Biblical Economics Manifesto: Economics and the Christian Worldview* (Lake Mary, FL: Creation House, 2002), 31.

if one may default on a loan from a distant nameless corporation or with relative impunity, that is one thing. However, if eight or ten recipients are treated as an incorporated unit and the prospect becomes defaulting against one's near neighbor also, more incentive is placed on the recipients. Here the existence of a group or family makes the enterprise stronger. Such philosophical concepts or values make a difference.[18]

Capitalism, thus, presupposes certain conditions that will make it work. Its invisible glue is of a different sort than the imperceptible glue of statism, environmentalism, and other macroeconomic systems. Capitalism will often provide more explanatory power and more ability for productivity. If those are underlying values, then one should not be surprised if capitalism is viewed as more of a success than a failure. While Calvin himself did not write a formal economic treatise, we suggest that the worldview encased in his writings and interpretations has more lasting value than many short-lived economic fads. A five-century test of his ideas against other business or economic systems is worthwhile.

We are cautious to avoid making a stealthy endorsement of all types and expressions of capitalism, for we are aware of its various shortcomings. Accordingly, we remain cautious about abuses of materialism within many capitalistic contexts. Calvin himself knew and condemned such temptations or excesses in his own sixteenth-century environment; so there is nothing new under the sun in issuing a similar caveat. The temptations of individuals to abuse the fringes of any paradigm or specifically for individuals to engage in wanton hedonism within the capitalistic construct is present (and was present for Calvin) on the micro level. Still, socialism does not make a man more righteous or capable of resisting temptation. Nor does communism,

18. I am grateful to Mr. Guillaume Taylor of UBS in Geneva, who also serves on the board of ECLOF, for his information on this advance in accountability that certainly fits with the views of human nature of the earlier Genevan we wish to commemorate by this book.

libertarianism, or environmentalism make a man less of a sinner. Human sinfulness is a macro issue that persists throughout all systems and all of history. If the sinfulness of man is an inescapable axiom, then all economic or business systems can be aptly referred to as iron cages. It is only a question of knowing which cages confine us and which idols are being worshipped. Capitalism abused is rooted in the idols of materialism or greed. Socialism abused is devoted to the idol of self-righteousness or communolatry. Honest assessments of presuppositions must also equitably address idolatry where it occurs.

The Bible, of course, does not teach a complete, formal economic system. However, the Bible addresses and alludes to certain economic realities and policies. It also provides a moral framework within which business may be profitable, humane, and charitable. That is why this work will appeal to many biblical passages—as did Calvin. As we highlight economic themes in the pages below, one challenge will be to see which business system fits best with biblical teaching, a challenge that Calvin accepted and one that led to much commentary from his pen and counsel for his associates. Whether one agrees with the tenets of Calvinism or not, it is undeniable that modern business culture was transformed while Calvin, working at a crucial turning point in history, was fueling intellectual debate with new ideas. A proper understanding of his contributions is needed.

I

Creation

To commence, any proper understanding of Calvin on the subjects of money, wealth, and business must accept that these are all created entities. The Swiss Reformer knew that God was more important than material wealth, and Calvin's advice can serve to steer investors, entrepreneurs, and stewards in any century away from a chilling materialism. Money is—and ever will be—a creation; as such it should not be worshiped, overemphasized, or ignored. Like the creation itself, it has a place and is useful. However, outside of that designed space, Calvin warned that it can become an idol.

Calvin was clear that Mammon was not to be served. In his commentary on Matthew 6:24, he explained the dilemma well: "Where riches hold the dominion of the heart, God has lost his authority. True, it is not impossible that those who are rich shall serve God; but whoever gives himself up as a slave to riches must abandon the service of God; for covetousness makes us slaves of the devil."[1]

In earlier comments on the same chapter from Matthew he perceptively described how the devil plagued many with the worship of wealth:

> Men are grown mad with an insatiable desire of gain. Christ charges them with folly, in collecting wealth with great care, and then giving up their happiness to moths and to rust. . . . What is more unreasonable than to place their property, where it may perish of itself or be carried off by men? Covetous men, indeed, take no thought of this. They lock up their riches in well-secured chests, but cannot prevent them from being exposed to thieves or to moths. They are blind and destitute of sound judgment, who give themselves so much toil and uneasiness in amassing wealth . . . particularly, when God allows us a place in heaven for laying up a treasure and kindly invites us to enjoy riches which never perish.[2]

Instead of entangling oneself in this world's snares, Calvin commended the alternative of making it one's "business to meditate on the heavenly life," a theme that would be repeated throughout his work. He warned that if money becomes the chief good, "covetousness will immediately predominate."[3] Calvin knew—in ways that might be shocking to those who only refract Calvin's thought through the lens of Max Weber[4] or other hostile critics—that "if we were honestly and firmly convinced that our happiness is in heaven, it would be easy for us to trample upon the world, to

1. John Calvin, *Commentary on a Harmony of the Evangelists, Matthew, Mark, and Luke* (Grand Rapids: Baker Book House, 1979), 1:337.

2. Ibid., 1:332.

3. Ibid., 1:334.

4. Weber's disciples have argued that the Calvinist sought to prove his election by his capital accumulation. The elect, thus, were those who succeeded at business and were externally identified as prosperous.

despise earthly blessings, and to rise towards heaven."[5] He was emphatic that, while wealth has a place as a created blessing, it should never be confused with the Creator.

Moreover, his explanation of the law often echoed this teaching. Commenting on the first commandment, Calvin called for exclusivity of allegiance to God. If one is subtly tempted to put the acquisition of wealth above God, he is reminded that God is a jealous God who will not tolerate co-allegiance to God and Mammon. Later, in reference to the eighth commandment, Calvin warned against lusts that could lead to a variety of frauds. Since Calvin so strongly supported the holding of private property (which is implicit in that commandment), he also opposed any wrongful taking or seizing of others' property, insofar as such misappropriations are normally motivated by greed, which is itself a form of idolatry (Col. 3:5).

In similar comments on the tenth commandment, Calvin advised against setting our hearts on others' property or seeking "gain at another's loss and inconvenience."[6] Not only was greed condemned in this commandment, but Calvin perceived that through it God sought to "put a restraint on evil desires before they prevail."[7] He compared coveting and other temptations to "so many fans" that swirled human passions even higher. Perched at an early stage of modern economic development, Calvin certainly knew that wealth has its snares if one's inward dispositions are not rightly ordered.

Calvin's comments on the rich young ruler in Luke 18 reflect the same principle. It is not enough merely to divest oneself of riches ("he who deprives others, along with himself, of the use of money, deserves no praise"); one should also use wealth for the glory of God and love of neighbor. Calvin observed on this

5. Calvin, *Commentary on a Harmony of the Evangelists,* 1:334.

6. John Calvin, *Commentaries on the Four Last Books of Moses* (Grand Rapids: Baker Book House, 1979), 3:187.

7. Ibid., 3:188.

passage that to "renounce riches is not in itself virtuous, but rather an empty ambition." Referring to Crates the Theban from secular history, Calvin further noted that the rich young ruler was called to aid others with his income as an act of love: "And so Christ is recommending him not to simply sell but to be liberal in helping the poor."[8]

Calvin believed that Christ was teaching his listeners not to worship money or riches. He stated that this teaching warns both rich and poor to trust in God—the rich being warned of their danger, the poor being called to be satisfied with their lot—so that each can serve God. While Calvin realized that riches themselves do not preclude obedience to God, he perceived that, in view of mankind's incurable depravity, it is rare for those with abundance to avoid becoming intoxicated by riches.[9]

Calvin realized from his careful reading of Scripture that God does not want humans to worship wealth or any aspect of it. He has given humans the capacity to use wealth, but if the ever-present idol-factory of the human mind confuses Creator with creation, it inevitably leads to disaster. As he reflected upon the opening chapters of the Bible, Calvin noted a categorical distinction between the Creator, who is ever blest, and all other created things. In terms of economic matters or management, the Lord assigned persons a stewardship to care, first, for the garden, and then, by extension, for all of creation. It is noteworthy that this assignment came to man[10] in his native, pre-fall state, and thus has no part of the curse in it. It was, in other words, a positive good for man to care for many aspects of creation—animals, the garden, others, and wealth.

But the design of God is not to have money worshiped or served. No one, as Jesus would later say, can serve two masters.

8. André Biéler, *Calvin's Economic and Social Thought* (1959; repr., Geneva: World Alliance of Reformed Churches, 2005), 283.

9. Calvin, *Commentary on a Harmony of the Evangelists*, 2:401.

10. Using this older fashioned naming for "person," of course, is not intended to be gender specific.

One either serves money as a creator or uses money to serve the Creator; these two purposes are mutually exclusive. Calvin understood the difference, and his disciples put that economic faith into practice in many sectors.

While it is too much to claim that Calvin produced the principles of wealth development *de novo*, it is historically true that such development seemed uncannily to happen wherever Calvinists went for several centuries after the Reformer's death. Secularists might try to explain that phenomenon away, but we prefer to understand why and how Calvinism fostered the kind of business culture that it did.

Calvin and his business disciples knew that the Old Testament (hereafter, OT) was replete with wisdom on the subject of wealth. The book of Proverbs, for example, has much to say on this subject. To begin with, it teaches that the Lord may give wealth but that to acquire wealth by illegal means is sinful. Moreover, some riches will sour. "Ill-gotten treasures," wrote Solomon, are "of no value" (Prov. 10:2); however, "diligent hands bring wealth" (Prov. 10:4). The earnings of the righteous aid their life (Prov. 10:16), and "the blessing of the Lord brings wealth, and he adds no trouble to it" (Prov. 10:22). One may even be ruthless and gain wealth; however, ruthlessness is contrasted with virtues like kindheartedness (Prov. 11:16). Hoarding is also condemned (Prov. 11:26), and giving to others can lead to greater gain, refreshment, and blessings (Prov. 11:24–26).

Puritan descendants of Calvin noted the advice on work and business planning contained in Proverbs 12:11, which advocates the working of one's land instead of chasing fantasies or speculation. Proverbs 13 also warns against pretentiousness (v. 7) and issues a caveat about being owned by one's own riches or possessions (v. 8). Moreover, some income can come with a hangman's noose around it (Prov. 15:6). Calvinistic business practices would assimilate these teachings into a distinct corporate culture.

Readers of this OT wisdom also learn that dishonest gain has a way of dwindling away, while a gradual accumulation of wealth normally makes those assets grow more (Prov. 13:11). Prosperity can be a reward to those who serve God well (Prov. 13:21), and even a poor man, if he works the ground that is given him, may "produce abundant food" (Prov. 13:23). It is a sign of a man's goodness to "leave an inheritance for his grandchildren" (Prov. 13:22), but according to the contrast in the second half of that verse "a sinner's wealth is stored up for the righteous." The distribution of providence is one thing and it continues. Houses and wealth are inherited from the Lord (Prov. 19:14). Calvin and his disciples took these biblical truisms and applied them to the evolving business and economic practices of their day.

Again, one can identify the profit assumption of the Calvinistic business ethic in Proverbs 14:23–24, which promises that all useful work brings some kind of profit. In contrast, mere discussion or even elaborate planning devoid of action and work "leads to poverty" (Prov. 14:23). Wealth may even provide a protective buffer or a cause for societal admiration, while the folly of laziness and nonproductive behavior "yields folly" (Prov. 14:23).

Calvin also understood that oppressing the poor to increase one's own wealth is morally wrong (Prov. 22:16) and that one should not exhaust oneself in the pursuit of riches (Prov. 23:4–5). In fact, the allure of riches should be avoided. In other words, one should take care of wealth but not fall in love with it. For, as we read in Proverbs 27:24, "riches do not endure forever, and a crown is not secure for all generations." Also, one should avoid wearing oneself out to obtain status or fame that the Lord has not designed to give. Embracing these principles has led many nations and families to lasting wealth. God's Word, Calvin knew, has much to say to us on this topic. In summary, the application of OT wisdom supplies the following business premises:

1. Ill-gotten treasures are of no value.
2. Wealth per se is not condemned.

3. Wealth has a limited long-range advantage, but it should not be idolized.
4. Wealth does not endure.
5. Godly obedience or righteousness is more valuable than the acquisition of riches.

When one compares Jesus' teaching in Matthew 6 (which warns us not to store up corruptible treasures) both with the OT wisdom on wealth and with even a few of Calvin's comments, a harmonious chorus of voices can be heard.

Furthermore, all these voices affirm that wealth is given by God and can be used very productively to enhance his created order. Again, the distinction between the right and the wrong use of wealth is what makes the difference for Calvin, who surely could recount better than most of the numerous wealthy people recorded in the Bible who never received a rebuke from God for owning and accumulating assets. Among them are:

- Abraham, whose possessions are noted in Genesis 12:5 and who, according to Genesis 14:14, had over three hundred trained men born in his household. He must have had quite a business to have 318 trained soldiers (and most likely their families as well). This was a wealthy man.
- Joseph, who later rose to a position of great importance and wealth in ancient Egypt. He served God through economic acquisition and management.
- Solomon, who, of course, was the wealthiest person in the world of his time.
- Nicodemus and Joseph of Arimathea, both of whom became followers of Christ.
- Mary and Martha, who, according to the book of Acts, used their large home for church meetings.
- Barnabas, an unsung hero of the New Testament, who donated family lands to the cause of the gospel.

Like the OT, the New Testament (hereafter, NT) warns against love for money as a many-pronged root of evil (1 Tim. 6:10). Even so, as one surveys either the Scriptures or the works of Calvin, one can clearly see that wealth is presented as a providential creation from God. It may also become (either immediately or gradually) a means by which God tests the allegiance of a person's heart. Materialism, in contrast to Calvinism, fails to recognize the proper relationship between wealth, a creation, and God, the Creator.

God may bless a person with wealth or he may choose not to do so. If an individual is so blessed, then along with the blessing comes the call to share generously and to work for the glory of God rather than selfish ambition. Therefore, wealth summons a spirit of servitude to the Lord and stewardship of his gifts in order to glorify God. Furthermore, misuses of wealth can reflect insufficient theological or moral values. If one exclusively strives to save and never to enjoy, then he is not embracing the call to glorify God through spending. Similarly, individuals who are consumed by debt and continually live beyond their means demonstrate a lack of stewardship and responsibility. Both of these patterns represent an imbalance in one's attitude toward affluence. Calvin's view of wealth, giving, and affluence determines how persons live in economic settings. This is a matter not of abstract theology but of pastoral theology with macroeconomic content.

While wealth is to be shown proper respect and treated according to God's calling, it is never to be worshiped or treated as divine. Instead it is designed to be used as a tool for the glory of God and the betterment of man. Thus, money, wealth, or finance is always a tool—always a creation, never the Creator—and it is useful for the ends that God designed. The wise steward will seek to keep wealth in its place—never becoming mesmerized by its allure but always using it to serve God, his creation, our families, and society. Wealth is not eternal; neither is it an automatic identifier of the blessing of God. The Lord gives and he takes away. Wealth can be destroyed just as easily as it is created.

In his commentary on the book of Genesis, Calvin asserted that prior to creation there was only emptiness and formlessness. Accordingly, "the world is not eternal" but was created by God.[11] God took the shapeless chaos, the formless void, and imposed himself on it to create beauty and habitation. Thus, in his first revealed work, God is seen as an artisan—"the wonderful Artificer" (85, 105), who takes that which is not inherently useful and harnesses it for great usefulness. God takes the unstable mass and turns it into a biosphere where man, his chief creation, may thrive. The purpose of the creation is to serve and sustain man, a point with great ramifications both for economics and for ecology. Furthermore, Calvin noted that God provided for his creation without needing or depending on preexisting sources (for example, he did not need the sun to create light). The Creator, for Calvin, was originally and always above his own creation. And at the conclusion of each period of creation, God stamped his approval upon each day with the phrase, "And God saw that it was good." The creation, both as a whole and in each of its constituent parts, is good. Calvin put it this way, commenting on the final verse of Genesis 1: "On each of the days, simple approbation was given. But now, after the workmanship of the world was complete in all its parts, and had received . . . the last, finishing touch, he pronounces it perfectly good; that we may know that there is in the symmetry of God's works the highest perfection, to which nothing can be added" (100).

Calvin further observed that God added "a germinating principle" (82) to the now-formed creation. Because of his own created law of nature, God also created trees and herbs before the sun and moon. It was, the Genevan Reformer noted, for the purpose that "we might learn to refer all things to him [that] he did not then make use of the sun or moon" (82). Calvin realized that man

11. John Calvin, *Commentaries on the First Book of Moses Called Genesis* (1554; repr., Grand Rapids: Baker Book House, 1979), 70. In the section that follows, page numbers in parentheses refer to this edition of the commentary.

could easily ascribe to creation a self-generating power, and he wished to contradict that error early and often. He argued that it was necessary, "because we are wont to regard as part of their nature properties which they derive elsewhere" (82), that God should in his very creation clearly demonstrate to mankind that his initial creations were dependent directly on him and not on other creations. This proves, he thought, "that the First Cause is self-sufficient and that intermediate and secondary causes have only what they borrow from this First Cause" (82). Early in his commentary on Genesis he warned against thinking that God's creation was so poor or imperfect as to need to be "assisted by second causes" (82). God acts, to be sure, through his creatures but not "as if he needed external help, but because it [is] his pleasure" (82).

Along the way, Calvin also taught that various parts of creation were "endued with the power of propagation" (83), a feature that will later become important as we consider the multiplication of wealth. If wealth is a creation, then there is no reason that it may not be fruitful and multiply. Yet, just as "the sun is still a servant, and the moon a handmaid" (87), so again wealth as a creation is designed to serve or assist, never to be worshiped as or confused with the Creator.

Man as Created and Creator

One of the unique characteristics of man is that he is singled out in Genesis 1 as having been created in the image of God (*imago dei*). While some theologians have devoted volumes to explaining this concept, one thing is indisputable: in the context of Genesis 1, being in the image of God surely means that man is capable of creating and creativity. Modeled after God, man can take formlessness and convert it into form; he can take that which is non-useable and transform it, with industry, into something that has great usefulness. This harnessing of the creation for the use of humans is a prime part of the *imago dei*. Not only does this capacity give man dignity in terms of artistry, but it also allows him to use the creation to generate wealth and to promote his own comfort.

Entrepreneurial activity is an expression of creativity. God evidently did not intend for man to accept the creation and leave it merely in its native state—even though it was filled with beauty and perfection. He intended for man to enhance what was originally given. Adam Smith, a later economist raised in the very Calvinistic Scotland of his day,[12] put it this way: "The property which every man has is in his own labour, as it is the original foundation of all other property, so it is the most sacred and inviolable."[13]

Yet in his inventiveness, man was not intended to create false gods or to use his creativity to distort the image of God. Commenting on Isaiah 46:5, Calvin noted that God is "robbed of his glory, when he is compared to dumb and senseless things." And in reference to Jeremiah 10:6, Calvin described idolatry as "madness," "sottish," "beyond measure foolish," and "shameful," noting that "the very richest worshipped a wooden god, while despising the artificer." Calvin even spoke of idolatry as leading to "profitless deceptions" when he explained Jeremiah 2:8.

Acknowledging the premise that man is made in the image of God, most major economic systems would not debate the assertion that man is a creator or prone to create. However, the method of creation, the ownership of creation, and the ensuing benefits of creation are all issues of debate and disagreement. From these differences in various economic theories, applications arise within

12. Although Mark Skousen, among others, notes that Smith was part of the Scottish Enlightenment associated with the skeptic David Hume, he also states: "Adam Smith was greatly influenced by Calvinist doctrines favoring thrift and hard work while condemning excessive luxury, usury, and 'unproductive' service labor." Skousen, *The Big Three in Economics*, 39.

13. Cited in John E. Stapleford, *Bulls, Bears & Golden Calves: Applying Christian Ethics in Economics* (Downers Grove, IL: InterVarsity Press, 2002), 57.

nations, legal systems, markets, and cultural practices that are contrary to Calvin's view of creation. The ideal is an economic, legal, and cultural environment that encourages creation, values creation, protects the benefits and rewards of creation, and allows the marketplace to judge the appropriateness and validity of the creation methodology. Clearly, though, not all economic systems favor this ideal.

Grounded in the various socialistic theories, for example, is the belief that private property is not to remain private. Indeed, one of the primary tenets of Marx's *Das Kapital* is the abolition of private property. Property, Marx argued, should become an asset of the state. Initially referring to physical private property—land—this concept has migrated over time to include intellectual property and other created products. In the mid- to late-nineteenth century the agrarian economy was the prime focus, with those owning land dominating others. As a modern illustration, however, certain legal systems throughout the world do not fully protect the rights of patents and intellectual property. The creator of such runs the risk of losing some or even a majority of the benefits of his creation should it be fancied by another firm or industry in another country. New drugs that may have cost millions of dollars to research, devise, compound, test, and produce can be reverse-engineered at a fraction of the total cost of development by firms in countries without restrictions and then reproduced without consequences from that national legal system.

At issue also is the process of creation and its sometimes destructive nature. Throughout history, inventions and new processes have delivered short-term shocks to the labor and capital markets. In the Genesis creation and throughout the Bible, God's actions are often catastrophic, shifting paradigms and radically changing hierarchies, displacing individuals and causing disruption. Speaking in terms of business, the creation story is an account of a manager creating new methodologies of production, activating a new workforce, and introducing competitive markets into what was previously a benign and stable environment. This creative destruction[14] is also evident in the episodes of Noah, Moses, the Exodus, and so on—right up to the coming of Christ upon the earth. Creation in the business cycle is a case of the *imago dei*. Man, following his Creator, also creates; and when he creates, the creative process often has exponential effects.

Creative action many times can and will bring with it costs. The flood, of course, killed nearly all of mankind; the exodus displaced an entire people for forty years, forcing a generation of brick makers and construction workers into new occupations; and the life and death of Christ caused thousands to change jobs (e.g., Paul, Peter, and Andrew), to alter their living standards (e.g., Zaccheus), to relocate, and even to perish.

In more recent times, the advent of petroleum refining displaced an entire industry of whaling vessels, the creation of farm machinery transformed economies, and gunpowder toppled regimes. However, there are economic practices today that refuse the costs of creation in order to avoid pain. For example, some teachers' unions are fighting to keep the creative destruction of charter schools out of their industry, and the Realtors of America are fighting to keep online discount agencies out of theirs. The avoidance of the costs of creation is not just limited to tangible products or services; it extends also to the free flow of information, ideas, and commentary. In an article entitled "Olympics preview: Beijing's Internet censorship, surveillance" (June 25, 2008), Graham Webster, author of the blog Sinobyte, observed: "In the lead up to the Olympics, many online limitations have been relaxed. Access to BBC News was restored.... English Wikipedia is available, but Chinese Wikipedia is still blocked. After pressure from the International Olympic Committee, the Beijing committee has promised fewer restrictions." As the leaders of China may

14. The Austrian economist Joseph Schumpeter (1883–1950) made famous the term "creative destruction."

realize, ideas coupled with information and mass access can have costs—costs that they have been reluctant to pay.

In order to protect the business creator, an adequate legal system must be in place. A court system that recognizes the rights of patents, intellectual property, and property rights is the first line of defense. Concerning the costs of creation, who or what is to decide if they are worth the benefits? In a state-controlled, socialistic system, it would be the government that makes the final decision. However, these decisions are rarely paragons of objective logic. Rather than engage in rational cost/benefit analysis, it is the tendency of governments to be influenced by other forces, such as public polling, financial influences, and often pseudo-science.

Even within a business climate that legally protects the rights of creators and encourages creation, social and cultural mores may, in effect, undermine this tenet. One does not have to travel far down the information superhighway to see various arguments for free software. Travel further into other corners and "free" versions of Adobe Acrobat, Vista, Microsoft Office, and dozens of other programs are available for download. With names like the "Free Software Society" and "Software for All," a growing number of groups reveal a disdain for the product creator by demanding free software and open-source coding.[15]

The joy of creation, of conceptualizing, planning, forming, and launching something—the pride of authorship—is an undeniable high point in human existence. However, this joy is threatened and neglected throughout the world today by enemies ranging from adversarial economic policies to practical applications of sovereign judicial systems to informal cultural norms. The enlightened Calvinist needs to see the necessity of protecting the business creator and the benefits of his creation

15. Of course, these free products are also designed, in some cases, to create a need for a product, which will cost later. Moreover, some companies give "free" software, only to offset that "loss" by charging more for other products.

from the assaults of collectivism and socialism, whether those assaults arise from state-controlled economies, ineffective legal systems, or cultural attitudes.

This notion of creation, separate from but bearing the imprint of the Creator, is a signature of Calvinism. It also has many applications for business.

Creation a Time of Abundance and Wealth beyond Basic Needs

There were no material lacks in Eden and the seeds of future productivity inhered in the creation. Calvin repeatedly spoke of creation as possessing a quality of abundance. Commenting on Genesis 1:26, he noted that the purpose of all creation was that "none of the conveniences and necessaries of life"[16] would be lacking. "In the very order of the creation," Calvin wrote, "the paternal solicitude of God for man is conspicuous because he furnished the world with all things needful and even with an immense profusion of wealth before he formed man" (96). "Thus," Calvin opined, "man was rich before he was born." A little later in his commentary on Genesis 1 he would speak of the creation as being "abundantly sufficient for [man's] highest gratification" (100), even though both the fall and the Noahic deluge brought and accelerated deteriorating dynamics into the cosmos. God's original creation is still assessed as "abundant," "beneficent" (100), and of "the highest perfection," showing that God is an excellent Creator. Calvin construed Moses as describing a well-furnished house, "well supplied and filled" with nothing "wanting to its suitable abundance" (103). The language of creation conveys that God, "the Architect," created a beautiful house, which in its original state showed perfection to be "the fabric of the world." Thus, any

16. Calvin, *Commentaries on the First Book of Moses*, 96. In the sections that follow, page numbers in parentheses refer to this commentary.

deterioration or decay we may now observe is but a "corruption" of the "proper furniture" (104).

When Calvin expounded the quality of the Garden of Eden, he stated that no part of creation was barren, but that all was "exceedingly rich and fertile" (116). Observing the liberal blessing that God placed on his completed creation, Calvin noted further that not only was there an adequate provision of food but also that God gave it a palate-satisfying "sweetness . . . and beauty to feast the eyes" (116). Furthermore, as a consequence of his creation in the image of God, it was given to Adam not only to live in the dimension of the body but also to take pleasure in the blessing of his soul, with all its capacities and enjoyments. Thus, God intended for his creation to be enjoyed, and God cannot be accused of under-creating or providing.

The Creation was a time of abundance. God was not content with creating a desolate wasteland or a barren planet. In Genesis 2:9 we read that God "made all kinds of trees grow out of the ground—trees that were pleasing to the eye and good for food." There was lavish variety and substance, and included in this creation was all that was needed for living and the advancement of society, including the raw materials for clothing, shelter, towns, and buildings (the Tower of Babel comes to mind). Speaking of the Creation, John Schneider says, "The whole view is one of almost embarrassingly extravagant excess."[17]

Implied in this abundance, moving into current business, wealth is often created by excess profits. In the socialist paradigm, excess profits are "theft." Or as the French novelist Honore de Balzac put it: "Behind every great fortune there is a crime." The socialist and moralist of the day would have us live in a state of equal incomes, where our needs are met and any excess profit is given to the state for the benefit of the state. It should be noted

17. John R. Schneider, *The Good of Affluence: Seeking God in a Culture of Wealth* (Grand Rapids: Eerdmans, 2002), 59.

that God intended his creation to be personally experienced and managed by Adam and Eve. Consider, for example, the words of Genesis 2:16: "And the Lord God commanded the man, 'You are free to eat from any tree in the garden.'" At the heart of the conflict between socialists and capitalists is the question of how wealth should be viewed and treated. The Calvinist businessman should be comfortable with and unashamed of abundance and the personal experience of wealth.

A criticism from those who espouse the minimalist view of simplicity and the evils of personal excess is that God did not intend this abundance to go exclusively to the benefit of one man at the expense of another. Yet throughout Scripture God continues to shower abundance upon those whom he chooses to bless. The Creation, and specifically the Garden of Eden, is similar to the nursery that new parents create for a newborn child. It is a snapshot of the level of abundance that is intended for the child to grow up in and enjoy.

As another example, take a large corporation like General Electric (GE). Within the organization there exists a broad range of employees, from management to factory workers to truck drivers and so on. As GE profits from its endeavors all employees benefit to some extent, even if at a minimum level by keeping their jobs and having a source of support. However, if—as is often the case for GE—revenues are larger than the costs of employment and production, then the corporation must make a fundamental decision: what should it do with "excess" profits? In the simplest of terms they can choose either (1) to pay a dividend to their shareholders or (2) to reinvest in the company by buying new equipment, increasing compensation, introducing new product lines, escalating research and development, and the like.

Each decision will positively impact one group at the potential expense of another. What is the correct choice? If you are an employee you may lean toward the second option, whereas a shareholder may prefer the first option. In corporate finance theory, the decision should hinge upon the expected return of the reinvested profits and whether or not they exceed the current "hurdle" rate of capital within the organization.[18] Furthermore, under the capital structure irrelevance principle[19] the value of the firm is unaffected by the dividend decision. The choice is net neutral.

Now take this example and substitute GE with all of creation—let the earth, man, animals, and the entire created order represent a single large corporation. Everyone within that corporation participates in the production process and prospers at some level. The "corporation," creation, extends a common grace in which all "employees" can benefit. Periodically, though, the creation pays dividends to its shareholders. Admittedly, this analogy cannot be taken too far, because none of us can buy "shares" in creation. But the main point is that the "dividends" or "excess profits" that are "paid out" to those whom God elects (under his specific grace)[20]

18. For example, assume further that GE has an internal return goal of 11%, that all of the company's divisions are returning at least 12%, and that the risk-free return (as symbolized by the 10-year Treasury note) is 4.5%. If GE identifies an opportunity that has the potential for returns greater than 11%, the company should reinvest excess profits into that opportunity. If the potential is between 4.5% and 11%, then the decision is not as clear and without other potential motives or synergies, the profits should be paid out as dividends. If the expected return is less than 4.5%, then the firm should absolutely pay out the profits in the form of dividends.

19. The Modigliani-Miller theorem holds that in an efficient market without tax considerations the decision to pay or withhold a dividend is irrelevant to the present market value of the stock. The underlying assumption to this aspect of the theory is that 1) the firm is paying out "inefficient" capital, that is, capital that cannot deployed above the firm's hurdle rate and 2) that shareholders/dividend receivers will take their payments and seek the highest return by reinvesting the proceeds into other ventures that are deploying capital above the hurdle rate. See Merton Miller and Franco Modigliani, "Dividend Policy, Growth, and the Valuation of Shares," *Journal of Business* 34, no. 4 (1961): 411–33.

20. This does not imply that only Christians will receive wealth on this earth. Contrary to the grave error of the "health-and-wealth" gospel, God elects some to receive wealth and some not, but the election is his to make. Evil men can prosper on this earth, and righteous men can live in poverty.

do not devalue his creation. Nor do they represent an injustice. The creation is full of abundance that not only supports all under God's providence, but also showers additional wealth and blessing upon those whom he chooses, who are then called to reinvest. Companies that do not strive for abundance, or that do not factor that goal into their business model, fail to live up to the spirit of Calvin's business ethic.

Man Charged with Dominion over God's Creation

Calvin stated that it was part of the dignity that God decreed for man that he should have authority over all created things. As he put it in his commentary on Genesis, God appointed man as "lord of the world" (96), thus exhibiting the image of God. And this authority was given not only to the singular Adam but also to all his descendants. Man was created initially with dominion, but the command also to "subdue it" (Gen. 1:28) further emphasizes that God put this possession "of his right" (98), signifying that man had a calling to develop, tame, organize, harness, subdue, rearrange, and make useful all subservient aspects of the creation. In fact, Calvin taught that "it was [man's] business to nurture the things provided" (99). We may thus affirmatively say that Calvin taught that man was to improve and enhance the creation as part of his dominion.

Creation gives a pattern of hierarchies, too. All is not on the same plane. Some species are higher, more capable, than others. Others serve the higher orders. Dominion is God's assignment to take the creation as we find it and improve it. He does not invite Adam to leave the creation as it is or to let it deteriorate. No, God calls men to exert themselves to nurture and bring improvement. This fundamental notion of change for the better is an economic truism that accords with some business systems and practices more than others. For example, the notion of inheritance and improving one's estate for the benefit of future generations seems to be logically compatible with the dominion mandate.

God does not wish his creation merely to maintain stasis. Instead, he designed creation for growth, productivity, and maturation. Thus, in reference even to the opening chapters of Genesis one may ask, what business system fits with both the creation and the nurture mandates? Growth, development, productivity, and orderliness are features that God has woven into the fabric of human nature.

Dominion Infers a Work Ethic and Accountability to God

How does one take dominion over an impersonal asset? One does this first by recognizing its status as created; then by imposing man's good on it; and finally by yielding fruit that contains the seeds of future productivity.

The economics of Genesis 1–3 calls for wealth neither to dissipate nor to stay the same. Man is to work the garden; and with hard work, he will seek to tame parts of the creation to serve God and neighbor.

Calvin summarized these notions well in his comments on Genesis 2:9: "No corner of the earth was then barren, nor was there even any which was not exceedingly rich and fertile; but that benediction of God, which was elsewhere comparatively moderate, had in this place poured itself wonderfully forth" (116). He noted further that "not only was there an abundant supply of food, but with it was added sweetness for the gratification of the palate, and beauty to feast the eyes. Therefore, from such benignant indulgence, it is more than sufficiently evident how inexplicable had been the cupidity of man" (116). The state of creation was such that Adam not only had a mere physical existence but also excelled in the endowments of the soul (118).

With this abundance comes responsibility. In the creation man is charged with dominion. But what does dominion imply? It is a balance of tensions: on the one hand, it is a call to enjoy, rule, grow, and shape; on the other hand, it is a call to protect, defend, perpetuate, and work. Furthermore, dominion implies a relationship of order and status. There is a hierarchy in dominion.

An additional facet of dominion is that work is required and, correspondingly, that benefits are accrued. A foundational premise of any economic system is that work and effort are needed; therefore, Marx, Smith, Ricardo, Keynes, and others would have no disagreement with a mandate to work. However, some think that the work mandate has often been abused by the free-market system. Individuals who have reached a stage of comfort and sustainability from their investments and income may choose to remove themselves from work. The Reformed capitalist needs to be wary of this trap. The call to dominion was not a call to consumption and leisure.

The dominion mandate ultimately leads to a stewardship mandate. John Schneider in *The Good of Affluence* writes: "Eden set the man and woman free from servitude to want, it unleashed them to dream, to use their creativity, to work in productive and rewarding ways, to reap the fruit of their labor, and to take human pleasure in the whole of life, in the image of God, and in his good pleasure. Capitalism has brought us closer to recreating that condition than has any other economic system in the history of the world."[21] Without belaboring the point and definition of stewardship, the socialist would argue that stewardship is fine but that it is the job of the government or the planning board to make the allocation and input decisions. In response to this criticism, the track record of centrally planned governments speaks volumes. Consider, for example, the famines of North Korea, Cuba's industry and technology (dormant since the 1960s), and the fall of the Soviet Union. Ludwig Von Mises, an Austrian economist, identified the fatal flaw in state-run dominion as the

21. Schneider, *The Good of Affluence*, 59.

lack of personal, individual information about the true nature of costs and benefits.[22] Mises argued that in a socialist system the government owns everything—the capital, the land, the machinery, the labor, and the distribution process. If the government owns everything, then the "cost" to the government is a non-issue. Furthermore, in highly regulated economic systems, the markets are even controlled by the government, so that no one can get a true measure of the price of an item, because transactions are forced and/or manipulated.

The interrelationship of work and wealth is exhibited as early as the opening chapters of the Bible. Calvin sought to reconcile them, giving each a full place. Other systems all too often seek to subordinate work or wealth, often rejecting both hierarchies and hard work. However, Calvin saw both as good aspects of God's creation and providence.

Creation and the Balance between Work (Vocation) and Leisure (Sabbath)

Vocation

Calvin believed that the Bible taught much on the nobility of work. Work is a high calling and a God-oriented activity in its best sense. Excellence is sought and valued. There is a dignity to man's work and calling that is unique to him and fits with his strengths, talents, and bents. In a sermon on Matthew 3, Calvin noted that a calling was only good if from God, and he defined "vocation" as the calling that "carries with it that God is beckoning with his finger and saying to each and every individual, 'I want you to live this way or that.' This is what we call 'stations in life.'"[23] When preaching on Ephesians 4:28, Calvin spoke of "occupations," "crafts," and "a trade," advising that each of these should be embraced if "good

22. Skousen, *The Big Three in Economics*, 208.
23. Cited in Biéler, *Calvin's Economic and Social Thought*, 357.

and profitable for the common good." To Calvin, who revealed an outlook that can only be characterized as very progressive for a theologian of his day, calling, profitability, and philanthropy all worked hand in glove.

Commenting on Genesis 2:15–16, Calvin observed that human beings "were created to employ themselves in some work, and not to lie down in inactivity and idleness."[24] This calling, even labor itself, was, he believed, "truly pleasant, full of delight, and entirely exempt from all trouble and weariness." God both ordained productive work ("the culture of the ground") and condemned "all indolent repose." Wrote Calvin: "Wherefore, nothing is more contrary to the order of nature, than to consume life in eating, drinking, and sleeping, while in the meantime we propose nothing to ourselves to do" (125). So important is work for human beings that to remove work "would throw human life into ruin."[25]

Calvin understood that as humans breathe, they are also to be producing, working, devising, repairing, and creating. The Garden of Eden was not a leisure park; it was an incubator of human products. To Adam was given "custody of the garden," and this was, in part, to illustrate how God planned for work and workers to care for and use the creation. Or as the Genevan Reformer expressed it in his commentary on Genesis:

> Let him who possesses a field so partake of its yearly fruits that he may not suffer the ground to be injured by his negligence, but let him endeavor to hand it down to posterity as he received it, or even better cultivated. Let him so feed on its fruits that neither he dissipates it by luxury, nor permits [it] to be marred or ruined by neglect. Moreover, that this *economy* [emphasis added] and this diligence ... may flourish among us, let everyone regard himself as the steward of God

24. Calvin, *Commentaries on the First Book of Moses*, 125. In the section that follows, page numbers in parentheses refer to this commentary.

25. The quotation is from Calvin's sermon on Deuteronomy 24, cited in Biéler, *Calvin's Economic and Social Thought*, 362.

> in all things which he possesses. Then he will neither conduct himself dissolutely, nor corrupt by abuse those things which God requires to be preserved. (125)

Sounding a similar note, John Stapleford has written:

> For . . . the right to work to be exercised, the economy must be generating jobs (ideally with multiple possibilities of employment and reward, minimally with jobs that provide an adequate level of sustenance). Economic structures that inhibit employment growth, such as the concentration of economic power (e.g., monopoly or state ownership of the means of production), are to be challenged. Access of individuals to work should not be limited by discrimination (by race, gender, ethnicity, status), favoritism (e.g., political access to public jobs), or lack of competition (e.g., monopolists or entrenched unions).[26]

Victor Claar and Robin Klay also echo Calvin when they affirm that "human beings have an obligation to work, and their societies must afford them many opportunities to do so, since work is the principal means for exercising stewardship."[27]

Another of the culture-shaping aspects of Calvin's thought was his emphasis on the sacredness of ordinary vocations. Before Calvin and the Protestant Reformation, the doctrine of vocation or calling was thought to pertain exclusively to the clergy. However, Calvin's view of work as inherently dignified by our Creator elevated all disciplines and lawful vocations to the status of holy calling. After Calvin, laying claim to a divine vocation to work in medicine, law, or education was every bit as valid as laying claim to a call to church ministry.

Calvin's call for hard work did not necessarily equate success or prosperity with divine blessing. His views, though, did have

26. Stapleford, *Bulls, Bears & Golden Calves*, 22.

27. Victor V. Claar and Robin J. Klay, *Economics in Christian Perspective: Theory, Policy, and Life Choices* (Downers Grove, IL: InterVarsity Press, 2007), 22.

a persistent tendency to elevate certain areas of human calling and labor. Business, commerce, and industry were all elevated by Calvin's principles—a prioritization consistent with the emerging realities of modern enterprise.

Even with his strong view of providence (see chapter 5 below), Calvin emphasized that humans were to work diligently. While commenting on Matthew 6:25–30, he averred:

> The fields must, no doubt, be cultivated, labor must be bestowed on gathering the fruits of the earth, and every man must submit to the toil of his calling, in order to make his living. But all this does not hinder us from being fed by the undeserved generosity of God, without which men might break their body working and achieve nothing. We are thus taught, that what we seem to have acquired by our own industry proceeds from him. Though the children of God are not free from toil . . . yet . . . we do not say that they are anxious about life: because, through their reliance on the providence of God, they enjoy calm repose.[28]

Max Weber and others are correct to assert that Calvinism dignified work and callings of many kinds. Calvin taught that any area of work—for example, farming, teaching, governing, and accounting—could be a valid calling from God, every bit as sacred as a pastor's vocation. This was a radical change in worldview, which would ultimately alter many businesses, cultures, and human lives.

Through his robust affirmation of all callings and the establishment of schools of law, medicine, history, and education (not merely religion) within his Genevan Academy, Calvin helped to break down the boundaries that distinguished the sacred from the secular. He sought to teach Genevans to view human labor in a new way, namely, in light of the truth that a person can serve

28. Cited in Biéler, *Calvin's Economic and Social Thought*, 201.

and glorify God in any line of work. Calvin counseled with many leaders, entrepreneurs, printers, and merchants in his time, and he did not revile any lawful calling. The spirit of Calvinism ennobles all good work. Despite its emphasis on the hereafter, Calvinism calls its adherents to be leaders in all fields of human endeavor here and now.

Calvin's comments on the fourth commandment underscored the dignity of work also. Just as God commands people to rest on the seventh day, Calvin argued, so the Lord expects them to work on every other day. Insofar as work is vital for all people made in God's image, Calvin taught that all callings are important. His doctrine of work was further emphasized—not to mention widely popularized—by his explanation that the fourth commandment, which mandates rest on one day out of seven, calls equally for work during the other six days.

Business, commerce, and profit-making enterprises would take on a new cast after Calvin. His teachings liberated believers to use the market for God's glory. Of interest to historians, both sympathetic and unsympathetic to Calvin, Geneva was transformed during his time there into a visible and bustling forum for economic development. The locus of growing intellectual and commercial ferment, as evidenced by the founding of Calvin's Academy and the presence of modern financial institutions (e.g., a Medici bank), Geneva became an ideal center for perfecting and exporting reform.[29]

29. Several studies detail Calvin's Geneva. Among the best are: E. William Monter, *Calvin's Geneva* (New York: John Wiley & Sons, 1967); Alastair Duke et al., eds., *Calvinism in Europe, 1540–1610: A Collection of Documents* (Manchester, UK: Manchester University Press, 1988); J. T. McNeill, "John Calvin on Civil Government," in *Calvinism and the Political Order*, George L. Hunt, ed. (Philadelphia: Westminster Press, 1965), 22–45; William A. Dunning, *A History of Political Theories: From Luther to Montesquieu* (New York: Macmillan, 1919), 26–33; W. Fred Graham, *The Constructive Revolutionary: John Calvin, His Socio-Economic Impact* (Richmond: John Knox Press, 1975); and William G. Naphy, *Calvin and the Consolidation of the Genevan Reformation* (Manchester, UK: Manchester University Press, 1994). Two recent biographies also add to our understanding: William J.

Wherever Calvinism spread, so did a love for free markets and capitalism. If one valid measure of leadership is its impact on its immediate environment, one might well compare Geneva *before* and *after* Calvin. The differences are striking. Prior to Calvin's immigration in 1536, for example, Geneva had fifty merchants, three printers, and few, if any, nobles. By the late 1550s Geneva was home to 180 merchants, 113 printers and publishers, and at least seventy aristocratic refugees who claimed nobility.[30]

It is certainly erroneous to think, as Weber did, that Calvinists believed that material success served as proof of their election. To rebut that idea, one may simply consult Calvin's teaching on the eighth commandment in his great work *Institutes of the Christian Religion*.[31] In his interpretation of that commandment, which forbids stealing, Calvin perceived that the holding and protecting of personal property was by implication perfectly normal. In fact, the commandment contained for Calvin a clear call for each person to avoid covetousness and greed and required every person to "exert himself honestly in preserving his own [property]" (*Institutes*, 2.8.45).

He warned believers not to squander what God has providentially given and also to care for their neighbors' well-being. He also wrote:

> This commandment, therefore, we shall duly obey if contented with our own lot, we study to acquire nothing but honest and

---

Bouwsma, *John Calvin: A Sixteenth-Century Portrait* (New York: Oxford University Press, 1988); and Alister McGrath, *A Life of John Calvin* (Oxford: Basil Blackwell, 1990).

30. Monter's numbers, of course, may be challenged. It is possible that records were kept better after 1536, which could explain some of the rise of the merchant class (Monter, *Calvin's Geneva*, 5). However, even if that should be established, the astronomic rise of printers and nobility is certain. Nobles, mainly from France, fled to Geneva because adhering to Protestantism at home could have meant their death.

31. John Calvin, *Institutes of the Christian Religion*, ed. John T. McNeill, trans. Ford Lewis Battles (Philadelphia: Westminster, 1960). Throughout the present work, all quotations from the *Institutes* are from this edition.

> lawful gain; if we long not to grow rich by injustice, nor to plunder our neighbor of his goods . . . if we hasten not to heap up wealth cruelly wrung from the blood of others; if we do not . . . with excessive eagerness scrape together whatever may glut our avarice or meet our prodigality. On the other hand, let it be our constant aim faithfully to lend our counsel and aid to all so as to assist them in retaining their property (2.8.46).

Had Weber factored those words into his theory, his conclusions might have been more accurate.

A prayer by Calvin makes Weber's hypothesis crumble to the ground even more rapidly. The commonly mistaken caricature of Calvin as a crass capitalist should be contrasted with the prayer he suggested for the taking up of work. In that prayer, which is included in the 1562 Genevan Catechism, he led the people in asking God to bless their labor, noting that if God failed to bless it, "nothing goes well or can prosper." He prayed for the Holy Spirit to aid workers in their calling "without any fraud or deception" and he exhorted all who work to "have regard more to follow [God's] ordinances than to satisfy our appetite to make ourselves rich." Along with this, Calvin prayed that workers would care for the indigent and that the prosperous would not become conceited. He prayed that God would diminish prosperity if he knew the people needed a dose of poverty to return them to their senses. Far from callousness toward the less fortunate, Calvin prayed that workers would "not fall into mistrust," would "wait patiently" on God to provide, and would "rest with entire assurance in [God's] pure goodness."[32]

32. Duke et al., *Calvinism in Europe, 1540–1610*, 34. The 1562 prayer to be used prior to work is included in full in Biéler, *Calvin's Economic and Social Thought*, 345: "Gracious God, our Father and Saviour, since it has pleased you to command us to work, to answer our poverty, so bless our labor through your grace that your blessing reach as far as us, without which nothing can prosper in good; and that your favor may bear witness to us in your goodness and aid, thus letting us know your fatherly care for us. Also, Lord, may it please you to assist us through your

Moreover, he warned against "eagerly contend[ing] for riches and honors, trusting in our own dexterity and assiduity, or leaning on the favor of men, or confiding in any empty imagination of fortune." Instead of relying on these false supports, urged Calvin, one should "always have respect to the Lord." The prosperity ethic that followed Calvin's time in Geneva is one of the wide-ranging effects of his thought and practice. But he also advocated reliance on God—not wealth! The "Calvinistic work ethic" is a topic that many researchers study and discuss. In essence, certain historians and scholars have ascertained a historic and pervasive trend. That trend suggests that wherever the character of Calvinism takes root, a flourishing culture of industriousness and hard work ensues. Despite the centrality of what some might consider a divine disincentive to work, i.e., the Reformed doctrine of salvation by grace alone, Calvinism actually encourages a very strong work ethic.

One of the societal overflows of Calvinism is the view that its adherents derive about work. German social theorist Max Weber was partially correct in his analysis of this view in his famous 1905 work, *The Protestant Ethic and the Spirit of Capitalism*. In its baldest form, Weber's argument contended that Calvinists confused earthly and heavenly prosperity. He ascribed to Calvinists the alleged belief that material prosperity could be taken as a sure

---

Holy Spirit, so that we may faithfully fulfill both our station in life and our calling, without duplicity or deception, but rather strive to follow what you have ordained rather than to satisfy our desire for riches. If nevertheless your pleasure is to prosper our work, give us also a mind to aid those in need according to the power you will have given us, keeping us wholly humble so that we do not set ourselves higher than those who have not received such a generous share of your open-handedness. But should you wish to have us poorer and needier than our flesh would desire, may it please you to be gracious to us by adding faith to your promises, to assure us that you will always sustain us through your goodness, so that we do not fall into lack of trust; but rather let us wait patiently for you to fill us with not only your temporal but also your spiritual graces, so that we may always have the greater opportunity to thank you, and may rest wholly in your goodness alone. Hear us, Father of mercies, through Jesus Christ, your Son, our Lord." So popular was this prayer that it was contained in many versions of the Geneva Bible (see the 1599 edition) in an appendix on prayers "to be used in private houses every morning and evening."

sign of divine blessing. If Weber's assessment were correct, then Calvinists would certainly be incentivized to be the hardest of workers. Labor and business would take on eternal significance but one that could be measured in this life by coins. In the estimation of André Biéler, Calvin assigned "human labour a spiritual dignity and value it did not have either among the schoolmen or . . . in the ancient world. This fact was to have huge effects in the economic development of Calvinist societies."[33]

In his *Institutes,* however, Calvin also asserted that any endeavor that ceased to have charity as its aim was diseased at its very root (3.8.50). Moreover, he warned that luxury could incite great problems and produce "great carelessness as to virtue" (3.10.4). In another passage Calvin clearly explained his view of the relationship between prosperity and work:

> If we believe that all prosperous and desirable success depends entirely on the blessing of God, and that when it is wanting all kinds of misery and calamity await us, it follows that we should not eagerly contend for riches and honors, trusting in our own dexterity and assiduity, or leaning on the favor of men, or confiding in any empty imagination of fortune; but should always have respect to the Lord, that under his auspice we may be conducted to whatever lot he has provided for us. (3.7.9)

In that same section, lest Calvin be misunderstood, he called for a "curb to be laid on us" to restrain "a too eager desire of becoming rich, or an ambitious striving after honor." Thus, Calvin called for hard work but did not necessarily equate success or prosperity with divine blessing. His views, though, did have a persistent tendency to stimulate various areas of human calling and labor. Weber and others are correct to recognize that Calvinism dignified work and callings of many kinds.

33. Biéler, *Calvin's Economic and Social Thought,* 365.

With respect to the doctrine of calling, from 1 Corinthians 7:20 Calvin deduced that a vocation was a "lawful mode of life." He did not, however, consider this mode immutable. "Now it were a very hard thing," Calvin wrote, "if a tailor were not at liberty to learn another trade or if a merchant were not at liberty to betake himself to farming."[34] Calvin did not believe that one had a burden of vocational necessity, as if one could never change jobs. At the same time, however, he did reiterate that the providence of God resulted in "different ranks and stations in the world."[35]

Calvin believed that humans were "governors of the world," albeit subject to the Almighty.[36] This belief expressed itself in action, in business, in development, and as an unquenchable motive to create and multiply. This doctrine of calling continues to fuel investing and financial concerns.

The Sabbath: A Forgotten Key to a Successful Entrepreneurial Model

Calvin also taught that the Sabbath was a regular, continuing, and important part of creation. Contained in this was also the commendation of proper leisure for man's enjoyment, as well as a release "from all other business."[37] Not only was no part of creation to be worshiped or excessively adored, but also work itself was not to be enshrined as an absolute. For Calvin, work had its place in God's economy; and so did rest and worship, as the fourth commandment taught.

In his commentary on the fourth commandment, he noted several purposes for this mandate, among them: to provide relaxation for workers, to encourage believers not to depend on their work, and to remind them that, with only 14% of the week set

34. John Calvin, *Commentary on the Epistles of Paul the Apostle to the Corinthians* (Grand Rapids: Baker Book House, 1979), 1:248.

35. Ibid., 1:249.

36. Calvin, *Commentaries on the First Book of Moses*, 125.

37. Ibid., 106.

aside for rest from labor, there was yet "plenty of time, exclusive of the Sabbath, for all their business."[38]

One may wonder how taking one day away from business and creativity could possibly maximize results. From a purely mathematical point of view, to formulate a business plan that automatically sacrifices over 14% of the workweek might seem like business suicide. However, as is the case in other matters of faith, it is in giving and sacrificing that we often find blessing and prosperity. The commandment to keep one day in seven as a holy rest from industry flies in the face of most entrepreneurial schemes, whether ancient or modern. After all, few believers keep this commandment anymore; it is perhaps more often transgressed than are the prohibitions against adultery, stealing, and lying. It may even closely rival the tenth commandment for selective ignoring, perhaps because the behavior proscribed in the fourth commandment has some relationship to the covetousness that is dealt with in the tenth.

But things were not always so. For centuries, many Christians honored God, served their fellow man, and provided time for worship by keeping the Sabbath. Many businesses flourished without slavishly being concerned about work twenty-four hours a day, seven days a week.

If business owners or entrepreneurs are to obey the ancient commandment, though, certain commonsense objections must be met. Chiefly, we can think of three hurdles that must be overcome:

1. Isn't the Sabbath commandment an outdated vestige of an ancient, agrarian society that has no compelling application to business practices today?
2. Isn't the Sabbath, if business owners practice it, inefficient at heart and unprofitable?
3. Since so few Christians keep this commandment today, are there any large traditions that justify it?

38. Calvin, *Commentaries on the Four Last Books of Moses*, 2:438.

What must be regained is an appreciation of God's order, man's own finiteness, and the ethical limitations on entrepreneurship. The points below speak to those three challenges.

Is the Sabbath commandment an outdated vestige? As one examines the transcultural basis of the Sabbath, it becomes clear that it is not merely a Jewish custom. It is certainly not an anti-business invention. Neither is it, as revealed, only for one epoch of history. A review of the biblical development of the Sabbath is necessary before it can be applied to any business model. Such a review also implies that the Sabbath is based on a creation ordinance, where God is depicted as the model for inventiveness.

The Sabbath is, in fact, a central symbol of biblical teaching. Referenced dozens of times throughout Scripture, the Sabbath is a crucial concept that incorporates two central ideas:

1. God does not wish to enslave us to work and productivity; there are times to rest. By resting we take time to enjoy creation. God does not mind us enjoying creation; in fact, he commands us to enjoy, as well as to glorify. The commandment to cease from normal labor and productivity is a gesture arising from God's grace and mercy. Just as man does not live by bread alone, neither does he live by work alone. We are free to put down our tools. In fact, if one arrives at a position of self-importance that denies relaxation and rest, one may have created an idol. We may tell ourselves that we are essentially indispensable to some task, but God does not share that opinion. We are free to rest.
2. The Sabbath temporarily sets aside human labor for a larger purpose: to permit God's people to worship him in holiness. Worship and fellowship with God's people are activities that are vitally important. We need to do these regularly, and God provided for that. The Sabbath

> also doubles as a divine scheduling mechanism, if we'll allow it. God structures our week, telling us when we have times for certain things. Business is not the only activity of importance.

Rooted in creation before the fall, the Sabbath as a concept is a merciful token of God's work. He cares for us greatly, and he shepherds us by means of this great idea. Only a person consumed with worldly obligations or acquisition could fail to love God's provision of the Sabbath.

Since it is such a central concept in biblical teaching, we should not be surprised that the Sabbath appears in a variety of contexts with different nuances.

God's Sabbath is described in Genesis 2 as a resting from his creative labor. He also commends the pattern to humans. Other religions later copied this institution, but the divine pattern of seven is derived from Scripture. The next large concentration of teaching on the Sabbath occurs in the context of the Ten Commandments. This signals that God's purpose for the Sabbath is enduring. The Sabbath custom, evidently, was neither temporary nor provincial. It pertained to all ages.

If anything, the institution is broadened by the fourth commandment, which begins by reiterating the injunction to keep the Sabbath day holy. The rationale is that one is to work for six days (a couple more than the average American; if a person wished to work more than sixteen hours per day for six days, he could work one hundred hours per week, every week, and still keep the Sabbath), but that the seventh day is reserved for God. Not only is the head of the household not to work, but all non-necessary work by every member of the household is prohibited. Even those with no standing or rights ("aliens") are to have the day off. In other words, the divine pattern established in creation is to include all people—a universality that Exodus 20:11 supports with this unassailable argument: If God can do all he did in six days, humans too should confine themselves to a fixed period of labor, punctuated by a day of rest.

Throughout the remainder of the OT, God stressed that this practice was to continue. There is nothing in the issuance of these commandments that in any way indicates that they are only to be kept at certain times or in some locales.

As codified in the Decalogue, the command is a dual one: (1) one is to work on six days and (2) one is to rest on the seventh day. The purpose of this day is to rest and keep the day holy. That provides an opportunity simultaneously to rest laborers, care for our families, and stimulate believers. God required all of these for humane culture.

The OT also contains a further enlargement of the Sabbath concept to include a Sabbath of years. This does not abolish the weekly pattern of six days of work followed by one day of rest; it merely takes that seminal concept and extends it more broadly. If all humans are to follow a Sabbath custom in their week, then the Israelites thought that they should apply the custom to their land and life cycles. The Jubilee pattern (which is unique to Israel; see Deut. 26) enlarges the concept even further. The point of each extension of the Sabbath concept was to remind people, first, that God is the ultimate owner of all things and, second, that humans need to have stated release or rest times. All of creation needs this. Constant slavery to labor is not virtuous.

As OT history progressed, however, numerous abuses and corruptions of the Sabbath recurred. Toward the end of the OT, Isaiah taught the people that whenever they kept certain festivals commanded by God, they should do so without hypocrisy. That also meant that they should care for the poor and downtrodden whenever they fasted.

As Isaiah reminded the Israelites, pleasing God involves a moral component with attitudinal expectations. It is not a matter of ceremonies alone. So when the Israelites kept the Sabbath, they were to refrain from "doing as you please on my holy day." They were also to view "the Sabbath as a delight . . . and honorable." People were to honor it by serving God, not by going their own way or "doing as you please or speaking idle words." If the people kept God's day holy with joy, delight, and honor, and without hypocrisy toward their neighbor, God would bless them incredibly (Is. 58:13–14). Isaiah's words tell us much about how to view the Sabbath.

After several centuries of practice, the originally revealed custom began to be warped by the crafting of human hands. The Pharisees, one of the major religious parties of Israel, had taken the original and distorted it nearly beyond recognition. They had taken a good creation of God and transformed it into a beast. They had created numerous, onerous laws that strangled the life out of the Sabbath. They would not let people use fire, walk more than a mile, or use medicinal ointment on the Sabbath, classifying these activities as labor. Calvin referred to these practices as injurious and a foolish attempt to overturn an institution that God had designed to help, not crush, man. Noting the malice and superstition of the Pharisees, Calvin wrote: "It was hypocrisy, therefore, that made them so exact in trifling matters, while they spared themselves in gross superstitions. . . . It is the invariable practice of hypocrites to allow themselves liberty in matters of the greatest consequence, and to pay close attention to ceremonial observances."[39]

Jesus had to rescue the Sabbath and return it to its intended design. He did not overturn the Sabbath in the NT; rather, he confronted the Pharisees over their misuse of the day. With their legalism and small-mindedness, they had placed too many restrictions on the institution. They were crucifying something good that God had created. A person could not even be healed on the Sabbath or retrieve his ox from a ditch. In opposition

39. Calvin, *Commentary on a Harmony of the Evangelists*, 2:46.

to the Pharisees, Jesus taught the people that the Sabbath was made for man, not vice versa (Mk. 2:27). The original plan was not to enslave man to a new taskmaster but to free him to rest and worship. The Sabbath, intended to be a merciful gift from God to man, had to be liberated from man-made restrictions. That is the error that Jesus sought to correct, all the while personally attending synagogue and keeping the Sabbath himself.

However, he did not do it as the legalists thought he should. Neither did he lessen or change the Sabbath from its original, divine design. He sought to restore it as a day of rest, a day for man to be replenished by worship and leisure. It was a foretaste of the coming eternal rest that is discussed in Hebrews 4.

Jesus and the NT authors never make the kind of argument so often heard today—namely, that once a person is saved, he can ignore the law of God and make up his own moral standards. Jesus kept the Sabbath and never tried to overturn it. The early church followed him in this, merely changing the day from the Jewish seventh day to the Christian first day. All Jesus corrected was the Pharisees' distorted version of the custom.

The later NT teaching in Hebrews indicates that the original weekly pattern also has a spiritual meaning. The day for worship each week should be a wonderful foretaste of what we will have in heaven. That experience is portrayed as an eternal rest. In heaven unending Sabbaths will unfold, work will be completed, and the redeemed creation will be enjoyed forever. The Sabbath rest, then, became a symbol for heaven in Hebrews 4.

The Sabbath commandment, thus, is far from being a vestige of an ancient, agrarian society that has no compelling application to us today.

Moreover, it may be a forgotten key to business and economic planning that both allows for leisure and also forbids turning work into a god or an absolute. Work has its place, but it is not the *summum bonum*.

Isn't the Sabbath, if business owners practice it, inefficient at heart and unprofitable? Why should anyone, especially a business owner, observe God's Sabbath today? Several good reasons that Calvinists identify are listed below; there are doubtlessly many others.

It defines limits on certain activities for the owner; i.e., work is good but not God. A regular observance of the Sabbath is a needed braking mechanism for humane existence. It prevents us from being enslaved to labor. The scriptural teaching maintains that work is good and an essential part of healthy humanity. However, owners and workers are both under the command to avoid ceaseless work. The Sabbath is a divine "no," which undergirds the divine "yes" pronounced on human joy. Keeping the Sabbath also precludes the conquest of raw acquisitiveness.

It requires the owner to plan ahead. If an owner is both to succeed and to keep the Sabbath, it is necessary for him to plan ahead. Indeed, this imperative requires that future planning be a regular activity. The steward must see that Monday's supplies, work, and personnel are prepared by the end of Saturday, if he is to keep the Sabbath. The sabbatical year (Ex. 23) and Jubilee require even more long-range planning. Should the executive constantly be late, behind, inefficient, or lacking in forethought, it will be impossible for him to stay afloat *and* set aside a day for refreshment. Thus, planning is a requirement implicit in the divine mandate. Keeping the Sabbath, in the end, may actually enhance an executive's organization.

It means that the owner must pay heed to sacred things and meet (as must others) with God's saints. He, too, needs worship. The owner is not ontologically superior to the worker when the Sabbath commandment is recalled. A distinct leveling effect is borne within the bosom of the Sabbath. Owners and laborers become equals on this day. No one is superior in the Lord's house; with parity all approach a greater Sovereign. Further, each rests, engages in ministries of mercy, and worships devoid of class distinctions on this day. Social harmony is furthered the remainder of the week if owners and workers alike recall that the Sabbath is the pattern for eternal rest and a respite from the Curse. Keeping the Sabbath also prevents the wrongful deification of other humans. A weekly reminder that all have sinned and fallen short of the glory of God is an essential part of worship. Such anthropology carries over into one's business ethic.

It provides an opportunity for a distinctive witness. When Christians abstain from normal chores, recreations, and employments on the Lord's Day, it becomes an opportunity for witness. A healthy heavenly-mindedness is presented. Admittedly, by keeping the Sabbath one may garner frowns similar to those directed at the Amish because of their unfashionable customs and conduct. However, our witness is often strengthened when there is something about it that is distinctive and difficult to dismiss. Those who are materialists, for example, may be stunned to meet an entrepreneur who honors God more than clutching wealth, thus giving rise to his gentle explanation for his hope (1 Pet. 3:15). Entrepreneurs should be as concerned about their communal witness as any others. In fact, to those who have been given much, much in the way of public witness is required. Keeping the Sabbath is one of those ordinary means to give witness; its observance may be more necessary for owners than others.

It identifies for the owner opportunities to show charity (to aliens, servants, etc). The original command in Exodus 20 singles out several groups who are protected from an unending labor demand and who also might not have legal protection. This command prevents immigrants and the poor from being mistreated; they, too, have a Sabbath and equal protection to its blessing. The owner is to be charitable, and this small incursion on a weekly basis will probably serve to sensitize the executive to other charitable needs. Moreover, the Sabbath day is an excellent day to devote to charitable and diaconal ministries.

It necessitates work for the able-bodied (for six days). The Hebrew work ethic was stronger than that of the modern West. Not only does the Sabbath commandment require a full day of rest, but it also stipulates that all people should work for six days—not five days or the average for the industrialized West (about thirty-four hours per week). Keeping the Sabbath, if both parts of the commandment are kept ("for in six days shall you labor"), may actually increase productivity.

Of course, if this imperative is taken as transcendent, it may also call into question one of the idols of our day—a false view of retirement. Too many of us idolize an existence in which there is no work—a time of life when we will merely coast on our capital or a pension. The Exodus commandment, however, does not say, "Work six days if you're under sixty-five or unless you did really well in the stock market." It is a universal command. That long-distance horizon affects one's planning and investments significantly.

Since so few Christians keep this commandment today, are there any large traditions that justify it? One nagging challenge is frequently set forth: "If most other Christians ignore the Sabbath, why shouldn't we?" Note, however, that the question, as frequently formulated, assumes either that (1) North American Christians provide a normative standard of conduct; or (2) earlier voices from the church must be discounted. The universal church is certainly much wider than our own limited cultural experience.

To reflect the transdenominational agreement on this subject, one can compare the Reformed Protestant views outlined above with the 1994 Catechism of the Catholic Church (CCC). The Catholic Catechism refers to the Sabbath as a "sign of the irrevocable covenant" between God and Israel. It further describes the Sabbath as halting everyday work and as a "day of protest against the servitude of work and the worship of money." Agreeing with the traditional interpretation given above, the CCC affirms Jesus' respect for the Sabbath and points to him as the authentic interpreter of its activities.

The Catholic Catechism speaks of a "rhythm and spirit" developed by Sabbath observance. Of course, it also emphasizes the obligation to worship and celebrate the Eucharist on that day. According to this doctrinal statement, Christians are to refrain from works that hinder the worship, joy, physical refreshment, or ministries of mercy that are appropriate for the Sabbath. In keeping with Jesus' teaching, the CCC also recognizes that the Sabbath should not smother family needs or appropriate diaconal ministries. On the other hand, believers "should see to it that legitimate excuses do not lead to habits prejudicial to religion, family life, and health."

Following Augustine's maxim, that "the charity of truth seeks holy leisure [and] the necessity of charity accepts just work," this recent Catechism summons Christians to remember the needs of others as they rest. The Sabbath lends itself to works of mercy and care for the truly needy. In sum, the CCC states: "The institution of Sunday helps all to be allowed sufficient rest and leisure to cultivate their familial, cultural, social, and religious lives. Every Christian should avoid making unnecessary demands on others that would hinder them from observing the Lord's Day."

From the time of the Puritans in England right up to the most recent Catechism of the Catholic Church, the Sabbath has been recognized as a moral duty with distinct benefits.

As with all the other commandments, the instruction to keep the Sabbath contains much grace. It actually offers "freedom" to rest. With this command, the sovereign Creator does not merely give permission to rest (which permission would later be extended to a Sabbath of years and the Jubilee in Leviticus 25); he positively mandates that workers take a day to rest and refocus. Such a mandate shows that matter is not all that matters. This is part of the enduring moral law, which cannot be minimized except to our own hurt.

Truett Cathy, the founder of Chick-fil-A, is an impressive model of this. Despite the prevailing culture, his company has been closed 14% of the workweek from its inception. Yet its profits are astounding. His sole reason for closing all those "eat-mor-chikin" franchises is to obey and honor God. In the meantime, he provides a humane workplace and proffers a witness that is matched by profitability. Could it be that God would use business folks to call the church home? In any case, one thing seems clear: if certain factors—e.g., creation, the supernatural, morality, and Christ—remain in the front of our economic minds, then our businesses will be different from those within other economic systems.

For example, in Marx's contrasting theory of labor, the value of an item is best weighed by the amount of labor used to produce it. Consequently, labor becomes the most valuable input into production. Marx even classified machinery capital as stored-up labor that could be released by operating the machine. As a result, in Marx's paradigm, the worker is encouraged to constantly keep producing; he is enslaved to the things that bring worth to the production equation—his time and energy. On the other hand, some capitalist attitudes make little or no provision for the Sabbath and can breed a certain "hyper-capitalist" who is inclined to work seven days a week. In either case, the Sabbath is not honored.

The honoring of the Sabbath is ultimately efficient and responsible for increased productivity Monday through Saturday. It also boosts inventiveness and entrepreneurship. Without modernization and entrepreneurship, the Sabbath keeper would be reduced to a flurry of activities on Saturday that are now made unnecessary. Power, heat, water, and food storage are just a few examples of the amenities that allow believers to enjoy the Sabbath without, as Brian Schwertley states, a "return to the stone age every Lord's day."[40] An item as basic as the refrigerator allows the believer the comfort of fresh food on the Sabbath; the advent of the electrical power plant and distribution frees up the individual believer to better worship and enjoy the day of rest. Markets that allow new technologies to efficiently reach the masses are supportive of furthering the practice and enjoyment of the Sabbath.

Wealth Is Not Morally Evil

While some economists strive to raise wealth from its bad reputation or establish it as an aspect in neutral territory, it is certainly not morally evil and may be good, if used under grace.

Wealth may actually be used very positively. It potentially has numerous salutary effects. So important is business that one author suggests that it is the best method for lifting folks out of poverty. Wayne Grudem avers that "starting and maintaining productive, profitable businesses" is the only "long-term solution to world poverty."[41]

Grudem also realizes that several barriers prevent the flood of business's benevolent overflow. Excessive governmental regulations often inhibit entrepreneurs in poorer countries. Governmental confiscation of private wealth is another strong disincentive to entrepreneurship. Weak governments that do not punish crime or protect against fraud also dash cold water on the business climate. Notwithstanding these hindrances, one of the largest barriers potential entrepreneurs must overcome is a negative attitude toward business and profit in general. Grudem asks:

40. Brian Schwertley, "The Sabbath and Modern Industrial Civilization: A Critique of Gary's North's 'The Economics of Sabbath Keeping,'" Reformed Online, http://www.reformedonline.com/view/reformedonline/sabbathciv.htm.

41. Wayne Grudem, *Business for the Glory of God: The Bible's Teaching on the Moral Goodness of Business* (Wheaton, IL: Crossway Books, 2003), 81.

> If people think business is evil, they will hesitate to start businesses, and they will never feel real freedom to enjoy working in business, because it will always be tainted with the faint cloud of false guilt. Who can enjoy being an *evil* materialist who works with *evil* money to earn *evil* profits by *exploiting* laborers and producing material goods that feed people's *evil* greed and enhance their *evil* pride and sustain their *evil* inequality of possessions and feed their *evil* competitiveness?[42]

He later argues against one of the ultimate lies of "the Enemy who wants to keep God's people from fulfilling his purposes," suggesting that "if the devil himself wanted to keep people created by God in the wretched bondage of lifelong poverty, it is hard to think of a better way he could do it than to make people think that business is fundamentally evil, so they would avoid entering into it or oppose it at every turn."[43] His alternative as a modern Calvinist is for believers to invest themselves and their talents in subduing the earth and using the materials from God's good creation to earn profits and then to use those profits to produce more jobs and to care for real needs.

Economists rarely address the moral quality of wealth. However, in much of society wealth has become a convenient punching bag. During the 1980s, the standard bad guy in the movies was a Russian or a Nazi. In the 1990s Hollywood looked to the Chinese, the drug cartels, and the Vietcong (as popular cinema relived the Vietnam War) to provide the villains. In this decade the rich, the powerful, and greedy oil companies have become the "new" villains. Daily doses of moralistic economic theory courtesy of Aerosmith and their song "Eat the Rich" were often preached on radios during the 1980s or 1990s. Such cultural catechizing has accumulated and yielded predominantly negative views of wealth.

42. Ibid., 82.
43. Ibid.

To better understand today's vilification of wealth and the wealthy, we might begin with David Ricardo (1772–1823).[44] Ricardo presented a model, called the corn model, according to which wealth serves as *prima facie* evidence of the exploitation of labor. In the model, there are three entities: (1) the landlord, (2) the employer who leases the land, and (3) the workers whom the employer hires to grow and harvest the corn. According to the model, any excess profits eventually end up with the landlord. As corn is grown and labor demands a higher wage, the demand for corn also increases and the price is able to increase as well. The employer and his workers remain locked in a cycle of increasing demand, increasing wages, and increasing prices. The landlord, however, is able to adjust his rents so that any excess profits within the system are paid out to him. In the end wealth is presented as a zero-sum game in which labor and management are fighting over a smaller and smaller portion.

From Ricardo, Karl Marx picked up the theme and called the common working man to arms with his rallying cry, "workers of the world, unite!" Although Marx is referred to as the "father of communism," he was not a lone voice crying out in the wilderness. *The Communist Manifesto* was published in 1848, yet for several years prior to its appearance the themes of socialism and equitable redistribution of wealth had been introduced to the public courtesy of the American press. Horace Greeley, one of the leading journalists of the day, was recognized in 1844 by "fellow communalists as the man who had

44. First published in 1817, Ricardo's *On the Principles of Political Economy and Taxation* was the first major economic work to arrive on the scene following Smith's *Wealth of Nations* in 1776. Ricardo was a theorist in his approach, characterized by abstract and deductive reasoning. Touching on a broad array of subjects, one of his most concentrated efforts and impacts was on the study of income distribution or what is referred to as the "functional distribution of income." See Harry Landreth and David C. Colander, *History of Economic Thought* (Boston: Houghton Mifflin Company, 2002), 108–16.

'done for us what we could never have done. . . . He has done the work of the century.'"[45]

Like two streams converging, Greeley's forceful writings and editorials from 1841 to 1848, which "reached 10 percent of all voters in the Northern states . . . and often the most socially involved 10 percent,"[46] joined together with the passionate writings of Marx to create a surging river that quickly shaped the economic and sociological thinking of the day. Many times ideas from one discipline take years, decades, or generations to expand into other arenas and the public discourse, like a slow osmosis with fits and starts that can mutate the original ideas into mere shadows of themselves. However, the themes of exploitation, of the theft of surplus value, and of the pitfalls of private property exploded to the forefront of society's influencers and intellectuals, spilling over rapidly into the work force. Within months of the release of *The Communist Manifesto*, "worker revolts spread throughout Europe—in France, Germany, Austria and Italy."[47]

At the turn of the century Max Weber's *The Protestant Ethic and the Spirit of Capitalism* introduced readers to the concept of his "iron cage." According to this concept, the Christian capitalist is trapped by capitalism, addicted to its benefits yet trapped in an immoral paradigm. Weber, according to one modern economist, asserted "that capitalism by its very nature had to grow into a culture of worldliness and of the worldly acquisition of things, the pursuit and enjoyment of non-necessities (luxury)."[48] Undergirding Weber's argument is the notion that even the most righteous Puritan was unable to escape the temptation and moral dilemma of wealth. Weber paints the picture of well-

45. Marvin Olasky, *The Tragedy of American Compassion* (Wheaton, IL: Crossway Books, 2008), 51. Horace Greeley (1811–1872) was the editor of the influential *New York Tribune* and founder of the Liberal Republican party.

46. Ibid., 56.

47. Skousen, *The Big Three in Economics*, 76.

48. Schneider, *The Good of Affluence*, 24.

intentioned believers being corrupted and caged by the shiny baubles of wealth.

Closer to our day, in the 1960s Christian socialists and theologians turned up the volume in their denouncements of the evils of abundance and wealth. Citing Acts 2 out of its canonical context, they called for a simpler lifestyle, a feature often commended by collectivist theorists. Even faced with the myriad benefits that capitalism brings to society—enhanced employment and liberty to mention only two—they still felt trapped in Weber's "iron cage." Commenting on this phenomenon in his book *The Good of Affluence*, John Schneider has noted that "economists like Robinson and moral thinkers like Hauerwas feel the same is true of capitalism—that while it may bring about enormous good in the form of prosperity, its inner human workings are not good, but quite immoral."[49] The great twentieth-century social experiment needed villains who ostensibly threatened its ideals of free love, peace, social liberties, and unrestricted expression. Fueled by a century of suspicion and attacks and gaslit by the new liberation theology, the 1960s and 1970s cemented the concept of the immorality of wealth, making it part of the mainstream cultural consciousness.

Even today there is a prevailing tendency to despise wealth; one need only listen to the various criticisms of the latest vilified violator—big oil. Over the past three years, the leaders of Exxon and other oil companies have been summoned before Congress to defend their "excessive profits." Almost as an annual rite, Congress berates Exxon and the other members of the cabal they call "big oil." But are their profits truly excessive? In 2007 ExxonMobil made $40.6 billion after taxes—a staggering sum. However, based upon their revenues of $358.6 billion, the net profit margin for 2007 was 11.3%. The table below shows financial data for the top ten stocks in the S&P 500 based upon market capitalization.

49. Ibid., 23.

Company	Net Profit Margin	Dividend Yield	Dividend $ Distributed
Exxon	11.3%	1.5%	$7.62B
GE	12.5%	3.3%	$11.49B
Microsoft	27.5%	1.2%	$4.01B
AT&T	15.5%	3.8%	$8.7B
Proctor & Gamble	12.6%	1.9%	$4.2B
Google	29.9%	0%	$0
Chevron	8%	2.5%	$4.79B
Johnson and Johnson	19.9%	2.5%	$4.67B
Wal-Mart	3.3%	1.9%	$3.58B
Bank of America	27.5%	6.2%	$10.87B

Financial data courtesy of Baseline database, compiled by Thomson Financial, New York, New York.

Comparing Exxon's profit margin to that of the other nine companies in the top ten, we can see that Exxon is actually the third least profitable. If Exxon is guilty of excessive profits, then what of Microsoft, Google, and Bank of America, which have established corporations that withhold over 20% of the consumer's dollar? Note also that Exxon paid out over $7 billion in the form of dividends in 2007, whereas Google paid absolutely nothing. Once the playing field is leveled by the magic of analysis, Google, Microsoft, and other corporations earn more than Exxon per dollar spent and return less to shareholders. If Congress is truly concerned about excessive profits, then they should mandate that every firm limit its profit margin to that of Exxon and redistribute the excess to the people of the United States.

Furthermore, ExxonMobil uses its wealth to reinvest in activity throughout the world, employing hundreds of thousands of individuals. For example, twenty-two thousand employees are employed by Exxon in Chad. Is not that national economic system bolstered by Exxon's presence? What is the ultimate value to thousands of homes in Chad because of the trickle-down effect of Exxon's profits? To take a snapshot of prof context is always prone to distortion or manipulation wealth, when not hoarded, has a multiplier effect t value. The political circus is at best a sideshow, but it illustrates the thought of our time, that wealth and profit are in large measure bad and may be subjected to redistribution. However, under an efficient market system that operates in accordance with biblical economic principles, the power of wealth as a tool of reinvestment and grace can be understood not as evil, but as good, creating value, impacting lives, developing communities, and advancing the abundance of God's creation to all men as an extension of his providence.

The point is that God created wealth and gave humans the ability to manage and exchange currency. Rather than restricting humans to the barter or exchange of goods alone, we should recognize that the free flow of capital is actually an exercise in dominion. It is another way that the crown of God's creation, humanity, can practice good stewardship over the rest of creation. The use of wealth to enrich the lives of our families and others is one way to glorify God. One cannot conclude from a study of Scripture that wealth is inherently evil; instead, it is a part of creation. While human envy, greed, and avarice may cast doubt upon the management of wealth, those covetous desires can also be oriented toward other things that are not inherently evil. Calvin had a balanced enough view to understand that the Creator created even wealth. He saw that wealth, while it must never become an idol, can and should be used properly to comfort God's creatures.

Wayne Grudem puts it well when he affirms that money is a fundamentally good human invention that "sets us apart from the animal kingdom and enables us to subdue the earth by producing . . . goods and services that bring benefit to others. Money enables all of mankind to be productive and enjoy the fruits of that productivity thousands of times more extensively than we could if no human being had money, and we just had to barter with each other."[50]

In revealing the splendor of God, the creation account had important implications for the Reformer's understanding of wealth, man, dominion, and the Sabbath. As one considers Calvin's comments on the creation and God's plan, one notices not the visage of a heartless merchant, a furious taskmaster, or an isolated monk. Instead, Calvin unfolds God's designs like a gentle shepherd directing members of his flock to worship the Creator above the creation, while maintaining the energy and diligence needed to care for the creation entrusted to them. Between the tension of Creator and creation, Calvin crafts a mosaic in which man has dominion over an abundant garden, is inclined to create, is empowered to enjoy the benefits of his labor, and is responsible to reap and sow for the glory of God.

These benefits are balanced by a certain work ethic that requires accountability and a proper use of the Sabbath in order to honor the Creator. The tools of man's sustenance include not only the creative drive, but also the wealth and financial profits that have been ordained by God not as instruments of destruction or evil, but as instruments of mercy, reinvestment, and ministry. Calvin's thought on the creation had an impact even in his day within Geneva, and it still influences those business systems that encourage creation, protect the business creator, and view wealth without disdain, envy, or anger. Seeing wealth and property as created by God and in light of the stewardship mandate, one is able to take a positive view of such things as profit, business, wealth, and assets. However, along with these also come temptations to misuse, as the next section shows.

50. Grudem, *Business for the Glory of God*, 47.

2

Fall

Before any economic prescriptions are given, a correct diagnosis of the patient's condition must be made. That means that Calvinists and others should assess the nature of man before advocating remedies for economic scarcities. While Calvin's biblical faith was clear about the status of wealth as a created entity, it was equally clear that all of creation, including man, had changed dramatically and substantially from its original state. Calvin noted that prior to the fall, the world was "a most fair and delightful mirror of the divine favor," whereas afterwards it and human beings were "cursed."[1] Characterized by a "dreadful alienation" (173) and servile conditions, the fallen world was the antithesis of the Garden of Eden. Concerning work in the Garden before the fall, Calvin spoke of the "pleasant labor in which Adam previously employed

1. John Calvin, *Commentaries on the First Book of Moses Called Genesis* (1554; repr., Grand Rapids: Baker Book House, 1979), 173. In the section that follows, page numbers in parentheses refer to this commentary.

himself, [so] that in a sense he might be said to play; for he was not formed for idleness but for action" (174). In the cursed conditions after the fall, however, the "sweet delight" of cultivation was exchanged for "servile work . . . as if he were condemned to the mines" (174).[2] Once sin entered the world, economic realities changed too. Thenceforward it would be impossible to make an assumption of man's goodness, fairness, righteousness, or benevolence. To the contrary, because of the fall man's depravity must be factored into business. The resulting thorns that pained Adam would make work hazardous and less enjoyable.

André Biéler has noted the fluctuation of the primitive economy away from superabundance and toward disorder. The underlying cause, he writes, was a spiritual one, and in support of his interpretation he cites Calvin's comments on the effects of the fall. Calvin explained that the hunger of men and animals "must be attributed to the corruption of nature." Nature went from the "fair order" that had once subsisted "by God's original appointment" to a condition that was subject to barrenness, crop failure, inclemency, drought, hail, and "whatever is disorderly in the world, [which] are the fruits of sin."[3] In contrast to the perfect economy before the fall, our inherited economic culture is characterized by corruption, travail, oppression, vengeance, and divine wrath. The once-harmonious economic order now suffers major inequities and disruptions. In a sermon on Deuteronomy 24 Calvin explained the underlying anthropology in these words:

> Without any doubt, God here wanted to correct this unbelief that prevails too much in us, when everyone thinks he will never have enough. That is why men always seize things and

2. It is in this context that Calvin also views work as far more than manual labor. He condemns those who would "rashly impel all men to manual labor" and argues that there is a legitimate place for "mechanical arts" and many forms of work. Ibid., 175.

3. Cited in André Biéler, *Calvin's Economic and Social Thought* (1959; repr., Geneva: World Alliance of Reformed Churches, 2005), 211.

> can never be satisfied; and the more they have of them, the more their covetousness flares up, as with someone having drunk who has dropsy. And what is the cause? That devilish unbelief when we do not recognize that God's true concern is to feed us. . . . And this is why men are so insatiable and burn with such envy that they seize large quantities for themselves and store them and are never content. . . . Let us have recourse to God and recognize that when he blesses us we shall have plenty with which to be fed and sustained.[4]

A definite anthropology (or view of man's nature) flows from Calvin's progressive teaching. In a sermon on Galatians Calvin said, "*If we were all like angels, blameless and freely able to exercise perfect self-control, we would not need rules or regulations.* Why, then, do we have so many laws and statutes? Because of man's wickedness, for he is constantly overflowing with evil; this is why a remedy is required."[5] If men were sinless, no fiscal accountability or external structures would be necessary. Each person would work hard, produce more, steward with excellence, and benevolently share. However, the unavoidable fact of human selfishness requires us to anticipate the following truths as effects of the fall on business.

Depravity Requires a Work Ethic

Calvinism is as unique in its view of human motivation as it is in its view of human potential. Following Scripture, it views humanity as having radically declined from a once-high state. Whereas humans once tilled the Garden without external imposition or constraints, since the fall workers have had to be motivated. Sloth and selfishness, in the changed universe, have become more normal than industry and stewardship.

4. Cited in ibid., 215.

5. John Calvin, *Sermons on Galatians* (Edinburgh: Banner of Truth, 1996), 313. Emphasis added.

Thus, not only is work called for, but a distinctive work ethic is also required. The calling to work is one that conforms to expectations that humans might do otherwise. The innate and twisted selfishness, inborn since the fall, must be offset or restrained by a powerful work ethic and by incentives.

The Calvinist work ethic recognizes that seldom will individuals work hard for nothing. Some stimulus is normally needed to impel humans to work long or hard. The Calvinist recognizes this and so might, for example, schedule payments at the end of a completed job (instead of before) or require workers to show productivity before allowing them to receive benefits. The book of Proverbs teaches that "the worker's hunger drives him" (16:26), and that principle is embedded in the Calvinist work ethic.

If humans still lived in the pristine Garden, such strictures would not be needed. However, the reality of depravity requires a work ethic that motivates as well as rewards. Employers and employees alike will understand that depravity affects the motivational level of the work force. As such, requirements, incentives, and rewards (along with the withholding of them) are parts of reasonable accountability in this fallen world.

If We Recognize Depravity We Will Not Tolerate Non-productivity

It follows from our comments above that a Calvinistic work ethic does not reward or tolerate non-productivity. In fact, a depravity-sensitive work ethic will recognize sloth as a symptom of sin and will seek to ward it off wherever possible. Of course, one way to do this is to withhold rewards from those who do not work or who do not work well. Rewarding only those who are productive seeks to nullify where possible one of the effects of the fall.

Any business system that recognizes the realities of the fall and human sin, therefore, will strive to motivate workers toward productivity. In the process, it will not assume that they will be productive on their own, whether for the good of the state or for the good of others. Successful businesses will make this a factor in their planning. One of the reasons for such grandiose failure among socialist communities is that non-productivity is relatively tolerated. Because high goals are not held out, because minimal work performance is acceptable, because workers are not motivated to enhance their own standards of living, and because all assets are redistributed regularly, such Sisyphean economies do not encourage multiplication, enhancement, and the increase of wealth or assets. Those dynamics are understandable in terms of the Calvinist work ethic and assumptions. What is not reasonable is to expect that human beings will work otherwise.

Owners and workers who understand that productivity is called for and expected will make this a part of their business life. The recognition of human weakness in this area may be one of the first steps toward fixing the fallen nature of workers. Workers who fail to enhance and produce should not be rewarded; their job performance is not acceptable. Workers who do enhance and produce should be rewarded; that in turn will lead to more productivity.

God did not envision, for example, that Eden would remain in stasis. It was designed for beautification, growth, productivity, and enhancement. The conditions of Garden economics, admittedly, are different from the conditions of thorns-and-thistles economics.

Depravity Necessitates Limited Trust and Requires Accountability in the Marketplace

With the foregoing discussion in mind, accountability in the marketplace becomes essential. If human beings were not fallen, they might be trusted to act and work on their own without any external rewards or punishments. However, once we understand that the fall has introduced sin into human culture, our business practices and investment strategies will seek to build in regular accountability.

Owners and managers may trust, but that trust will be limited. Man requires accountability because he is sinful. Because he is sinful he has to work. Work is given as a consequence, not a punishment. It sanctifies man and helps provide for man's needs. Again, because he is sinful he needs accountability, personal and structural. A well-constructed business system provides that structural or systematic accountability.

The institutionalized foundation for this systematic accountability has two pillars. The first is a strong legal and moral system. This is crucial; it should never be forgotten when we talk about business or economic systems. At the heart of his argument for capitalism in *The Wealth of Nations*, Adam Smith discusses how the ideal system must have robust laws and must protect property and the rights of property owners.[6] Many times capitalists have been mistakenly generalized as exploitative, greedy, and destructive. Those adjectives may be accurate for people who adopt capitalism apart from its Calvinistic spirit. However, even principled capitalists in a free market must be constrained by appropriate legal and moral systems. Without that, the economic system is distorted, a mutant of capitalism.

Moreover, there are examples of distortion whereby those who are powerful and bureaucratically connected can actually use the government for their own purposes at the expense of others. In this perversion, firms and industries can be directed to hire certain individuals or groups, compelled to pay above-market wages, and forced to elevate workers above their competency in the name of appeasement. This behavior is often little more than sophisticated, polished socialism that acts under a banner of sovereign

6. For a complete understanding of Adam Smith's theme see book 4 of *An Inquiry into the Nature and Causes of the Wealth of Nations*, entitled "Of Systems of Political Economy."

immunity as it directs the actions of entrepreneurs and business owners. In their book *A Biblical Economics Manifesto*, James Gills and Ronald Nash warn Christians not to fall prey to the cabal of various types of excessive centralization. "The new class of Christians," they write, "who support American-style liberalism and the Big Government that goes with it insist that the state use its coercive powers and take whatever it regards as properly excessive and use it in whatever way seems best to the elitists who happen to control the state at that particular time."[7] The text is not a political statement pitting liberal against conservative or Republican against Democrat. Implicit to it is the understanding that the governing elite are always changing from one party to the other in the White House, Congress, and Senate. Regardless of party, however, the distortion lies in the ability of elitists to direct policy to fit their purposes at the expense of market freedom. If anything, this persistent willingness to harness market efficiencies to political agendas may have created disillusionment toward politicians of both parties.

An extreme example of an inefficient system is one in which the government is allowed to extend its powers and authorities beyond its constitutional limits for the purpose of benefitting individuals or groups that are well connected. The most egregious form of overextension is the misuse of eminent domain—the forcible taking of an individual's property for the benefit of the common good. In the past, eminent domain has been exercised for the construction of dams, airports, roads, and infrastructure. However, in 2005 the case of *Kelo v. City of New London* set a new precedent for the expanding use of eminent domain. Essentially, the city of New London, Connecticut condemned privately owned real property in order to use that property for the purposes of a redevelopment program that would include a conference

7. James P. Gills and Ronald H. Nash, *A Biblical Economics Manifesto: Economics and the Christian Worldview* (Lake Mary, FL: Creation House, 2002), 56.

center, a new state park, new homes, and various commercial and retail spaces. The government was required to provide "just compensation" for the taking of property, but how can one determine the complete value of the property that is lost by an owner when eminent domain encroaches? Often, the infringement of property rights is hidden under the disguise of environmental laws mandating "open space." Zoning, planned communities, and even homeowners' associations have also contributed to the erosion of property rights. Commenting on this phenomenon, Thomas Sowell has written that "the erosion of property rights has allowed affluent and wealthy communities to keep out people of moderate or low incomes and prevent the building of housing for ordinary people that would change the character of existing upscale communities."[8] How ironic that those who hold to the liberal environmental political agenda are indirectly responsible for increasing the cost of housing for lower- and middle-class citizens and even perhaps for increasing the problem of urban sprawl and homelessness. "Where thousands of acres of land are taken off the market around an upscale community" in the name of open space or green zones, Sowell maintains, "millions—or even billions—of dollars worth of land is made unavailable to others for *the benefits of the existing residents* [emphasis added] of that community."[9] When supply is reduced, prices go up, which forces individuals at the margin to seek for other alternatives. The primary alternative for residential property in neighborhood x is typically property in neighborhood y, which is more likely than not further away from town and in a more "rural" setting.

The chipping away of property rights is a dangerous trend and should be viewed as a major hindrance to a biblical economic system. The ability to have ownership in real property—and to sell, buy, and protect that property—is vital to developing markets and

8. Thomas Sowell, *Economic Facts and Fallacies* (New York: Basic Books, 2008), 33.

9. Ibid., 34.

wealth. The legal ability to establish title is more than a technicality and should be carefully protected. As Sowell observes:

> Perhaps the easiest way to understand the role of property rights is to see what happens in their absence. Even in countries where property rights have not been formally abolished, the costs of legally validating ownership of a home, farm, or a business may be prohibitively expensive, relative to the average income level in a given country. This is in fact a common situation in Third World countries. The *Economist* magazine has estimated that, in Africa, only about one person in ten works in a legally recognized enterprise or lives in a house that has legally recognized property rights.[10]

The second pillar for systematic accountability is the unrestrained/unrestricted movement of wages, rewards, and employment choices (on the employee's side), and consequently the unrestricted ability to hire and fire (on the employer's side). The key word here is "unrestricted," meaning "free of distortion." A distortion of the second pillar of accountability is found in institutions and organizations—whether unions, trade guilds, cartels, or other collective bodies—that inhibit the free flow of employment. The tenure system within major universities offers a prime example. Once a teacher reaches a certain status, suddenly the employer's ability to fire or release that worker is greatly diminished. As a result, universities are unable to dismiss underperforming professors, and tenured faculty possess both the ability to teach whatever they desire without fear of repercussion and the right to demand higher pay, regardless of performance. Sowell notes:

> The extraordinary protections and prerogatives of faculty members permit not only much self-indulgence but even corruption. . . . The unique position of college and university faculty

10. Ibid., 201.

> members as both labor and management offers many different kinds of opportunities to serve their own interests, rather than the interests of the students or of the academic institution.[11] . . . Professors are able to confine the ideological spectrum to those views consonant with their own, not only in selecting reading material for their own classes but still more so in deciding whom to hire as fellow faculty members, leading to situations in which it is not uncommon for the ratio of Democrats to Republicans to be dozens to one in some departments, even through supporters of the two parties are relatively evenly divided in the country at large.[12]

Economic mobility needs to be present in order to provide systematic accountability. In this instance, the term "economic mobility" is intentionally ambiguous so as to refer to and include unrestricted movement of wages and rewards, as well as a vast array of employment options and an unrestricted right to hire and fire employees. When such mobility is truly unrestricted the system is virtually distortion free. However, distortions are numerous within even the most laissez-faire economies.

These distortions reduce the amount of mobility and in turn prohibit systematic accountability, ultimately delaying economic sanctification. It is easy to identify the negative effects of economic systems that only benefit the bureaucratically connected. It is also easy to spot a system in which the government has overextended its powers with the intention of exploitation. However, less explicit distortions and their effects on economic sanctification are often more difficult to perceive.

In order for social mobility to remain unrestricted, individuals must have the right to pursue opportunities either to advance in or even to change their occupation. The process of rewarding an educator who achieves a certain status greatly diminishes the

11. Ibid., 90–91.
12. Ibid., 94–95.

employer's ability to fire or release that worker. As a result, the university becomes increasingly inefficient and may reach the point where it lacks the budgetary means to hire new—possibly more gifted—educators. Furthermore, these experienced professors require higher salaries for jobs that could often be performed at a lower cost by younger, but equally talented, employees. Therefore, the cost of education rises (even at public universities) and higher education becomes more selective.

Other distortions with regard to employment include laws that limit the employer's ability to fire employees or to hire without restriction. While there may be superficial benefits to such laws and restrictions, a true capitalist transcends such needs.

The authors live in the state of Georgia, which is considered a right-to-work state. In a right-to-work state employers can hire and fire at will. This unrestrained ability also provides an accountability structure that is not hindered externally. However, in many states around the nation and certainly in many foreign countries, employers cannot fire at will, and most are required to show cause, even when firing untenured, nonunionized employees. Even more extreme is the concept of lifetime employment, which exists in France, Japan, Korea, and elsewhere. The negative effect is that employers are hesitant to hire new employees. Therefore, the unemployment rate for fresh college graduates is high. For example, in France and Japan the unemployment rate rarely falls below 10%. Thus, young people face tremendous pressure and competition in their efforts to secure jobs. The end results are higher unemployment and a further dislocation of trained workers from the workplace.

Other distortions include the mandatory use of unionized labor and the governmental enforcement of affirmative action for universities and business. In both cases, business decisions are being affected by factors unrelated to overall performance and efficiency. If employers are forced to sacrifice performance to considerations of bureaucratic connections, gender, race, or sexual orientation, while also being forced to pay the prevailing wage, their cost of business escalates. Combining reduced production with an undiminished wage equals an increase in cost. Hence, the inefficiency becomes systemic and affects others outside the organization as well. As Gills and Nash write: "Capitalism also presupposes a system of morality. Capitalism does not encourage people to do anything they want. There are definite limits, moral and otherwise, to the ways in which people should exchange."

Man Is Not by Nature a "Socialist"

Calvinism, when applied to business matters, quickly affirms that socialism is not mandated by creation. Nevertheless, a recent study offers these observations:

> Certainly communism, except in recalcitrant Cuba, North Korea and China, is dead. Nevertheless, socialism, where citizens through the expression of their collective will determine the allocation of resources and the resultant goods and services, is very much alive. While direct government ownership of the means of production is on the wane, central planning, substantial redistribution of income, and social engineering through regulations and the law will occur in the more socialist nations. A mixed capitalist economy such at the United State where central government expenditures account for 22 percent of GDP stands in sharp contrast to such nations as Israel and Italy (48 percent of the GDP), France (47 percent of the GDP), Sweden (44 percent), Hungary (43 percent), Denmark and Portugal (41 percent), and the United Kingdom (39 percent).[13]

13. The World Bank, *World Development Indicators 2000* (New York: Oxford University Press, 2000), table 4-13. Cited in John E. Stapleford, *Bulls, Bears & Golden Calves: Applying Christian Ethics in Economics* (Downers Grove, IL: InterVarsity Press, 2002), 81.

In the state of nature, if no systems are imposed, man will accumulate and distribute as an individual. His interest in a "community of goods" is rarely observed in a state of nature. Confiscation, violence, theft, and prodigality may occur, but seldom does philanthropy of a scope larger than the family appear in primitive society. That may be a commentary on the fallen nature of man. It also may be a clue for businesses and economies, indicating how they will best function in reality.

John Stapleford summarizes the point this way: "Communal property rights encourage overuse and abuse of property and reward shirking one's obligations. Private property rights encourage property to be treated as a long-term asset and provide a direct link between individual effort and economic return."[14] Moreover, one need look no further than the parable of the two sons to illustrate the slothfulness that accompanies guaranteed employment (Mt. 21:28–31).

Due to the fall, an economic golden age in which all humans glorify God with their wealth is not anticipated prior to establishment of the New Jerusalem. Instead, we expect selfishness, conflict, theft, destruction of property, and strife in economic and business sectors. Rather than living in denial of such realities, we should seek enduring solutions that take them into account. Anyone who begins with the expectation of a utopia will quickly become frustrated by the fallen nature of our universe. Realism in business and profit sectors is a better beginning point than utopianism. Thus, Calvinism explains what and why to expect in the marketplace because it has a realistic understanding of the nature of man. The children of Calvin will be profoundly and inevitably dystopian.

For our own times we can also glean much about the right view of work if we explore Calvin's views on social welfare. Calvin and his colleagues thought that work should be required of all who received a subsidy. As Jeannine Olson comments:

14. Stapleford, *Bulls, Bears & Golden Calves*, 58.

> There was an effort in Geneva to maintain the image of the *Bourse française* as a fund to help people who were considered worthy, rather than as an institution that indiscriminately aided everyone. The funds were intended for those who were in genuine need, particularly those who were ill or handicapped. The deserving poor were numerous in this age before modern medicine or surgery, when a simple hernia or poorly aligned broken bone could render one unable to work. The limited funds of the *Bourse* were not intended for derelict poor, those who are considered unwilling to work, lazy and slothful vagrants and vagabonds, to use the popular English terminology of the era. The assumption that welfare recipients should be worthy of aid had long been common in Europe, but the definition of worthiness varied from one milieu to another.[15]

There were instances in the records of the *Bourse* (the French term for the treasury of the church) when the deacons declined to give assistance to individuals because of laziness. Social relief did not call for subsidies that discouraged personal industry and responsibility. Recipients of subsidies from the church were expected to uphold Christian standards of morality, and the deacons attempted to use the *Bourse* as a means of discipline and encouragement.

Furthermore, Calvin and his followers seemed to understand that private property could help individuals and families climb out of impoverished conditions. He seemed to understand how private property could benefit the poor—a theme echoed by Thomas Sowell when he notes: "Where property rights prevail in a free market, housing circulates regularly among different classes of people."[16]

Calvin's views, as we are beginning to see, formed a fabric of thought. His view of the value of work—not to mention the role

15. Jeannine Olson, *Calvin and Social Welfare: Deacons and the Bourse Française* (Selinsgrove, PA: Susquehanna University Press, 1989), 139.

16. Sowell, *Economic Facts and Fallacies*, 35.

of private and religious charity—was not ignored as he and his disciples in Geneva formulated protocols for welfare.

The Role of Wealth

It may be an opportune time to synthesize some of the points discussed above and to make some initial comments on the role of wealth, as defined by both Scripture and Calvin. To set the context, many in the modern West begin with notions that wealth:

- is inherently bad;
- is a sign of exploitation;
- provides an outward identification of villains (consider the term "robber baron");
- should not be allowed to be passed down to subsequent generations;
- should be redistributed periodically to keep the villainous from amassing more.

Wealth, then, in many circles is seen as inherently bad—one commentator calls it the last remaining kind of bigotry, the bigotry against the successful—instead of a possible blessing. Our contention, however, is that wealth can be morally neutral or good, depending on use, productivity, and stewardship. A few simple biblical examples will amplify our thinking.

At the outset, one may ask whether the Scriptures offer examples of the "righteous rich." Having already made the case that Adam was, at one time, blessed with nothing but plenty, one can easily list believers who not only had much but also gained and used much. After the flood, for example, Noah and his family virtually owned the world. Moreover, the NT describes the deeds of several affluent individuals who used their wealth for the Kingdom of God. And, of course, throughout church history numerous wealthy people have aided the church in its expansion, helped to build hospitals and schools, assisted in the building of churches, and contributed to wide-ranging ministries of mercy.

In an attempt to offset the frequently negative view of wealth, the following biblical examples illustrate *positive* uses of wealth.

Wealth Is Given to Help Shape Lives: Boaz

Boaz is an unlikely hero. He was not from a priestly line; nor was he a warrior or a prophet. He was just a landowner and businessman—a shrewd businessman at that. But the wealth God had blessed him with was the key ingredient that separated Boaz from the crowd. The story begins with Ruth and her mother-in-law, Naomi, both widows, living together and destitute, returning to Israel as poor beggars. Ruth spends her days gleaning in the fields and catches the eye of Boaz. By the end of the story, Boaz has "redeemed" Ruth and lifted her and Naomi out of poverty. Furthermore, from Ruth's relationship with Boaz the grandfather of King David is born, thus maintaining the line that runs from Adam through David and eventually to Jesus. What is notable about the story is that, throughout it, God's will unfolds through the instrument of Boaz's wealth. Boaz is in a position to own land (upon which Ruth gleans), to have an abundance of crops (which he shares with Ruth), and to have the shrewdness and capital to buy the land and title of Naomi's dead husband (which entitles him to marry Ruth).

Wealth Is Given to Support God's Work on This Earth: Barnabas

Barnabas was from the priestly line but his family had accumulated enough land that he was able to sell it and devote the proceeds to the early church when it had no assets. The profits from his real estate liquidation came at a most opportune moment and provided for the church in a time of expansion. His wealth, then, was used to aid charity. It was private, voluntary giving that from an initial investment eventually bore much fruit. One gets the feeling from the narrative in Acts that his gift might have been viewed as a life-saving rescue, without which the church might have floundered. In any event, his compassionate use of his wealth ("money" is mentioned in Acts 4:34, 37) was blessed and greatly used to support the most robust charitable institution in history during a critical period. Believers with wealth may use the material blessings of God to support God's work; and without such wealth, many of those culture-enriching ventures could not occur. To put it inversely, if the church had never had any wealth and if it had been confined to poverty only, many good things would have been left undone.

Commenting on Acts 4:32–37, Calvin noted that discord within the church was remedied not by an equalization of wealth, but by a spirit of unity. He also observed that only what was needed was sold and that the proceeds were "not equally divided" but were rather "distributed as every man had need." Amidst his commentary on these verses, he also warned against the selfishness that invents "a thousand subtle shifts to draw all things unto us by hook or by crook," and he commended the early church for selling "past their possessions."[17]

Calvin further used his comments on this passage as an occasion to reiterate his rejection of communal ownership and to warn against pride, greed, thanklessness, hypocrisy, and "even the poor themselves [who have] blame for some part of this evil."

The early church relied on the wealth of families who shared their resources. Had those wealthy families not possessed or shared their resources, the early church might have moved toward extinction. Moreover, when the wealthy tithe to their churches, large resources accrue that may be used for large charitable projects designed by trusted local leaders. Wealth given by God's

17. John Calvin, *Commentary on the Acts of the Apostles* (Grand Rapids: Baker Book House, 1979), 1:193.

providence sustained the early church, and the principle of tithing (see below) holds continuing promise.

Wealth Is Not Condemned, Selfishness Is: Ananias and Sapphira

In contrast, the next chapter of the book of Acts contains a different tale. Noting the esteem given to Barnabas, a couple apparently sought to replicate his charitable giving—albeit with significant differences. Ananias and Sapphira followed Barnabas's act of generosity (Acts 5). But whereas he gave his entire property and gave it freely—not in search of recognition—they gave theirs partially and in search of notoriety. Rather than giving in secret and in the spirit of Matthew 6:3 (do not let your left hand know what your right hand is doing), Ananias and Sapphira gave with great pomp and display. They wanted human applause instead of the divine smile, and their punishment is surely a warning about wrongly motivated charitable giving. Not only was their motive wrong, but they were deceptive in their representation of their giving, and the Holy Spirit revealed to the apostles the deception. When the apostles confronted the couple with their deception, Ananias and Sapphira both suffered a stroke of some kind, and their bodies were removed.

However, what is instructive for our purposes is that the wealth itself is not condemned. Ananias and Sapphira were not reviled for having property; they were condemned for holding some back deceptively, when they could have kept it all. This passage indicates that wealth could have, in this case, been retained entirely with no divine condemnation. The condemnation comes for both the selfishness and the misrepresentation.

Calvin commented perceptively on Acts 5:4, affirming (as he had in his remarks on the previous chapter in Acts) the right of believers to own and hold private property:

> We gather out of this that no man was enforced to sell his goods or lands. For Peter saith, that Ananias had free liberty to keep both his land and his money; because, in the second member, the field which was sold is taken for the price itself. Therefore, he should nevertheless have been counted faithful, though he had kept that which was his own. Whereby it appeareth that they are men destitute of their right wits, who say that it is not lawful for the faithful to have anything of their own.[18]

Profit Is Praised and Countenanced by the Bible: Parables

Many OT passages imply that making more wealth or adding to one's estate is a good activity. While charity is commended in the OT, wealth is not condemned in the Hebrew Scriptures. When the NT has opportunity to advocate either the redistribution of wealth or the equalization of incomes, it does not. Several of Jesus' parables allude to this.

In one well-known parable, Jesus spoke of units of currency given to servants to use or invest (Mt. 25:14–30). One servant took five units, put it to work, and yielded five more units. The second servant was given or loaned two units to be put to work in the market (which seems to have been assumed to be fairly unhindered or unregulated), and his labor and investment yielded two more units. The profits of both servants were accepted, approved, and praised by the Savior, who described the ventures positively as "well done," "good," "faithful," and worthy of the master's "happiness" (v. 21). In addition to this blessing, the faithful investors received a promise that they would be put in charge of other tasks for their master.

However, this parable contains an important contrast. Unlike the two industrious servants, a third servant garnered no increase. This servant took his master's beginning stake and neither put it to work nor even made the minimum effort to generate interest

18. Ibid., 1:197.

on it. This person offered no gain or profit to his master and was definitely criticized for this loss of potential profit. The words of Jesus make this clear. Besides calling the servant "wicked" and "lazy," the master accuses him of not trusting in the Lord's power (v. 26). Accordingly, Jesus' view of interest and profit may be partially discerned from his words in verse 27: "You should have put my money on deposit with the bankers so that when I returned I would have received it back with interest."

One of the lessons that Calvin drew from this parable was that God "does not bestow on all indiscriminately the same measure of gifts . . . but distributes them variously as he thinks proper."[19] It is clear from this and other passages that Calvin's work ethic did not include the assumption that unequal outcomes and distributions were wrong. On the contrary, Calvin recognized that, in principle, different people could be given differing amounts without violating justice. What was expected of each, however, was that "whatever gifts the Lord bestowed on us," that seed fund was to "yield some gain" (441). Calvin went so far as to term it supremely "unreasonable" that we would allow our capital to remain buried by failing to invest it, since its value "consisted in yielding fruit" (442).

When Calvin commented on Matthew 25:15, he recognized that the "master of the house," or God, "has assigned to everyone his place, and [having] bestowed on him natural gifts, gives him also this or the other injunction, employs him in the management of affairs, raises him to various offices, furnishes him with abundant means of eminent usefulness, and presents to him the opportunity" (442). He even used this parable to compare, not

19. John Calvin, *Commentary on a Harmony of the Evangelists, Matthew, Mark, and Luke* (Grand Rapids: Baker Book House, 1979), 2:441. In the section that follows, page numbers in parentheses refer to this commentary. See also 2:401. Grudem concludes from the Lucan version of this parable that "there will be inequalities of stewardship and responsibility in the age to come. This means that the idea of inequality of stewardship in itself is given by God and must be good." Wayne Grudem, *Business for the Glory of God: The Bible's Teaching on the Moral Goodness of Business* (Wheaton, IL: Crossway Books, 2003), 51.

negatively, the Christian life to "trading," in which "exchange," "barter," "merchandise," and "industry" are all approved (443). Far from denouncing increase, he stated further that the goal of the "gain" in this parable is "to yield profit" (443). At the same time, he also warned against the opposite of profitableness—sloth. He noted that the rebuke contained in this parable was reserved for those unprofitable servants who have been given gifts but then do not use them. Calvin believed that such a slothful disregard of God's gifts would lead to being "deprived of them all, and that [the slothful person's] wretched and shameful poverty would redound to the glory of the good" (444). Such slothful people "hide either the talent or the pound in the earth, because while they consult their own ease and gratifications, they refuse to submit to any uneasiness; as we see very many who, while they are privately devoted to themselves and to their own advantage, avoid all the duties of charity and have no regard to the general edification" (444). At a minimum, these individuals should deposit their money "with a banker that it might at least gain interest" (444).

Thus we see in Calvin an early advocate of the idea that wealth can be used beneficially. It is viewed as a tool. Like the Apostle Paul before him, Calvin knew that life could be full, whether under conditions of plenty or of want. Writing on Philippians 4, he warned both against the prosperity that can inflate one's sense of importance and against the depression that can color one's adversity. Calvin described the "peculiarly excellent and rare virtue" that is stronger than either prosperity or poverty in these words: "If a man knows to make use of present abundance in a sober and temperate manner with thanksgiving, prepared to part with everything whenever it may be the good pleasure of the Lord, giving also a share to his brother, according to the measure of his ability, and is also not puffed up, that man has learned to excel and to abound."[20]

20. John Calvin, *Commentaries on the Epistles to the Philippians, Colossians, and Thessalonians* (Grand Rapids: Baker Book House, 1979), 2:124.

It is not, Calvin understood, the amount that brings contentment, but the stewardship and use of what God provides. Thus, for Calvin and his followers wealth was neither automatically sinful nor a sign of unfaithfulness—any more than its absence was a sign of reprobation. Calvin did teach, however, that if a person is given much under God's providence—as Boaz and Barnabas were—he should use his wealth charitably, strategically, and faithfully.

While he never condemned profit and monetary gain, Calvin issued this stern and balanced warning on the difficulty of a wealthy man entering heaven:

> It is an evil almost common to all to trust in their riches. Yet this doctrine is highly useful to all: to the rich, that being warned of their danger they may be on their guard, and to the poor, that being satisfied with their lot they may not so eagerly desire what would bring more damage than gain. It is true, indeed, that riches do not, in their own nature, hinder us from following God, but in consequence of the depravity of the human mind it is scarcely possible for those who have a great abundance to avoid being intoxicated by them.[21]

The Scriptures consistently discuss business and economic matters without revealing an expectation that all activities will yield the same results. Paul's first letter to the Corinthians summons competitors to run the race in such a way as to get the prize (1 Cor. 9:24). Even in this illustration, all do not win a prize; but that does not make the competition unfair. The Bible does not depict every instance of plowing, sowing, farming, and investing as a success. There are failures in the Bible. So it would appear that, if not sanctioned outright, competition and the rough-and-tumble of the markets are assumed in the Scriptures to be economic realities.

21. Calvin, *Commentary on a Harmony of the Evangelists*, 2:401.

Interest or Usury?

Calvin also helped shape attitudes on another topic that had long troubled the church—the subject of lending with interest. Prior to the Reformation, a hyper-literalism in most Christian communions prevailed on this point. John Calvin had a good bit to say about the subject of interest-bearing commerce. He and the other Protestant Reformers both clarified and revolutionized how profit could be used to restrain theft. "Usury" is an old term, and it may be defined in one of two ways: (1) charging any interest at any time on a loan; or (2) charging such a high percentage of interest that it amounts to stealing or exploiting the poor.

Calvin commenced his discussion of the eighth commandment with this axiom: "Since charity is the end of the Law, we must seek the definition of theft from thence."[22] Rooting himself firmly in the golden rule, he called for each person's rights to be safeguarded and for all believers to treat others as they themselves wish to be treated. Applied to the eighth commandment, that view of the law would classify as "thieves" not only those who secretly steal property but also those who seek "gain from the loss of others [and] accumulate wealth by unlawful practices and are more devoted to their private advantage than to equity" (110–11).

Typical of Calvin's approach to applying the law, the Reformer classified many different sins under the heading of a single sin (in this case, theft), and he warned about the crafty ways that depraved individuals might seek to cheat the system, while still reducing another's property. He warned against "false pretexts," "craft," "rapine," and "cunning" (111). He also noted that God's law "pronounces all unjust means of gain to be so many thefts" (111). Moreover, employing his hermeneutic of the law—according to which "an affirmative precept . . . is connected with the prohibition"—Calvin

22. John Calvin, *Commentaries on the Four Last Books of Moses* (Grand Rapids: Baker Book House, 1979), 3:110. In the section that follows, page numbers in parentheses refer to this work.

called for stewards to utilize liberality and kindness as vaccines or antidotes for theft. In short, each person "should safely keep what he possesses, and our neighbor's advantage should be promoted no less than our own" (111). Those preliminary principles would dictate Calvin's view of usury and defend the propriety of capitalistic lending.

His commentary on Exodus 22:25 offers one of his fullest discussions of usury, as understood in the second sense above. Calvin warned that, although the goal of profit is generally sought in lending, the practice of charging exorbitant rates is wrong. He added that "we neglect the poor" if lending is restricted only to the wealthy who can repay (127). In addition, he noted that lending without interest depends on the "rule of charity" more than on the Jewish political law (127). He also recognized that Jewish law itself had permitted interest-based profit from loans to the Gentiles.[23] However, the transcultural absolute for Calvin was "that our brethren who need our assistance are not to be treated harshly" (128). Calvin was savvy enough to note that many kinds of commerce could be a "mode of extortion." Further, he wrote that "crafty men are forever inventing some little subterfuge or other to deceive God" (129).

Calvin understood the market well enough to realize that "no creditor could ever lend money without loss to himself," if opposition to usury entailed an absolute prohibition of charging interest (130). His view of human nature kept him from endorsing such a prohibition, for he perceived that borrowers would "cheat" under that scheme and use "false pretences . . . to inconvenience the creditor"(131). Creditors could be victims too, Calvin knew. His argument was that if interest were absolutely forbidden, then

23. See Deuteronomy 23:19–20. "God permitted his people to receive interest from the Gentiles since otherwise a just reciprocity would not have been preserved" (128). Calvin also noted the difference between borrowing for personal consumption and borrowing to fund a business, which is tantamount to rent.

loss of property would occur in some cases. This in itself would be a violation of the eighth commandment. Still, he interpreted Exodus 22:25 to apply only to the poor and noted that usury should be freely permitted in instances where borrowers are able to repay.

In reference to this verse, Calvin stated that not all usury was condemned. He argued:

> If the debtor has protracted the time by false pretences to the loss and inconvenience of his creditor, will it be consistent that he should reap advantage from his bad faith and broken promises? Certainly no one, I think, will deny that usury ought to be paid to the creditor in addition to the principal to compensate loss. If any rich and monied man, wishing to buy a piece of land, should borrow some part of the sum required of another, may not he who lends the money receive some part of the revenues of the farm until the principal shall be repaid? Many such cases daily occur in which, as far as equity is concerned, usury is no worse than purchase (131).

André Biéler confirms that Calvin drew an important distinction between "consumer lending on the one hand and lending to promote production on the other."[24] Following the views of Aristotle, as Roman Catholicism frequently did, an eighth-century church council in Nicea had condemned lending at interest. Various papal decrees and major theological works had similarly denounced profits that came from interest alone.[25] Calvin, however, based his seismic shift in exegesis on two principal ideas: (1) in a fallen world, it is possible for persons to borrow with ill intent, and if the lender is never repaid that constitutes theft; and

24. Biéler, *Calvin's Economic and Social Thought*, 402. On pages 400–420 Biéler provides a thorough discussion of theological views on usury.

25. Ibid. Biéler also reports that Geneva allowed a ceiling on interest at 5% in 1538. By 1546 Calvin's colleagues were publishing defenses of interest-charging as a catalyst for trade (ibid., 421).

(2) in a growing economy, if one wishes to loan money to another person who is producing or developing, that is a fruitful use of assets.[26] Freedom to invest found a theological buttress in Calvin, who showed that lending at interest could be moral after all.

André Biéler summarizes seven moral conditions that need to be present for interest to be ethical:

1. The poor should not be disadvantaged.
2. Charity should be exercised first; then if one's estate contains surplus, that may be used to loan with interest.
3. The golden rule should be invoked—i.e., one should not lend at a rate that he himself would not accept.
4. Interest should only be charged for profit-making ventures.
5. Neither common custom nor worldly standards decide the right of charging interest.
6. Benefit to the broader community is to be made possible—i.e., "one must properly determine that the contract is of service generally, rather than harmful."
7. Interest charging must be legal or permissible by the civil laws of the region.[27]

Calvin's argument, in short, was this: the ethic of love calls for us to value and protect our neighbor's property and estate. When one has the resources to pay interest, to borrow from a neighbor without interest is to use part of his wealth for one's own benefit with no repayment. For Calvin, the attitude "I win, he loses" (if no interest is charged) violated the commandment "thou shall not steal." In fact, if I win and the neighbor's children lose—by a reduction in estate—the charging of interest actually has an instrumental value to curb property loss.

Calvin continued his exposition on Exodus 22:25 to note that if one lends money to a fellow believer who is needy, money

26. Ibid., 411.
27. Ibid., 406–7.

lenders still need to keep in mind the call to compassion. These OT laws—contrary to many misapprehensions of them—call for charity. The poor should, if possible, be helped by people with resources. Similarly, if a poor person tenders his cloak as collateral, it should be returned to him for the night, for that might be all the cover he has (Ex. 22:27). Holding on to the little that a poor borrower owns—especially if he has need of it—can be abusive, if for no purpose.

Calvin consistently plied this interpretation, even calling for other OT verses to be harmonized with "the rule of charity" (132). Based on his interpretation of Exodus 22:25, for example, he boldly concluded that "usury is not now unlawful, except insofar as it contravenes equity and brotherly union" (132). Love for neighbor was Calvin's standard, and "how far it may be lawful to receive usury upon loans, the law of equity will better prescribe than any lengthened discussions" (132).

In sum, Calvin construed that a person violates the eighth commandment (whether by theft or usury) when "another is made poorer" (149). He called for restraint and encouraged believers to respect and protect the property of others. From a Calvinist perspective, therefore, the purpose of the eighth commandment is that "no one should suffer loss by us, which will be the case if we have regard to the good of our brethren" (149).

How many times have parents urged caution in their children's spending patterns by reminding them that "money doesn't grow on trees"? Similarly, we may say that "there is no free lunch." In the sense that someone always pays for the lunch, Calvin had a similar attitude toward usury. He realized that we live, in one sense, in a zero-sum world. In other words, he understood that things always have some cost, somewhere. To presume on a neighbor's goodness is to get a free lunch. It is also to rob that neighbor. Since money does not grow on trees and since there is no such thing as a free lunch, all consumers should share in the real costs for things. Calvin's new theological perspective, which allowed lending with interest, accepted the reality that handouts are never really delivered freely, that loans cannot be extended indefinitely without loss, and that money does not grow on trees. The ensuing changes in the practice of usury, as well as in the minds of men, led both to a more equitable distribution of costs and to the avoidance of theft in the form of interest-free loans. For Calvin realized that in such no-interest loans, someone was paying for the lunch after all.

Poor and Rich Are Here to Stay

One of the things that becomes clear as we proceed through this study is that Calvin understood that God has not decreed a classless society. The rich and the poor alike are here to stay. Jesus asserted that we would always have the poor among us (John 12:8).[28] Furthermore, God does not seem committed to rendering to all persons the same income or assets. The humanistic idea of radical economic equality (which dates back at least to Plato)—the idea that economic disparity is an abnormality that should disappear—finds very little if any support from the comprehensive testimony of the Scriptures. To the contrary, it may be an economic reality to accept that people will indeed have differing amounts of wealth and profit. Whether they are the result of inheritance, hard work, good fortune at certain times, or unusual seasons of blessing, the Bible does not indicate that economic classes will or should disappear.

This may be another key to accepting and appreciating God's providence, rather than envying what others have or bemoaning the fact that one has less than another. Calvin was astute to comment several times on this expectation. On one occasion, while commenting on Philippians 4:12 he exhorted believers to "accus-

28. From this verse Calvin inferred that alms given to the church's diaconate for the poor were appropriate.

tom themselves to the endurance of poverty in such a manner that it will not be grievous and burdensome to them when they come to be deprived of their riches."[29]

The realistic recognition of human depravity has much value for business theory and practice. To fail to anticipate it is to beg for multiple mistakes based on seriously flawed assumptions. Put another way, realism about one's neighbor entails the expectation that sin, crime, harm, oppression, evil, aggression, and war will occur. Businesses and individuals are prudent to factor this expectation into their plans. Calvin's picture of fallen man requires nothing short of a productive work ethic supported by accountability. This accountability needs to be undergirded by a strong legal system and the free movement of wages, labor, opportunities, and consequences. A Calvinistic grasp of man's depravity reveals the weakness inherent to the concept of socialism. Human sinfulness is incongruent with the socialistic requirements of self-sacrifice and altruism. Economic systems are advanced by the providence of God, who uses wealth, the work ethic, and the open market as a few of the visible means to advance his will upon this earth.

29. Calvin, *Commentaries on the Epistles to the Philippians, Colossians, and Thessalonians*, 2:125.

3

Redemption

If we took only part of the scriptural testimony into account, we would perhaps become needlessly pessimistic. The same might happen if we concentrated exclusively on that part of Calvin's teaching that deals with the ineradicability and pervasive effects of depravity. However, one of the wonderful and confidence-building aspects of biblical economics is that the concept of redemption is not restricted to the salvation of the soul. Following that great and overwhelming change in personality is also the truth that persons may use their wealth, businesses, and assets to do good. They may redeem assets and put them to good use. Thus, a mature understanding of the whole of Calvin's teaching on this concept will keep people from becoming unduly dour.

In fact, throughout Scripture and the best commentaries on it, one may find encouragement to view business, investing, and wealth as areas subject to human dominion and also as arenas in which God's providence, goodness, and creativity may be seen.

Redemption itself is actually a term that is used in both testaments. In the book of Ruth, for example, a kinsman-redeemer is mentioned (originally drawn from the Hebrew *Go'el*). In the Ruth narrative, the kinsman-redeemer was, in keeping with the legislation in Leviticus 25:25ff., to repurchase family land, if a relative was about to lose it. To keep the ownership within the extended family was an aspect of redemption. In OT times, redemption involved making an exchange that was equivalent or "a bit extra to avoid dishonest exchanges."[1] The concept was so important that God took that name to himself in prophetic material (e.g., Is. 43:1–3), and Calvin would also note that God employed the term Redeemer for himself in Exodus 6:6–8.

Later in the NT, the Greek word *apolutrosis* (redemption) is used several times. It is used in Romans 3:24 to refer to what Jesus Christ does through justification—he provides redemption. Also in Romans 8:23, when believers receive the full benefits of adoption, their bodies are redeemed. Christ himself becomes our redemption (1 Cor. 1:30), meaning that he is exchanged in our place; as a result of that, he calls us to be involved in the ministry of redemption (which in 2 Cor. 5:17–18 is also translated as 'reconciliation'). In the seventh verse of the opening chapter of Paul's epistle to the Ephesians, the apostle again compares salvation to redemption—originally an economic term. The meaning, however, is clearly spiritualized, referring to God's buying. The term also frequently takes on an end-times nuance, as in Ephesians 1:14. There Paul speaks of the Holy Spirit, who is a "deposit guaranteeing our inheritance until the redemption" (note the multiple economic terms in this single verse). Similarly, in Ephesians 4:30, Paul refers to God's continuous work

1. R. Laird Harris et al., *Theological Wordbook of the Old Testament* (Chicago: Moody Press, 1980), 144.

until "the day of redemption." The authors of the NT epistles seldom hesitated to use business or economic terms—subtly showing that they were hardly associated with immorality—to refer either to the salvation of the believer (Col. 1:14) or to the end of human history (see the chapter on eschatology below). So distinguished was the commercial term for redemption that Jesus himself used it in Luke 21:28 to refer to the end of the age. Toward the end of the NT, the work of Christ is presented as "having obtained eternal redemption" (Heb. 9:12), with Christ himself being the ransom price to secure our eternal inheritance (Heb. 9:15).

Other market terms are drafted into service by the NT authors as well. The Greek term meaning "to buy at the [agora] market" (*agorazo*) is employed in Acts 20:28 to describe how God purchased the entire church. This transaction was based on Christ's sacrifice. God's purchasing work is also mentioned in 2 Peter 2:1. In his commentary on another occurrence of this term in 1 Corinthians 6:20, Calvin spoke of God as paying the price of our redemption, and he alluded to two different nuances of the word "price": (1) the common meaning of cost; and (2) "a dear rate" for things "that have cost us much."[2] When thinking of God's redeeming work, he preferred the second interpretation. Commenting a little later on 1 Corinthians 7:23 and 30 (where the same term occurs), Calvin warned against an excessive preoccupation with things. Believers were to buy as though they are not addicted to material things. Still, they were not instructed "to part with their possessions"—only to behave in such a way "that their minds be not engrossed in their possessions."[3] The economic term *agorazo*, which can also be translated "to purchase," is used frequently in the final book of the Bible, for example, in Revelation 3:18, 5:9, 13:17, 14:3–4, and 18:11.

2. John Calvin, *Commentary on the Epistles of Paul the Apostle to the Corinthians* (Grand Rapids: Baker Book House, 1979), 1:220–21.

3. Ibid., 1:258.

The Pauline epistles build on this market concept and do not find fault with the notion of exchanging goods in the marketplace. God himself does not hesitate to employ overtly economic metaphors to convey some aspects of the meaning of salvation. Galatians 4:5 speaks of Christ redeeming his people at the right time, Titus 2:14 depicts Christ as one who redeems his people from wickedness, Galatians 3:13 speaks of Christ "redeeming us from the curse of the law," and 1 Peter 1:18 offers the following assurance: "For you know that it was not with perishable things such as silver or gold that you were redeemed ... but with the precious blood of Christ." Each of these passages employs economic terminology, thus lending validity to the practices of commerce and business.

With the understanding that the concept of redemption itself has economic nuances and with the further insight that creation allows for development and multiplication, the discussions below consider how wealth may be used positively, redemptively, and profitably. Before turning to those discussions, however, we should note two other important prerequisites: (1) the need for liberty, as Calvin properly defined it; and (2) the need for a long-range horizon to sustain believers during the trials and troughs of this life.

Christian Freedom

To make business engines run smoothly, Calvinism has historically also expected the presence of a particularly crucial condition—personal freedom. The freedom that Calvinism enhanced in the marketplace also sought to yield the following for investors, workers, and owners:

- A free market where goods could be exchanged directly with potential purchasers and where red tape and interference were minimized

- Honest currency, which facilitated the free exchange of goods
- Stability, such that future ventures could be planned and pursued
- Profit, which incentivized others to participate in markets
- A legal environment in which entrepreneurs were neither punished nor subjected to recriminations for developing their products
- Personal ownership of businesses
- Access to necessary natural resources

Underlying these features was a personal freedom that allowed an owner—whether of a field, or of a factory, or of intellectual property—to cultivate his property as he saw fit.

As we have already had occasion to note, many economic realities are not matters of business alone. Instead, they are matters of morality or value. In this instance, the freedom that is needed to sustain the markets is buttressed by John Calvin's explanation of Christian freedom. Despite the frequent identification of him with a crippling kind of determinism, Calvin actually furthered the human understanding of liberty. He did so precisely against the backdrop of medieval and Catholic thought. In his thinking, Christian freedom could best be understood in contrast to the law.

John Calvin lived in a day when the freedoms most of us cherish were uncommon. In two different spheres, he was challenged to work out an enduring view of liberty. First, in the civil sphere, he lived in a society that had until recently known only monarchies. There was no long history of liberty. Before Calvin's time, most European cities were under the rule of a king, and citizens had few civil liberties. Calvin's writings would help lay the foundation for the modern tradition of civil liberty. The second form of authoritarianism that he inherited was in the sphere of church government. Prior to the Reformation, under the dominance of the Roman church, believers were only granted liberties as the church recognized them. These liberties were, at times, few and far between. As such, the idea that a Christian could be truly free and at liberty to serve his own conscience was a new concept that Calvin aided substantially by his teaching.

In book 3 of the *Institutes,* he took up this subject of Christian liberty, and his insights are still unsurpassed today. To begin with, a key distinction must be introduced from the conclusion of chapter 19 of that book. Calvin spoke of two species of liberty, civil and spiritual (*Institutes,* 3.19.15). In the same fashion, he taught that human government is twofold: spiritual government is internal and trains the conscience in matters of piety and worship, while civil government refers to external matters. The church is to teach and handle the spiritual order, and political rulers are to manage affairs relating to the civil order. Calvin suggested that if we pay attention to this distinction, "we will not erroneously transfer the doctrine of the gospel concerning spiritual liberty to civil order." This division of labor would become an essential building block of stable modern societies; it would also supply ample protection for proper freedom.

With that in mind, it should be clearer that both church and state have valuable roles to play in human life. However, they should not interfere with the proper jurisdiction of each other; God intended them to operate in separate spheres.

As Calvin began his groundbreaking chapter on Christian liberty, he first sought to explain why it was so important. He argued that it was necessary for people to understand this, even if only on an elementary level, lest they have their consciences burdened by the threat of endless rules and stifling captivity. Indeed, he asserted, this topic was a "proper appendix to justification," which is to say that even as one is justified by God alone, so one experiences liberty only as a consequence of following God alone. Thus, from the outset, Calvin's view of liberty should be distinguished from any humanistic view of liberty.

He believed that liberty was a gift, and one that should be used as God designed it.

For Calvin this spiritual or Christian liberty comprised three parts. First, believers should have their consciences free in regard to the law of God. Having been justified by God and freed from the demands of the law, believers should learn to look to the mercy of God continually and to turn away from any thought of saving themselves by works. Not that the law was unimportant to Calvin, but in terms of conscience he understood that believers must find their assurance in Christ, not in any ostensibly self-perfecting acts of legal obedience. Freedom of conscience was as important to Calvin as civil liberty, and it began with a right understanding of justification.

The second part of Christian liberty was that believers were to obey the law from a different motive. Being regenerated by God, they should "voluntarily obey the will of God" (3.19.4). Instead of obeying out of a servile fear, believers should act gratefully in response to the love of God, from which true liberty flows. This also meant the end of various perfectionist schemes. Calvin's followers were to be perfect in Christ, not in themselves. That also implied the end of legalism.

The third part of Christian liberty was that believers were not obligated to observe external rituals only or to keep the ceremonial customs of the Old Testament. Instead, Christians were permitted either to use ceremonies as helpful or to omit them, as long as they did not seek to overturn the moral law. Accordingly, there were many things in life that Calvin classified as "indifferent." To fail to make that distinction would, he thought, mean "no end of superstition" (3.19.7). God's Word was the authority for believers, but many things in life had to be decided in terms of principles and deduction. Believers were free to use the good things that God had created. They were only to use them as he had designed them and for his glory. As long as that was done, liberty was a good rule of thumb. The goal of this liberty was to "give peace to trembling consciences" (3.19.9). Of course, Calvin is not rightly understood as encouraging libertinism or using liberty as a "cloak for lust."

To further bolster his interpretation, Calvin also offered a hierarchy of norms to help people make decisions. Matters of Christian liberty had to be subjected to the law of charity (3.19.13). In other words, Christians must sometimes voluntarily restrict themselves so that they do not cause others to stumble. Thus, liberty is not absolute in Calvin's scheme. It is good and a gift from God, but even liberty must be kept in perspective. Moreover, just as the law of liberty must be subject to the law of charity, so also the law of love "must in its turn be subordinate to the purity of faith." Thus, for Calvin a finely nuanced view of liberty and ethics valued the purity of the revealed faith to the utmost. Following that, the rule of charity trumped, and after that came Christian liberty.

Keeping things in that delicate balance—a balance that was a signature of Calvinism, I might add—would also help in periods of reform. An incremental approach to reform is consistent with this theory. Indeed, Calvin did not condone "the intemperance of those who do every thing tumultuously, and would rather burst through every restraint at once than proceed step by step" (3.19.13). Change could come slowly and steadily in his opinion, and he wanted neither Christian liberty, nor love, nor the purity of the faith to be sacrificed in the process. "We are not at liberty to deviate one nail's breadth from the command of God," wrote Calvin (3.19.13). And with these words he set a proper boundary for liberty, even as he stayed true to his liberating principle that "consciences were exempted from human authority" whenever that authority disagreed with the will of God.

This view of liberty, wherever it spread, gave citizens confidence and protections. Within a century, the American colonies would exhibit this Calvinistic distinctive. Not incidentally one of America's first law codes was named the Massachusetts "Body of Liberties." So close were law and liberty that Calvin's disciples could call a law code a table of liberties. The reason was that a proper understanding of liberty is essential for any successful venture, whether it is commercial, civic, or religious. In the persecution of Protestants in Paris, Calvin had seen the effects of oppression. He'd seen the same effects in the eyes of the many Roman Catholic refugees who arrived so regularly at Geneva's walls. Certainly his view of liberty was framed in reference to what he had witnessed. However, it is important to note both that his teaching was founded upon God's Word and that he presented it in a fashion that cautioned against the misuse of Christian freedom.

Later views of liberty were influenced by Calvin's groundbreaking ideas. Adam Smith in *The Wealth of Nations* advocated "natural liberty," which he viewed as the freedom to work, invest, or act apart from any hindrance by the state. Smith sounded like a disciple of Calvin when he wrote: "To prohibit a great people ... from making all that they can of every part of their own produce, or from employing their stock and industry in the way that they judge most advantageous to themselves, is a manifest violation of the most sacred rights of mankind."[4] One of history's finest capitalist thinkers, Smith also concluded that, according to the principles of natural liberty, "every man, as long as he does not violate the laws of justice, is left perfectly free to pursue his own interest his own way, and to bring both his industry and capital into competition with those of any other man or order of men."[5] Calvin would have uttered a hearty amen. However, he also taught that liberty was not given by God to encourage sloth or preoccupation with this world.

4. Quoted in Mark Skousen, *The Big Three in Economics: Adam Smith, Karl Marx, and John Maynard Keynes* (Armonk, NY: M. E. Sharpe, 2007), 10.

5. Quoted in ibid., 18.

n against Selfishness and Shortsightedness

n began a widely read section of his greatest work by reminding his readers that one of the objects of God's saving power is to bring the ethics of believers into accord with the holiness of God (*Institutes,* 3.6.1). He also affirmed that one of the keys to life is the self-denial that can only come if a person realizes that he and all his abilities are owned by God. Calvin said that one "should not speak, design, or act without a view to God's glory. . . . We are not our own; therefore, neither is our reason or will to rule our acts and counsels" (3.7.1). That kind of trust in God necessarily calls for abandonment of self. From a Calvinist perspective the first step of Christian maturity involves replacing selfishness and natural impulses with a renewed mind that follows God in obedience. The "laying aside of private regard" means that we are not our own persons but are called to serve God. When one lives and leads this way—when one learns "to look to God in everything"—one is also "diverted from all vain thoughts" (3.7.2).

Once this attitude lodges itself in our habits, it "leaves no place for pride, show, or ostentation." On the other hand, Calvin realized that when people pursue selfishness first, they normally hit their target, and the result is vice or "a depraved longing for applause."

Calvin also warned against collecting "all those frivolities which seem conducive to luxury and splendor" (3.7.8). He knew that when we focus on these frivolities our minds become restless and unfocused. Thus, a person should not hope for "any kind of prosperity apart from the blessing of God" (3.7.8). Rather, one must entrust all outcomes to the true Sovereign, who controls all and in whose goodness we should love to depend.

Calvin realized that his disciples needed to trust less in their own will and more in God's. Nothing, he wrote, whether it was poverty or exile (and he was an expert on that) can happen except by the will and providence of God (3.8.11). If one remembered that, one would be led to meditate more on the future. That was, and remains, a very helpful exercise for believers facing tribulation in this life.

He also warned against the dazzling "glare of wealth, power, and honors," and he urged us to be sensitive to the vanity of the present life (3.9.1). Consistency would never be achieved otherwise. "For," Calvin wrote, "we must hold that our mind never rises seriously to desire and aspire after the future, until it has learned to despise the present life" (3.9.1). We should not, in other words, be so infatuated with this life that we ignore eternity.

However, we must be careful to take Calvin's words "despise the present life" in the full context of his thought. There was a balance to be found, which involved both distrusting this life and also being thankful for it. The principle he advocated was this: we should use the gifts and things of this life for the purpose that "their author made and destined them" (3.10.1). We should neither overvalue nor undervalue what God gives. The phrase "to use this world as if he used it not" summarizes the proper attitude; by bearing it in mind believers can avoid overindulgence and vice. "Luxury," Calvin knew, can cause "great carelessness as to virtue. Those who are much occupied with the care of the body usually give little care to the soul" (3.10.4). Contentment, then, has always been a great indicator of the spirit of Calvinism.

Commenting elsewhere on Luke 10:42, Calvin wisely expressed his sentiments this way: "Whatever believers may undertake to do, and in whatever employments they may engage, there is one object to which everything ought to be referred. In a word, we do but wander to no purpose, if we do not direct all our actions to a fixed object." Few mystics or devotional speakers will ever muster the depth of spirituality present in this paragon of Christian living. No reader of these words can justly vilify Calvin as a heartless rationalist.

He knew that man does not live by bread alone. There is an eternity ahead, and that fact informed all that Calvin did and thought. Calvin's biblical and economic conclusions call for the wealthy to give generously. Just as OT law required unharvested grain to be left for gleaners, so Calvin called the rich to make provisions for the poor among them. The wealthy are called to be rich in good deeds. John Schneider in *The Good of Affluence* mentions numerous examples, including calling for all persons but especially for those who are in the best financial position to act mercifully. For all men are elected to their economic status. Each has a calling to an occupation and is encouraged to work diligently. John Wesley in his sermon entitled "The Use of Money" aptly summarizes the sentiment in these words: "Having, first gained all you can, and, secondly saved all you can, then give all you can."[6]

Calvin's writings on redemption and stewardship would lead to such views, which spread extensively as colonization developed and modern society unfolded. With these philosophical building blocks in place, we may now appreciate Calvin's views on the use of private property.

Stewardship and Private Property

As already noted in several places, private ownership of property is supported throughout the Bible. Early in the book of Genesis, various believers were awarded tracts of land, engaged in productive ventures, passed on their wealth within the family, and had unrestricted use of private property. Nowhere does the OT imply that property should be surrendered to the collective. The earliest Hebrew patriarchs used their wealth to provide for many generations, and while government is sometimes depicted as taking measures to stave off disaster (e.g., during the extreme famine described in Genesis 41–42), its right to confiscate private property is never taught.

6. John Wesley, "Sermon 50: The Use of Money," in *The Works of the Reverend John Wesley, A.M.*, 1:446; also posted at: http://new.gbgm-umc.org/umhistory/wesley/sermons/50/.

Furthermore, as Calvin and many others have seen, the eighth commandment—"thou shall not steal"— both sanctions and explicitly protects the private ownership of property, estates, and businesses.

Elsewhere in the OT, the callous rich are rebuked (Prov. 21:13), and those who are insensitive to the valid needs of the responsible poor are told that to hate the unfortunate is akin to despising their Maker (Prov. 22:2). What is criticized consistently, however, is not the providential blessing of wealth but the uncharitable use or abuse of it. What drives the Jubilee statutes in Leviticus 25 is the concern to care for the poor and not have them lose their land permanently.

It is quite clear that the strongest consensus of Christian teaching on this subject supports the freedom to hold private property. The prophetic expectation, which is nowhere condemned, was that each person would one day dwell in his own lodging and own his own property (Mic. 4:4).

As one peruses the pages of the NT, it also becomes clear that Jesus did not call for his followers, except for a few during his earthly ministry, to turn over their property to a centralized unit. Nor did he intend to have them absent themselves from all business, enterprise, and productivity.

The call to stewardship is equally clear. Christ uses the term *oikonomos* for steward, and this is picked up elsewhere in the NT. The term is used frequently in the parables of Jesus (Lk. 12:42; 16:1–2). It also appears in Romans 16:23 in reference to a Roman comptroller. Calvin knew well that when Paul speaks of a "trust" (1 Cor. 4:1–2), he is using—and implicitly embracing— an economic concept to describe Christian stewardship. Later in that same epistle (1 Cor. 9:17), the ministry itself is described in fiduciary terms, as "discharging the trust committed" to Paul. In Galatians 4, Paul speaks at length about a trust, in which a child awaits the full assumption of his assets. In radical distinction from the Marxist view, Paul never denounces the concept of a financial trust. On the contrary, he uses it as a metaphor for the waiting period until Christ the Messiah returns (Gal. 4:2–4). The trust described by Paul is administered by guardians or trustees, much like modern instruments. Toward the end of Paul's ministry, he would call young Timothy to follow him and to "guard the good deposit that we entrusted to you—guard it with the help of the Holy Spirit who lives in us" (2 Tim. 1:14).[7]

The term for economics, or an orderly arrangement of possessions, is commended by its use in Ephesians 1:10, and in Ephesians 3:2 it is used of Paul's ministry. Colossians 1:25 also uses this term to refer to apostolic service, and the apostle Peter thought it was good economics for "each one [to] use whatever gift he has received to serve others" (1 Pet. 4:10). Believers have different gifts and abilities, but all are to be used to serve.

When we catch this vision and apply these terms to our own lives and estates, it becomes even clearer that we are to work, save, invest, and prepare for the future. The end goal is to improve one's estate; the process of achieving the goal is a form of redemption that entails a call to stewardship. Business, honest profit, and economics are far from evil or immoral as the NT uses these terms.

As stewards, wise investors seek return, profit, enhancement, or a higher net yield. Not only is property (the font of such increases) acceptable in general, but growth in assets (or profit) is also a goal—a goal that God praises, not denounces. The desire to serve the Master, coupled with the teaching in various epistles and parables, leads one to aspire for a net increase on the property and assets that the providential Lord has loaned to his servants. Conversely, his servants do not wish to diminish the Lord's seed fund; nor do they wish to leave it in a condition of stasis. Gain is sought and not rebuked.

7. Paul's instructions to Timothy also assume that hardworking farmers deserve to profit from the crops (2 Tim. 2:6), that large houses filled with nice articles exist (2 Tim. 2:20), and that a crown of righteousness (2 Tim. 4:8) is not a sign of evil.

Redemption and gain, thus, seem to be profoundly good and desirable. Awareness of that forms certain expectations among servants.

Wealth as an Overflow of Thanksgiving and Praise for Salvation

Servants who view themselves as stewards or managers of God's resources in search of lawful gain and true benefit will also use their wealth, benefits, and property for the good of others and as tributes to God's blessings.

The spirit of Calvinism, once imbibed, has led many to view wealth as a providential lever, given by God for the purpose of benefiting others. Accordingly, a distinctive view of charity (see below) arose among early Calvinists. In keeping with this view, successful entrepreneurs were expected to give back. This type of redemption was another facet of the faith that stirred the industry of Geneva in the sixteenth century.

The opposite view endorses something akin to hoarding. If an individual views himself (or his family) as the end-all of life, then wealth may accrue only in a self-interested fashion. However, if an individual feels a strong calling with regard to blessing and responsibility to be charitable, then prosperity can be turned to the benefit of others. Such charity, moreover, is not so much a voucher for future payment as it is a token of gratitude, offered in the realization that one only has what God wishes to give and that, when God gives abundantly, the gift is a mechanism for caring for the needs around us. Rather than instilling a Silas Marner complex, the spirit of Calvinism calls those who profit to use their material blessing to bless the church, the community, and those who are truly needy. The Calvinist investor will keep both multiplication and charity in mind.

There is a fine balance here—one we may illustrate by an example showing that believers may be pious and well paid at the same time. In the late 1990s a Christian baseball pitcher was conflicted about the size of his contract, because of its overwhelming value. He privately discussed the guilt he felt with a leading Calvinist minister, who admonished the pitcher that had he failed to get the highest value for his work, he was potentially guilty of sin. The justification for the minister's counsel was that all men are given talents and abilities and are called to pursue them so that they can make as much as possible (within the law), so that they can in turn save and give frequently. With regard to biblical economics, anything that impedes or reduces the three key activities of earning, saving, and giving is an inefficiency. Calvin would have been proud of the pastor's advice.

In fact, according to Max Weber, one Calvinist pastor who lived about a century after Calvin, Richard Baxter, taught similarly:

> If God shows you the way . . . on which you may legally earn more, without injuring your soul and that of others, and you refuse to choose the lesser profitable way; then you obliterate one of the objectives of your calling, you refuse to be a steward of God and to accept his gifts for the possibility to use them for him, if and when he wishes so. Of course, not for the pleasure of the flesh or for sin should you work, but to get richer in the name of God.[8]

Investment as a Calling of Redemption

Although seldom thought of in these terms, investment may even be seen as a calling of redemption. Just as Christ's disciples are summoned to go into all the world and increase the church (Mt. 28:18–20), so they are also called to take what he gives by

8. Quoted in Sergey N. Bulgakov, "The National Economy and the Religious Personality," *Journal of Markets and Morality* 11, no. 1 (Spring 2008): 171. (Orig. pub. 1909.)

his providence and seek to increase it, whether it be church ministry or private property. Ideally, of course, both of those should go together.

Investment is an exercise in taking what God provides and redeeming it to become better. That is what Adam was charged to do before the fall from Eden and that is what faithful believers have done for centuries. Investment, which is the taking of a stake and seeking to increase it, draws upon the propensity for creativity and the goal to be faithful stewards. Just as the steward is responsible to enhance (as well as preserve) his master's estate, so the investor takes what he is given and redeems it for even more. Christian investors are called not only to "be fruitful and multiply," but also to use a greater asset base for the glory of the Lord. Such investing may help believers provide for their own families and for others in their community, all without outside help or hindrance.

Investors have a goal to increase their estate; and this is a virtue. Such increase allows for numerous benefits, among them the ability to: hire more workers (who might not otherwise be employed), build educational and cultural centers, establish endowments for future spiritual needs, and provide security for a family or for future generations. All of these activities involve taking what exists in an original state and redeeming or improving it.

When a person takes earnings or profits and then seeks to increase them, a multiplication of the original is possible. This both fulfills the dominion mandate and provides greater potential for charity. To put it simply: if a person earns a net $100,000 per year from investments and later tithes on that income or gives additional charity above that, charities would receive at least $10,000 per year; however, if a person earns a net $1,000,000 a year from investments and then tithes on that or gives additional charity above that, charities would receive at least $100,000 per year. Ask any charity which it prefers for and from its donors. Thus seen, greater material prosperity will result in more dollars available for charity. And if more dollars are available, more charitable activities may be funded from greater amounts.

One possible motivation for good investing, then, is to earn more charitable dollars to care for others. However, we should reiterate that if returns on investment are either hoarded or selfishly consumed, then the conditions above are not met and charity will not increase. Faithfulness to biblical standards of giving must be paired with good investment, if charity is to be multiplied along with returns. Hence, not only is personal investment a virtue in Scripture but it also provides a mechanism for charity. As John Stapleford writes, "Through investments wealth allows for the improvement in the material well-being of all persons by facilitating economic growth. Through charity, wealth allows for the relief of poverty."[9]

In terms of useable charitable dollars, societies that have less government intrusion, less taxation, growing economies, and freer markets customarily generate more assets for charity. While Calvin did not, of course, comment specifically on macroeconomic issues like this, he did frequently speak of the need to treat one's neighbor with charity. He seemed cognizant of both the opportunities and the responsibilities for members of a free society to seek the welfare of their neighbors.

The spirit of Calvinism, if properly applied, continues to hold great promise for addressing a wide range of charitable needs. One also might be helped in that pursuit by having a comprehensive view of charity. Again, the Genevan Reformer will aid our understanding.

Charity and the Law

Charity should guide the use of a believer's assets. Calvin, though frequently misunderstood, actually had much to say about charity

9. John E. Stapleford, *Bulls, Bears & Golden Calves: Applying Christian Ethics in Economics* (Downers Grove, IL: InterVarsity Press, 2002), 25.

and the charitable use of a Christian's assets. We have seen how, for Calvin, Christian liberty was subordinate to the law of charity. We have concluded from this that liberty was not an absolute for Calvin. Indeed, he once noted that while freedom is more advantageous than servitude, nevertheless "liberty of the spirit is greatly preferable to the liberty of the flesh."[10] With this in mind, we can now examine Calvin's treatment of charity as it relates to the law.

Calvin honored the notion that the Ten Commandments (the moral law) contains two different sets, or tables, of commandments. The first table includes the first four commandments, which apply to God, while the second table includes the last six commandments, which apply to our fellow man. According to Calvin, this arrangement provides a "complete rule of righteousness," insofar as believers are instructed in both the duties of religion and the duties of charity (*Institutes*, 2.8.11). If ever conflicted, the believer was instructed by Calvin to honor the first table over the second. That instruction would eventually become a pillar supporting a just resistance to an evil magistrate, if he commanded disobeying God.

Moreover, Calvin perceived that the aim of law is charity and that the fruit of obedience is purity of conscience. He concluded his treatise on the use of the law by affirming that this right understanding of law "searches out and finds in all its precepts all the duties of piety and charity," and he warned against any who would "merely search for dry and meager elements, as if [the law] taught the will of God only by halves" (2.8.51).

So, charity, as will be shown in more detail when we examine his teaching on property ownership, factors heavily in Calvin's thought. Moreover, for Calvin some variables ranked above others, providing certain hierarchies.

In book 2 of his *Institutes*, Calvin provided an exposition of the eighth commandment ("you shall not steal") that serves as one

10. Calvin, *Commentary on the Epistles to the Corinthians*, 1:250.

of his primary teachings on wealth, property, and use of assets. He began his treatment of the commandment with a general condemnation of injustice as an "abomination to God." That being the case, an ethical responsibility is placed to render to each man what belongs to him. Theft, thus, is taking away from one what belongs to him. An attitude is incumbent as well: "We are forbidden to pant after the possessions of others" (2.8.45). So from the outset Calvin railed against an acquisitiveness that lusted after others' possessions. Conversely, Calvin believed that this law carried with it an implication that each person is to "strive faithfully to help every man keep his own possessions" (2.8.45).

Calvin emphasized that what each person possesses comes not merely by chance but by the distribution of God's providence. As a result, it should be construed as an "evil device" to deprive someone—in any manner—of the possessions that God has assigned to him to use. That involves tampering with God's wise plan. Calvin wisely noted that there are numerous kinds of theft (2.8.45), and that each is an assault on providentially supplied property. He observed that some thefts occur by violence, while others stem from fraudulent deceit. Yet a third kind of theft occurs when a man's property is taken from him by legal means. He categorically included under theft—i.e., as violations of the eighth commandment—"all those arts whereby we acquire the possessions and money of our neighbors." Even if our neighbor's property is acquired through court action, Calvin noted that God is not fooled: "For he sees the intricate deceptions with which a crafty man sets out to snare one of simpler mind, until he at last draws him into his nets" (2.8.45).

Exhibiting a sensitivity that may surprise many, Calvin warned both against the "hard and inhuman laws" that allow powerful oppressors to seize another's property and against the wily "lures" that catch the unwary in theft. Even though some of these escape human discernment, Calvin classified as theft of property any method that removes part of one's providential estate to another without proper exchange or recompense. Injustice, he noted, occurs not only in terms of money or merchandise, but also when a neighbor's property is taken, since we carry an obligation to protect each other's property. That obligation to increase others' property is a distinctive contribution of Calvin, and the degree to which he applied the concept is seen from his words below:

> If a shiftless steward or overseer devours his master's substance and fails to attend to household business; if he either unjustly spends or wantonly wastes the properties entrusted to him; if the servant mocks his master; if he divulges secrets; if in any way he betrays his life or goods; if the master, on the other hand, savagely harasses his household—all these are deemed theft in God's sight. (2.8.46)

With these things forbidden by the eighth commandment, Calvin further considered obedience to the commandment to include contentment with one's lot in life—note how obedience begins internally—and a zealous commitment to make gains honestly and lawfully (2.8.46). Accumulation of wealth through injustice is theft, argued Calvin, because it entails increasing one's wealth by depriving one's neighbor of his goods. He warned against gaining by the blood of others, by foul means, and by avarice. He also warned against seeking gain in order to satisfy prodigality. In essence, he called for those seeking gain to have an eye toward other persons. Calvinists have an important ethical burden, namely, to constantly help our neighbor keep and improve his property "in so far as we can" (2.8.46). This burden may require Christians in business to give something up when they are dealing with faithless men. But in any case, when blessed with abundant returns, the Calvinist investor has always been called to assist others with their needs.

With respect to civil society, Calvin emphasized that debtors are to pay their debts and that politicians are to keep the peace and ensure order. Churches and parents are to "nourish, govern, and teach" their children in these matters, and employees are to work diligently for their employers. Each person has a "rank and station" (2.8.46), and all men are to "strive to protect and promote the well-being and interests of others" (2.8.46).

While explaining the eighth commandment, therefore, Calvin not only showed the highest respect for property, but also extended that respect to the property of others. Of course, one finds nothing in Calvin in support of socialism or state-controlled property.

Calvin on Property and Business Ethics: Exodus 21–24

Exodus 21–24 provides commentary on and amplification of God's intention for giving the law on Mount Sinai (Ex. 20:1–17). The Lord in these chapters, like a merciful parent, takes the Ten Commandments and expands them; he takes time to apply them, lest the original and subsequent audiences should miss the message. He provides instructions as a long-suffering parent might give rules to a group of teenagers, who very soon act as though they don't know what the parent means. They rapidly begin to look for loopholes. They may even take the letter of what a parent has said and ignore the spirit of the law.

Calvin's view of business and property matters will be most clearly detected in his comments on an amplification of the eighth commandment. Other glosses from his commentary in this section will also, however, delineate his views further. Calvin, in a format that is somewhat sophisticated compared to most commentaries, provided a harmonization of the pentateuchal commentary by collating verses from Exodus, Leviticus, Numbers, and Deuteronomy as they amplify each of the commandments.

Exodus 21:2–11 contains laws applying to Hebrew servants and workers. This is largely an amplification of property laws. Not surprisingly, Calvin did not advocate slavery. Neither Calvin nor Scripture treats persons, slaves or otherwise, as subhuman or lacking the image of God. Abuse or murder of slaves was wrong and prohibited by the sixth commandment. However, this and other OT passages do allude to a pattern of working relationships that allowed servitude in ancient Israel. No passage from the Hebrew Scriptures later outlaws slavery. It was an accepted practice. What the Bible does, however, is to show how God wanted humane treatment, and this issue rests at the intersection of business and property matters.

There was a Sabbath pattern to servitude in ancient Israel. The Lord did not want Hebrew slaves to be forced into slavery indefinitely. A person could buy a Hebrew for up to six years but in the seventh year the worker was to be freed (Ex. 21:2). Verse 3 of this passage also illustrates how God wanted the society to respect the family. If the indentured servant came alone (even if he married during the six-year period), then he would leave alone. If he came with a wife, then the two would be freed together.

According to the fourth verse, however, if his master provided a wife for the indentured servant and she bore children, then the wife and children could remain with the owner. Why? Because each worker was valuable and essential to the estate. This case law was given to prevent the following scenario: Suppose a worker became a temporary slave and married a girl. If he took her when freed, he would take something of value/earning potential away from the owner. Of course, if he brought his own wife with him and left in the seventh year, he would not take away something that the owner had originally possessed. But if the worker came in, took an asset, and then claimed "we're family," the owner would be out of an asset. This casuistry illustrated how loss of property, even if a human resource, could decrease one's assets.

Obviously, the commandment "you shall not steal" is not only about physical property but also about things that have value and earning potential. God, in his law, knew that human beings would look for and quickly find loopholes—we are ingenious about finding ways to sin—so the Lord gave some protection to those who needed it. God seems serious about fairness to those who have farms, vineyards, and flocks. To allow workers to be taken away would hurt the farmers, vintners, and shepherds. So while the concept of Hebrew servitude may be foreign to our working relationships, please note God's intention to provide fairness to those who owned as well as to those who worked. Early on, at least, God is not a practicing socialist.

Similarly, if an ancient Hebrew bought a woman for his son, then once married, she was no longer under slave laws but was to be viewed as a daughter—as part of the family (Ex. 21:9). And her rights to care, including food and clothing, were permanent. They could not be cancelled even if a man took other wives. The principle that is being supported here is as follows: Don't diminish an estate but, at the same time, do treat people fairly, whether they work for you or are part of your family. Because the owner benefited from their work, he had an obligation to care for workers. It was a two-way street. As Exodus 21:11 puts it, "if the owner does not provide" a woman with her marital rights, then the contract is nullified and she "is to go free without any payment." Calvin understood Moses to be revealing that there are mutual burdens in the marketplace.

All of these laws and guidelines were given by the Lord in order to protect workers and owners. Calvin understood the divine law or the moral law as anticipating depravity and treated these OT precepts as moral strictures against the theft of property. His presupposition of human depravity, which has a tendency to seek to circumvent the law, led him to many other conclusions, one of which was his groundbreaking view of usury.

The next chapter of Exodus deals with the eighth commandment in more detail. Here the commandment "you shall not steal" is taken to mean that physical property is under private ownership and must be protected. Indeed, Exodus 22 shows how the Lord wisely protects personal property by a series of fines.[11]

The first verse of Exodus 22 treats the instance of a man who steals a farm animal and either slaughters it for personal consumption or sells it for profit. Since he has taken someone else's property, he must pay back five times the amount stolen, certainly a stiff penalty. Note that this penalty is not one-for-one, as in accidents or liability cases (e.g., habitual goring). In a case of theft, the thief must repay five times the amount he stole. The penalty is intended not only to repay the owner, but also to deter the thief from future crimes.

The second verse deals with the case of a thief who is caught breaking in at night and is struck and dies. The case is classified as legitimate self-defense, not intentional murder, and the defender is not deserving of the death penalty. God does not mind if we protect our property. However, the third verse provides fair balance: if the home invasion occurs in daylight, then the owner could be charged with a capital crime. He can, in other words, use lesser measures and avoid killing the thief.

What if the thief pleads bankruptcy or claims an inability to pay? The end of verse 3 teaches that he must make restitution; and if he cannot, he must pay with his own service—he will be sold into slavery. See how God closes and anticipates so many loopholes!

Verse 4 has a slightly different case and sentence. If a stolen animal is found alive in a thief's possession, then the animal is returned to the owner and the thief has to pay double the cost of the animal. Thus, the property is restored and a 200% damage claim is assessed. Calvin and his followers saw in these statutes additional support for private property ownership.

11. Note that not all offenses were capital offenses and that graded punishments were made to fit the crime.

There are very many ways to steal, too. Exodus 22:5 envisions two neighboring farms. If cattle or sheep stray from their field and graze on a neighbor's land, then the owner of the animals must repay "from the best of his own field or vineyard." Not the fringe grass but the best of the offending neighbor's field is to be confiscated.

According to the sixth verse, if a fire breaks out and destroys a neighbor's grain, the one who started the fire must make restitution. God holds us responsible and does not want our neighbors to suffer as a result of our irresponsibility. If harm is done, someone has to make it up. That, God knew, is how life works.

Note the sophistication of verses 7 through 9. This was not an unenlightened society. If a person places some goods with a neighbor for safekeeping, and a thief steals the goods, then once the thief is caught he must pay back double. Notice again the deterrent nature of the legislation.

However, what is to keep an owner from faking such a loss? After all, a lot of money can be made off of fraud. If the thief is never found, the safekeeping neighbor must appear before the judges to determine whether a theft has actually occurred or the holder of goods is profiting (Ex. 22:8). This is fairness, and God knew that human beings would take from each other if proper legislation were not in place.

Moreover, as verse 9 shows, in any claim of illegal possession, both parties must appear before judges. This assumes an early legal system. And when the trial is over the guilty person must repay double. That was the deterrent.

Verse 10 provides a case in which an animal is entrusted for safekeeping to a neighbor. If the animal dies, is injured, or disappears, the two parties must appear before the Lord (via judges) and swear by oath that "the neighbor did not lay hands on the other person's property" (Ex. 22:11). In this case, a man's word is his bond; and his oath must be accepted. If he is later found to be untruthful, other consequences will follow.

However, if it is determined that the animal was stolen, the thief must make restitution. In the case of a genuine accident, the remains are to be presented as evidence, and the neighbor will not be required to make restitution (Ex. 22:12–13).

Finally, according to verse 14, if a neighbor borrows an animal and it is injured or dies during the time of loan, the neighbor must repay the owner. Again, the owner suffers harm by the loss, so the borrower is held responsible. All of these and other similar verses unite to form the Calvinistic (and capitalistic) view of free markets and private ownership. Calvin's commentaries on this subject consistently support these ideas and do not undermine the major aspects of private property ownership.

A Pattern of Charity

With profit and ownership also comes responsibility for those in need. For Calvinists, charity became a widespread activity. It did not necessarily begin with and follow the same patterns of charity that one may associate with giving to the poor or downcast today. Charity in the spirit of Calvin is wide-ranging and begins with personal responsibility and giving to the church.

Tithing

Tithing to the church was both a personal discipline and a form of charity. With the onset of the Reformation, churches began to be supported more by their members than by state largesse. Although Calvin's Genevan church inherited prime property (the entire parish precincts were declared to be Reformation property when the citizens voted to support the evangelical religion in 1536), the ongoing support and work of that and other Protestant churches rested largely with the generosity of its membership.

Calvin realized that one of the essential aspects of wealth was for regular, charitable giving to be directed to one's church, which would then care for many spiritual and social needs. In reference to Abraham's tithing to Melchizedek (Genesis 14:20), Calvin asserted that the act was not done "wrongfully or rashly." Rather, Calvin saw tithing as a practice commanded by God, and he viewed Abraham's act as an early example of the kind of giving that is an honor to God and a useful tool for the ministries of the priesthood.

Elsewhere, in his commentary on the Hebrew prophet Malachi, Calvin made it clear that tithing is essential and should be treated as a routine part of financial management. He called the practice of retaining some of the tithe for personal use "fraud" and warned that "avarice so ruled among [the people of Malachi's day] that every one, bent on their own profit, neglected the temple."[12] In a strongly worded denunciation, Calvin referred to the failure of God's people to tithe as "perverseness," "hypocrisy," "impudence," and a violation of God's institutions.[13] The matter was so self-evident to Calvin that he commented: "God however deemed it enough to convict them by one sentence—that they defrauded him in the tenths and in the first-fruits ... [which] he rightly calls and counts ... his own."[14] Calvin underscored the importance of this by explaining that "God designed the first-fruits and other things to be offered to him, that men might thereby be continually reminded that all things were his."[15] In his commentary on Deuteronomy 26, Calvin spoke of tithing as "placing God, as it were, before [the Hebrews'] eyes, as if they paid them into his hand."[16] Moreover, he spoke of the correct motivation for this religious giving as the offering of a tribute to God, which was a "symbol of their emancipation ... as having been redeemed by

12. John Calvin, *Commentaries on the Twelve Minor Prophets* (Grand Rapids: Baker Book House, 1979), 15:585, 588.

13. Ibid., 15:585.

14. Ibid.

15. Ibid.

16. Calvin, *Commentaries on the Four Last Books of Moses*, 2:283.

the special mercy of God."[17] He also explained that believers are not masters of their money and property; instead, they hold their possessions "by no other title than as tenants at will."[18] Such was the importance of tithing to Calvin.

Tithing, in addition to providing for an ongoing priestly ministry, was also the base for charitable giving. Prior to Calvin's time, other than the church (which was largely Roman Catholic and prone to excess) and family inheritances, there were few, if any, institutions that gave charitable aid. Vehicles like today's plethora of foundations, private scholarships, and endowments were largely unthinkable in that day. In fact, one might argue that the spread of such multifaceted charitable outlets as we have in the West today followed the spread of Calvinism more certainly than did the spread of the Protestant work ethic of Weber's thesis. Perhaps there is a "Protestant charity ethic" that flowed from Calvin's work.

Beginning in Calvin's day, the church—with its care for refugees, the establishment of hospitals, and many other diaconal efforts—continued to radiate its scope of charity outward in larger circles. None of this would have been possible without tithing. In fact, there is likely a correlation between the percentage of tithers and private charity. State establishments do their fair share of charity, to be sure. However, the scope and efficiency of disestablished churches (supported by tithing, not taxation) is greater.

So tithing has offered a double benefit. In addition to supporting the churches' buildings and workers, it has also yielded charitable funds to care for the downtrodden and needy.

Personal Security

For Calvin, the next rung of charity was, surprising to some, personal security. In other words, Calvin upheld the view that

17. Ibid., 2:494.
18. Ibid.

one is responsible to provide for himself and his dependents. Calvin and other Reformers broke with the medieval pattern of almsgiving. Instead, they endorsed an ethic based on personal responsibility. Commenting on 2 Thessalonians 3:10, Calvin noted that while there are "different ways of laboring," each person should aid "the society of men by his industry, either in ruling his family, or by administering public or private affairs, or by counseling, or by teaching, or in any other way . . . [to] not be reckoned among the idle."[19] He also could not resist stating that "indolence and idleness were cursed by God," explaining:

> Besides, we know that man was created with this view, that he might do something. Not only does Scripture testify this to us, but nature itself taught it to the heathen. Hence it is reasonable that those who wish to exempt themselves from the common law should also be deprived of food [and] the reward of labor. . . . [Paul] forbade that the Thessalonians should encourage their indolence by supplying [idlers] with food.[20]

Calvin, thus, through his teachings on vocation and through the work ethic he cultivated, expected that a charitable outlook would lead individuals to eschew being drains on the resources of others. It is hardly loving to expect the financial support of others when one is capable of supporting oneself. Again, Calvin applied the words of 1 Timothy 5:8 generally, claiming that those who do not support their own families lack "piety towards God." Moreover, he said that such individuals deny the faith, rendering them "worse than brute beasts."[21] For Calvin, the "criminality of this conduct" was demonstrated by nature itself, since even "infidels are so prone to love their own." In light of the higher expectations

19. John Calvin, *Commentaries on the Epistles to the Philippians, Colossians, and Thessalonians* (Grand Rapids: Baker Book House, 1979), 2:355.

20. Ibid.

21. John Calvin, *Commentaries on the Epistles to Timothy, Titus, and Philemon* (Grand Rapids: Baker Book House, 1979), 127.

rightly placed upon those who profess to follow Christ's commands, Calvin found the conduct even more reprehensible. The work ethic was applied within the family of God.

In earlier remarks on 1 Timothy 5:5, he had noted the biblical distinction between a widow with a real need and one who either can care for her own needs or has adequate family assistance. Simultaneously, he cautioned against widows who give themselves over to "pleasant idleness," "convenience," or "excessive mirth."[22]

James Gills and Ronald Nash have suggested that when charity is taken out of the hands of the private sector and turned over to an invisible "Big Government," then it becomes easy for the recipients "to think that some goods and services, such as healthcare and prescription medicines, have no cost. The costs are still there, but the people who pay those costs often are out of sight and mind for those who not only take the result of government's redistribution of property but begin to act as though they are entitled to an increasing amount of such benefits."[23]

Each person has a divine calling to work—to use his time and resources for the glory of God and for the enhancement of his neighbor. One cannot give as charitably as possible if his own bills are passed to someone else. The essential building block for genuinely charitable giving can be laid only after a secure base is set. Moreover, it is only when these personal bases are secured that consistent planning may occur in long-term charitable projects. For example, if a group wishes to begin a denominational college or adopt a multiyear charitable effort, sustained giving is needed; that will normally come from mature and established givers who have first achieved their own financial security.

In his sermon on 1 Tim. 6:17–19, Calvin noted that one remedy to "correct a depraved attachment" to the world's wealth is "the right use of our possessions. A man's opportunities to do

22. Ibid., 125.

23. James P. Gills and Ronald H. Nash, *A Biblical Economics Manifesto: Economics and the Christian Worldview* (Lake Mary, FL: Creation House, 2002), 6.

good to others increase with the abundance of his riches, and because we are always more reluctant than we should be to give to the poor, he [Paul] uses many words in commending this virtue."[24] In another sermon on the Gospels, Calvin called for "contentment with what has been allotted to us," so that even those with means may see their greater responsibility. Similarly, those who are poor are called, under the doctrine of contentment, to accept their station and condition, without coveting or stealing. Calvin wrote:

> When a person has the means to increase his wealth, let this be done without doing an injury to others—and also without being consumed with envy. What is more: not only should the rich man be contented with what he has but he should also have the spirit of a poor man—that is, each and every day he should be ready to abandon all that God has given him, and not torture himself on that account; and if God wants to make him richer, he should take the blessing he is offered. If God wishes to give him less, he should realize that this is to his advantage.[25]

Calvin, in what may be curious to some, even described the materially poor as having a unique ministry to serve as "messengers" to probe the faith and love of those around them. They are "proxies" to test the compassion of the wealthy.[26] Calvin referred to the wealthy who failed to care for the poor as "murderers," who deprived others of what they should have: "For otherwise they are like murderers if they see their neighbors wasting away and yet do not open their hands to help them. In this, I tell you, they are certainly like murderers."[27] While interpreters of Calvin may differ on applications of this teaching, it seems that his point is to condemn the callous wealthy, not to advocate a system in which a

24. Quoted in André Biéler, *Calvin's Economic and Social Thought* (1959; repr., Geneva: World Alliance of Reformed Churches, 2005), 285.

25. Ibid., 286.

26. Ibid., 288.

27. Ibid., 299.

separate agency takes and redistributes their wealth to preclude them from being murderers.

Based on the prophetic denunciation of hoarding, particularly by Isaiah, Calvin identified the persistent problem of human discontent. Those who "never have enough, and whom no wealth can satisfy" are keenly covetous to "have everything just for themselves and reckon everything which others have to be something they are missing."[28] Calvin cited Chrysostom's opinion that the avaricious would confiscate the sun from the poor if possible. Those whose only "care is to swallow up a great deal" never have enough and never model moderation. Calvin saw this tendency to hoard even when he considered "the size and spaciousness of houses":

> For Isaiah points out the ambition of those who are desirous to inhabit magnificent palaces or spacious houses. There is nothing reprehensible if someone who has a large family has a large house; but when people, swollen with ambition, make superfluous additions to their houses, only that they may live in greater luxury . . . this is empty ambition and ought justly to be blamed. Such persons act as if they were to be the only ones that enjoyed a roof, and others should only have the sky for a blanket or must go somewhere else to find an abode.[29]

Calvin warned against lusting after wealth, but he also saw the need for the establishment of assets for family security and the ownership of personal property.

Family Estate

Following on the heels of personal security is the call to provide for one's household, dependents, and the future. Calvinists have

28. Ibid., 298.
29. Commentary on Isaiah 5:8, cited in Biéler, *Calvin's Economic and Social Thought*, 298.

long been associated with the notion of taking one generation's estate and increasing it; that is for good reason. Calvin, viewing wealth as a providential gift and creation of God, believed that estates should always be improved, provided that the means for improvement are legal and do not exclude charitable giving. Not only would that allow the family more liberty in the future, but it would also provide charitably for all the dependents. The modern notion that a state agency (or any other extrafamilial group) should assume the responsibility to provide for one's descendants was foreign to Calvin. Rather, he considered it an act of charity to provide for one's children and future progeny. Those who fail to provide for their own descendants, asserted Calvin, are worse than unbelievers. As he phrased it when commenting on 1 Timothy 5:8, they act with "inhumanity [that], therefore, is open contempt of God."[30]

Calvinism does not encourage the selfishness that fuels one merely to care for his own life. When God gives children and spouses, they, too, are to be cared for materially. It is hardly compatible with Calvin's teachings to exhaust all one's earnings during a lifetime and to fail to save anything for future generations. The biblical model he employed expected individuals to (a) tithe, (b) secure their personal material base through savings and investing, and (c) seek to provide for children and the family. To provide for children's education, whatever form that may take, is probably the first long-term investment toward this end. To assist children in beginning their life's race is a loving act of charity; such responsibility is lodged with no one else other than the family. To assist future generations by providing assets is not only charitable but also wise, if virtue is inculcated as well; for that means lower dependency ratios and a higher yield of funds from a higher asset base, if estates are invested well and consistently.

30. Calvin, *Commentaries on the Epistles to Timothy, Titus, and Philemon*, 127.

Through God's redemption, the believer is brought to a full understanding of Christian liberty that permeates all aspects of life. As such, Calvin would argue that Christian freedom implies market freedom, not as a coldly calculated means of survival, but as an extension of the worship and responsibility of the believer. Counterweighing the call for freedom is Calvin's censure of selfishness and his extensive teaching on the virtue of stewardship. Embedded in his argument for stewardship is a fierce defense of private property and of property rights that must be upheld and protected. A cheapening of property rights devalues the Christian act of charity and sacrifice that comes as a response to God's redemption. Having described wealth as a created tool for man to use (chapter 1) and as a visible means to advance God's will (chapter 2), we now see wealth as the wellspring of charity and giving that originates from a heart of thanksgiving and praise. In this sense, charity and investment share similar foundations. Both are symbolic of God's redemption and charity serves also as an advanced form of investment. The hierarchy of charity and investment, however, is founded upon the simple base of tithing.

Beyond providing for their churches and families, Calvinists have often exhibited some of the finest examples of charity. Throughout history, as the beliefs associated with the Reformed faith began to lodge themselves in the children of Calvin, and as wealth was created and increased, charity also found a wider circle. Calvinism's philanthropic spirit was tied to its business spirit.

4

Philanthropy

By now, the reader should understand that much of the customary criticism of Calvin is unwarranted, perhaps nowhere more so than in terms of his compassion toward the downtrodden or in terms of his philanthropic leadership in Geneva. Despite the numerous caricatures, Calvin knew how to help the truly needy in an effective manner.

Extrafamilial Charity

Calvin lived in a world that was as fraught with need as ours is today, if not more so. Absent massive social agencies and safety nets of many varieties, his world was much more of a tooth-and-claw world than ours. For him, as for many people today, it was always challenging to determine which needs should receive funding. While there are many attempts to classify worthy objects of

ity, we offer below a basic list of the opportunities for extrafa-milial charity. In other words, once the church has been supported by the tithe, and after a personal financial base has been secured and the family estate has been established, the following groups may rightly become objects of private charity.

Near neighbors. It is natural that compassion will flow to those seen most often. If their near neighbors are in need, as Jesus taught in the parable of the good Samaritan (Luke 10), believers will not ignore those needs. Assuming for our argument's sake that the near neighbors are genuinely needy or ill, Christ's strong rebuke was reserved for those who do not lend assistance. The calling to care for those closest to us is quite clear. According to Calvin, this parable also requires that we extend our charity far beyond our immediate neighborhood.

The working poor. After caring for one's nearest neighbors, it is prudent to care for the working poor. Those who labor long and hard but who do not have high wages, due to no fault of their own, may receive benevolent supplements if charities or individuals wish to subsidize them. It is no sin to be in a relatively low-wage occupation. For example, those who work in law enforcement and public education are frequently compensated little for much work and risk. If charities wish to subsidize individuals who work diligently in these necessary occupations, then that is a natural application of good charity.

Those with productivity prospects. Young students and beginning workers with promise may also become the objects of charitable scholarships or other subsidies until they assume full productivity. Obviously, not everyone will qualify for these grants but those who are helped normally express a gratitude that gives back to the next generation. As with any other type of charity, selection grids may be established by various groups to ascertain worthy recipients of charity. If the prospect of future productivity is targeted, then certain fields of work and certain income strata will likely become primary factors for consideration. Again, targeted, well-conceived charity is the best.

Institutions. Once some of these individual-focused opportunities have been addressed, there is also a place for long-term institutional development. The use of endowment funds to create charitable assets, if used wisely and regularly, is a macro project that may yield many benefits. Similarly, the establishment of schools—think of how much education Roman Catholics and Lutherans have provided over the years via their parochial schools—is one of the most enriching and necessary objects of religious charities. At the same time, these charities may help spread the theological values of a group. Such institutions require large seed funds to begin; and by nature they require sustained giving. However, they also touch many lives and may do so for generations.

The impoverished in general. After large philanthropic ventures have begun, then believers may attend to multinational poverty or need. By the nature of this case, few will be able to devote resources to this work other than the very wealthy (via private foundations) or international organizations.

Calvinism spawned and developed a number of these broader initiatives in charity. Chief among them—and a luminous example of institutional charity for centuries—was Calvin's Academy. Calvin broke with medieval pedagogy, which limited education primarily to an aristocratic elite. His Academy, founded in 1559, was a pilot in broad-based education for the city. Although Genevans had sought for two centuries to establish a university, only after Calvin's efforts did a college finally succeed.[1] By the time of

1. The most recent history of the University of Geneva recounts several abortive efforts, including one in 1420 under Roman Catholic authority and the attempt by François de Versonnex in 1429. See Marco Marcacci, *Histoire de l'Université de Genève: 1559–1986* (Geneva: University of Geneva, 1987), 17. For a prehistory of the Genevan Academy, see also William G. Naphy, "The Reformation and the Evolution of Geneva's Schools," in *Reformations Old and New: Essays on*

Calvin's arrival, city officials yearned for a premier educational institution, but in 1536 most Genevans thought this was a target too ambitious. Regardless of the unsuccessful initiatives that occurred between Geneva's adoption of the Reformation in 1536 and Calvin's return from his Strasbourg exile in 1541, it is clear that success in establishing a lasting university did not occur until Calvin set his hand to the educational plow after Geneva became settled in its Protestant identity in the 1550s. This lasting charitable accomplishment would not have happened without the vision to produce a multigenerational institution.

Calvin's Academy, which was adjacent to St. Pierre Cathedral, featured two levels of curricula—one for the public education of Geneva's youth (the college or *schola privata*) and the other a seminary to train ministers (the *schola publica*).[2] One should hardly discount the impact that came from this church-sponsored education of young people, especially in a day when education was normally reserved only for aristocratic scions or for members of Catholic societies. Begun in 1558,[3] with Calvin and Theodore Beza chairing the theological faculty, the Academy building was dedicated on June 5, 1559, with six hundred people in attendance in St. Pierre Cathedral. Calvin collected money for the school, and many expatriates donated to help its formation. The college, which had seven grades, enrolled 280 students during its inaugural year, and the Academy's seminary expanded to 162 students in just three years. At the time of Calvin's death in 1564, there were

---

the Socio-Economic Impact of Religious Change, c. 1470–1630 , ed. Beat Kümin (London: Scolar Press, 1996), 190–93. Until recently, Charles Borgeaud's *Histoire de l'Université de Genève* (Geneva, 1900) was the standard history.

2. E. William Monter, *Calvin's Geneva* (New York: John Wiley & Sons, 1967), 112. The *schola privata* began classes in the fall of 1558, and the *schola publica* commenced in November of 1558. Marcacci, *Histoire de l'Université de Genève*, 17.

3. Public records for January 17, 1558 refer to the establishment of the college, with three chairs (theology, philosophy, and Greek). Notice was also given commending the college as a worthy recipient of inheritance proceeds. See Henry Martyn Baird, *Theodore Beza: The Counsellor of the French Reformation, 1519–1605* (New York: G. P. Putnam's Sons, 1899), 104.

twelve hundred students in the college and three hundred in the seminary. Both schools, as historians have observed, were tuition free and "forerunners of modern public education."[4] Few European institutions ever saw such rapid growth.

To accommodate the flood of students, the Academy (in what would become characteristic of the Calvinistic view that faith should influence all areas of life) planned to add departments of law and medicine. Beza requested prayer for the new medical department as early as 1567, by which time the law school had already been established. Following the St. Bartholomew's Day Massacre (1572), Francis Hotman—and several other leading constitutional scholars—taught at the Genevan law school. The presence of two legal giants, Hotman (from 1573–1578) and Denis Godefroy, gave Calvin's Academy one of the earliest Swiss legal faculties. The medical school, attempted shortly after Calvin's death, was not successfully established until the 1700s.[5] Calvin's Academy became the standard-bearer for education in all major fields.

Historically, education, as much as any other single factor, has fostered cultural and political advancement. One of Calvin's most enduring contributions to society—a contribution that also secured the longevity of many of the Calvinistic reforms—was the establishment of the Academy in Geneva. Through his Academy, Calvin also succeeded where others had failed. Worth noting, none of the other major Protestant Reformers are credited with founding a university that would last for centuries. The university even became a sought-after property by some surprising suitors—among them, Thomas Jefferson.[6]

4. Donald R. Kelley, *Francois Hotman: A Revolutionary's Ordeal* (Princeton: Princeton University Press, 1973), 270.

5. Baird, *Theodore Beza*, 106, 113.

6. For this intriguing connection see my summary in *The Genevan Reformation and the American Founding* (Lanham, MD: Lexington Books, 2003), 2–4. I am indebted to Dr. James H. Hutson for this fascinating anecdote, which he presents in his work, *The Sister Republics: Switzerland and the United States from 1776 to the Present*, 2nd ed. (Washington, DC: Library of Congress, 1992), 68–76.

Philanthropy that spans many families and generations seldom occurs unless the following factors are present:

- A long-term view and horizon
- Personal discipline to save, preserve, and wisely use the resources provided by God
- A strong sense of responsibility to use wealth to care for those around us
- A repudiation of the idea that the state is responsible for the big projects of life
- A willingness to sacrifice to begin certain institutions
- A desire to inculcate virtue and value, based on beliefs
- A view of investing consistent with the above

One will be hard-pressed to identify any worldview, economic theory, or religious system that is more supportive of or consistent with these conditions of philanthropy than Calvin's Protestantism.

Calvin was also keen to counsel that excessive debt could annul charitable opportunities; thus, he warned against too much debt. He knew the multiple applications of Paul's teaching in Romans 13:8: "Let no man have debt except to love his neighbor."

Moreover, Calvin's philanthropic spirit—one that characterizes the best of business ethics—is seen in his care for the poor in Geneva.

Calvin's Philanthropy and Care for the Poor

To begin a consideration of this aspect of his work, we would do well to remember how Calvin reached out compassionately to homeless refugees by the thousands, as they arrived in Geneva in search of a place to rest their wearied consciences. This massive immigration maximally strained Geneva's resources. With the population nearly doubling because of this movement, the

Genevan church had to devise measures to care for the true needs around them. One of their first steps was to analyze the problem and distinguish between those who were truly needy and those who were not.

Second, a clearer view of the heart of Calvin may be seen from his development of ways to use the officers of a private agency (i.e., a non-governmental organization, an NGO) to care for so many. Calvin thought that the church's compassion could best be expressed through its deacons. Since God had ordained that office for the function of caring for the poor, Calvin's challenge was to arrive at practical protocols that would use the mechanisms already provided by God to maximize the efforts of these ministers of mercy.

It is an accomplishment well worth remembering that centuries ago Calvin pioneered principles and practices that were far ahead of their time. In fact, if most governmental agencies would implement some version of these principles, many people might be better off.

Jeannine Olson's able historical volume, *Calvin and Social Welfare: Deacons and the Bourse Française*, provides a study of Calvin's impact on Reformation culture, focusing particularly on the enduring effect of Calvin's thought on the institution of the diaconate. In her treatise, she notes that, contrary to some modern caricatures, the Reformers worked diligently to shelter refugees and minister to the poor. The *Bourse française* (the organized treasury of the church's deacons) became a pillar of social welfare in Geneva;[7] in fact, this was another of Calvin's contributions to Western civilization. This diaconal ministry may have had nearly as much influence in Calvin's Europe as his theology did.

Calvin's welfare program in Geneva was contoured to fit the theological emphases of the Reformers, providing an early illustration that welfare practice was (and is) erected upon definite

7. Jeannine Olson, *Calvin and Social Welfare: Deacons and the Bourse Française* (Selinsgrove, PA: Susquehanna University Press, 1989), 11–12.

principles that were religious or ideological in nature. Moreover, the theology of the Reformation was the guiding force for this welfare, just as the theology of medieval Roman Catholicism had been the guiding principle for almsgiving. Ultimate principles shaped the practice of welfare 450 years ago as they do today, which is to say, at no time is welfare truly divorced from underlying values.

The activities of the *Bourse* were numerous. Its diaconal agents were involved in housing orphans, the elderly, or those who were in any way incapacitated. They sheltered the sick and dealt with orphans and those involved in immoralities. This ecclesiastical institution was a precursor to voluntary societies in the nineteenth and twentieth centuries. But its inspiration was part of the genius of Calvin.

The *Bourse française* was founded under the leadership of John Calvin sometime between 1536 and 1541 (of course, not during his Strasbourg exile). Its initial design was to ease the suffering of French residents who came to Geneva, having fled sectarian persecution in France. It has been estimated that in a single decade alone (1550–1560) some 60,000 refugees passed through Geneva, a number large enough to produce significant social stress.

In the *Ecclesiastical Ordinances*, first proposed in 1541, Calvin had written a charter for the deacons, identifying them as one of the four basic offices of the church. This Reformation church order stipulated that there should be two types of deacons. "There were always two kinds in the ancient Church," Calvin wrote, "the one deputed to receive, dispense, and hold goods for the poor, not only daily alms, but also possessions, rents and pensions; the other to tend and care for the sick and administer allowances to the poor."[8] In addition, the 1541 charter assigned to the church deacons the duty of making sure that

8. John Calvin, *Calvin: Theological Treatises*, ed. J. K. S. Reid (Philadelphia: Westminster, 1954), 64.

the hospital "is well maintained, and that this be so both for the sick and the old people unable to work, widowed women, orphaned children and other poor creatures. The sick are always to be lodged in a set of separate rooms from the other people who are unable to work. . . . Moreover, besides the hospital for those passing through which must be maintained, there should be some attention given to any recognized as worthy of special charity."[9] In the conclusion of this section, Calvin noted that "to discourage mendicancy [begging without work] which is contrary to good order, it would be well, and we have so ordered it, that there be one of our officials at the entrance of the churches to remove from the place those who loiter; and if there be any who give offence or offer insolence to bring them to one of the Lords Syndic."[10] Begging without honest work was an affront to the tenets of the biblical Protestant work ethic. It was considered sinful and slothful by Calvin and others. Employing both a sophistication of administration and a discrimination of the root causes of physical needs, this model can still inform our practices today. In the 1541 *Ecclesiastical Ordinances* of Geneva, Calvin recommended a strong role for the church's deacons, who cared for a large range of needs, not wholly unlike the range of welfare needs in our own society.

Calvin was so interested in seeing the diaconate flourish that he not only left an inheritance for his family in his will but also provided for the Boys' School and poor strangers.[11] With a salary that was not exorbitant, Calvin exhibited both his personal frugality and his charitable commitments through his bequeathals.

After two decades, the *Ecclesiastical Ordinances* were revised in 1561. A recent translation of the 1561 *Ecclesiastical Ordinances*

9. Ibid., 65.

10. Ibid., 66.

11. Geoffrey Bromiley, "The English Reformers and Diaconate," in *Service in Christ: Essays Presented to Karl Barth on his 80th Birthday*, ed. James I. McCord and T. H. L. Parker (London: Epworth Press, 1966), 113.

shows the sophistication and refinement of the diaconate even prior to the death of Calvin.[12] The requirements of the 1561 revision clearly indicate that ministry to the poor was significant and well ordered in Calvin's time. It was neither a low priority nor slipshod in organization. In fact, the forethought and amount of detail for such philanthropy was nearly unparalleled in its time.

The deacons actively encouraged a productive work ethic. They provided interim subsidies and job training as necessary; on occasion, they even provided the necessary tools or supplies so that an able-bodied person could engage in an honest vocation. They were discriminating as they ascertained the difference between those who were truly needy and those who were merely idle. If necessary, they would suspend subsidy. Over time, they developed procedures that would protect the church's resources from being pilfered, even requiring new visitors to declare their craft and list character witnesses to vouch for their honesty.[13] Within a generation of this welfare work, the diaconate of Geneva discovered the need to communicate to recipients the goal that they were to return to work as soon as possible.

In sixteenth-century Geneva, there were cases of abandonment, and the *Bourse* was frequently called upon to raise children. Furthermore, the deacons supported the terminally ill, who also left their children to be supported. Special gifts were given to truly needy children. The *Bourse* also included a ministry to widows, who often had dependent children and a variety of needs. The church and other private institutions in Calvin's Geneva were not depending on governmental agencies to perform what they were equipped to do.

12. Cf. Mary Crumpacker, "Ecclesiastical Ordinances, 1561," in *Paradigms in Polity: Classic Readings in Reformed and Presbyterian Church Government*, ed. David W. Hall and Joseph H. Hall (Grand Rapids: Eerdmans, 1994), 148–49.

13. Olson, *Calvin and Social Welfare*, 39–40.

Still, it must be noted that although the *Bourse* resembled many other contemporary sixteenth-century welfare funds, it had its peculiarities. Naturally there were theological peculiarities, and these led to certain practical commitments. For example, there were no guaranteed food handouts. Furthermore, there were certain prerequisites for receiving care, including the possibility that certain moral deficiencies would nullify the opportunity to be assisted by the *Bourse*.

The *Bourse* was not concerned only with spiritual or internal needs. On many occasions the Genevan diaconate hired medical doctors to take care of the ill. Records indicate that the deacons oversaw medical care for the needy—clear evidence that the scope of diaconal ministry was not limited to evangelism. Those who led the *Bourse* were also prudent. In January of 1581, the *Bourse* adopted a set of constitutional rules underscoring the need to have a vital and well-considered, disciplined approach to the important task of alleviating poverty.[14] Calvin and the founders of the Genevan diaconate were also realists, who consulted the past and factored in Jesus' statement in Mark 14:7, "you will always have the poor with you." They lived on the cusp of a reform movement, learning from what had gone before them.

Modern advocates of philanthropy and charity might be better off exploring the past to see what it might teach them, rather than looking exclusively to the future. In fact, if we find ourselves advocating practices markedly different from those of Calvin's *Bourse* five centuries ago, then we should probably stop and ask ourselves why. Perhaps our novel methods should be deemed suspect precisely to the extent that they deviate from earlier sound practices in the area of public welfare.

In summary, we can identify the following principles of Calvin's welfare reform:

14. Ibid., 104–6.

1. It was only for the truly disadvantaged.[15]
2. Moral prerequisites accompanied assistance.
3. Private or religious charity, not state largesse, was the vehicle for aid.
4. Ordained officers managed welfare programs and brought accountability.
5. Theological underpinnings were normal.
6. A productive work ethic was expected.
7. Assistance was temporary.
8. History was valuable.

Illustrative of the philanthropy of Calvin, one of his fellow Reformers, Martin Bucer, went so far as to say of the diaconate that "without it there can be no true communion of saints."[16] Bucer also noted that "the first duty of the deacons is to distinguish between the deserving and undeserving poor, for the former to inquire carefully into their needs; [for] the latter, if they lead disorderly lives at the expense of others, to expel them from the community of the faithful. Care, next, is to be taken for needy widows."[17]

Both as confirmation of the affinity among Reformers and of the similarity of thought that Calvin passed on to his disciples, one need look only at the communities where the seeds of Calvinism blossomed to see how this movement of philanthropy developed. In the British Isles, almsgiving was emphasized as one means for poverty relief. John Knox, who spent several crucial years studying Calvin's Genevan model, continued this Reformation tradition of ministry to the poor in Scotland. In the *Second Book of Discipline* (1578), he established the office of deacon as a permanent function of the church.

15. The Genevan diaconate quickly realized that it must screen recipients. One reason was because the resources were finite. Charitable groups who realize that resources are not infinite also see the need to screen applicants, for every dollar given is an opportunity that is not necessarily renewable.

16. Basil Hall, "Diaconia in Martin Butzer," in *Service in Christ*, 94.

17. Ibid.

Hence the Calvinistic tradition was settled and fairly uniform in its institutionalization of the care for the poor. Such care was an ecclesiastical function to be carried out by spiritual officers according to biblical standards and principles. Effectively administered in Geneva and elsewhere, the diaconal ministry cared for the poor, employed the church's gifts, encouraged a productive work ethic, and relieved governmental stewardship in this area. As Geoffrey Bromiley summarizes, "The answer to poverty was still found in individual benevolence exercised either privately or through the Church."[18]

From this we can see that a number of welfare agencies began to blossom across Europe following the Protestant Reformation. Indeed, the Calvinistic diaconate was a model in its manifestation of consistent reformation of faith and life. Thus did these Reformation prototypes spread and become catalysts for welfare reform in the sixteenth century. Indeed, the Reformation "left stamped upon Christendom its idea of a properly coordinated and managed care of the poor and needy as the concern of the Church and as the responsibility of the Christian community."[19] That is an economic as well as a business concern, for poverty affects the entire society.

Calvin was atypical in advancing this particular social safety net. His philanthropy provides another instance of how his heart was compassionate toward the truly needy.

Charity and Poverty Accurately Defined

With the foregoing discussion of Calvin's praxis in mind, an informed discussion about charity may continue by more accurately defining what qualifies as poverty. In contemporary

18. Bromiley, "The English Reformers and Diaconate," 113.

19. James Atkinson, "Diaconia at the Time of the Reformation," in *Service in Christ*, 88.

society the question, who are the poor? has become a central point of disagreement both for relief agencies and for businesses that wish to contribute to ameliorating poverty. Much of what passes for "charity" in the United States today is in fact an attempt to legitimize wealth distribution. The attempt is made all the more appealing to citizens by framing the issue so that it holds maximum emotional appeal to those who will be losing income. Additionally, poverty is not as pervasive in the United States as the media might represent. The national standard of living has risen dramatically over the past century—for each socioeconomic group. The gap between what is considered impoverished in the United States and what is considered impoverished in other nations has grown dramatically since 1900.

The Heritage Foundation's paper "Understanding Poverty in America" reports the following facts about the "poor" as defined by the U.S. Census Bureau. It provides a good opportunity to consider the subjectivity of the definition of poverty since:

- 46% of the "poor" own their homes.
- 76% have air conditioning.
- Only 6% of "poor" households are overcrowded.
- The average "poor" American enjoys more square footage of living space than individuals living in Paris, London, Vienna, or Athens.
- 97% of the "poor" own a color television, and 62% have cable or satellite reception.
- 89% of the "poor" report that their families have enough to eat, while only 2% say that they "often" do not have enough to eat.[20]

20. Robert E. Rector and Kirk A. Johnson, "Understanding Poverty in America," Heritage Foundation Backgrounder, no. 1713, January 5, 2004, posted at: http://www.heritage.org/research/welfare/bg1713.cfm.

Compare the vision of the poor as presented in the Bible—men without homes, their bodies full of sores, hungry, owning only one tunic—to the circumstances of many poor people in the United States, and the social skewing of the definition of poverty becomes apparent. To be poor in America often means "having less than one's neighbor" instead of "lacking resources necessary for life."

For example, consider a man who owns a five-bedroom house, drives a large SUV, and wears an expensive watch. If his neighbor only has two bedrooms in his house, drives a used car, and cannot afford a watch, does that make the neighbor poor? While there may be a vast difference between the amounts of wealth the two men have, there is no historical context to label the neighbor as poor. His necessities—food, shelter, and clothing—are taken care of, as are other luxuries such as personal transportation and electricity. Moreover, his standard of living can be maintained through the opportunity for employment. While his socioeconomic status may be relatively lower than that of his neighbor, he has a much higher standard of living than the truly impoverished people of other nations around the world.

If an economist accepts the fact that the lower socioeconomic status and the higher socioeconomic status will always remain with us and that the elimination of poverty is unfeasible, then the question of charity's importance is actually complicated to some extent. It is easy to embrace charity and unquestioned giving to the poor when it seems as though it will make a difference or when it is given by an impersonal or state-subsidized institution. However, it is much more difficult to ascertain what can be done on an individual and personal level to aid poverty. At that level, one must address such questions as, What is the responsibility of the individual within an economic system to the poor, and how can charity be best expressed and most effective with regard to both biblical mandates and economic utility? Additionally, economic responsibility calls us to seek the most effective way to provide benefits and growth for the poor. Both the biblical and the economic requirements are met when the poor are assisted in a personal, non-institutionalized context that requires the highest amount of accountability and allows for progression through personal growth. Calvin certainly had the wisdom to pursue poverty relief in this spirit.

Furthermore, while lauding Calvin's earlier approach, it is also helpful and essential to briefly contrast both the theoretical models and the practical applications of other economic systems as they relate to poverty. In the first place, there is Randism, which views altruism as evil and finds no place for charity in a healthy society. Under the presuppositions of this perspective, the laissez-faire advocates of free markets would say that society benefits the poor more by encouraging them to pick themselves up by their bootstraps than by providing handouts. According to this view, there is no moral underpinning requiring charity, and the poor are left to themselves. Next, there is the firm capitalism that is often associated with the thought of Adam Smith. In this system, rank poverty is to be diminished and the poor are to be protected. Firm capitalism protects the poor by defending their legal rights and by providing them with a sound infrastructure, but not necessarily with monetary transfers. The capitalist is free to give charity to whomever he considers deserving and however he deems fit. Such independent giving is socially encouraged.

In a soft capitalist society (such as the present-day United States) charity is institutionalized and government bears a large portion of the responsibility to administer it. Businesses must contribute to this centralized relief by paying taxes. The government then acts as the main agent in the redistribution of wealth and strives to alleviate poverty and need through the allocation of tax revenues.

In a soft socialist system (such as that of Sweden or France) society has decided that politically, culturally, and even legally it is essential to have equalization of wealth and relief of deficiencies, even at the expense of economic growth as defined by the gross domestic product (GDP). Here the government is even stronger. It is actively engaged in income redistribution, and its allocation decisions are often made to the detriment of growth.

In a hard socialist (or Marxist) system there are no classes. In theory everyone is equalized and working for the state. There is no need for charity because there is no poverty. All are either rich together or poor together.

Practically speaking, there are multiple distortions within every economic system. For the continuation of this discussion, the emphasis will be on soft capitalism, which presently prevails in the United States. There are three evident (and prevalent) distortions within soft capitalism with regard to dealing with the impoverished. The first is that charity is often given too freely, which discourages growth for the poor. Secondly, there is a misallocation of money from individuals to a bureaucracy. When this occurs, the bureaucracy is prone to miss the target market. Therefore, the poor are not dealt with efficiently, and giving does not serve as a catalyst for their return to stable socioeconomic status. Moreover, such a system is liable to corruption. A large-scale example of the shortcomings related to the misallocation of money is the World Bank's giving to third-world countries. While very generous, the freely given money rarely alleviates poverty.[21] Lastly, there are wrong incentives and motivations being enforced by the government. This is a result of citizens allowing the government to institutionalize charitable giving and poverty aid, which should be an area for which individuals take personal responsibility.

Scripture states clearly that both the poor and the rich will always be present. Acknowledgement of this fact places severe

21. For more on this, see the recent works by William Easterly, *Reinventing Foreign Aid* (Cambridge, MA: MIT Press, 2008) and *White Man's Burden: Why the West's Efforts to Aid the Rest Have Done So Much Ill and So Little Good* (New York: Penguin Press, 2006).

limitations on poverty-reduction programs and makes total elimination unfeasible. Calvinists are suspicious of utopian theories, so they tend to prefer dystopian reality, even though that reality includes poverty. Of course, the attempt to eliminate poverty should not be criticized when it is performed by independent groups and individuals. But a holistic, institutionalized attempt to do so, or a theoretical paradigm that identifies poverty elimination as one of its primary objectives, should be carefully scrutinized. In fact, given the biblical principle that both wealth and poverty will always be present, such a systemic striving for total elimination of poverty is surely destined to frustrate itself and ultimately to fail to achieve its goal.

Furthermore, poverty associated with unemployment (often the most common cause of poverty) can be examined to indicate an economic (in addition to the previously discussed biblical) reality. When discussing poverty in terms of economic science many theorists maintain that the largest keys to poverty alleviation are strong property rights and employment. Therefore, we will further examine employment as a proxy for poverty, and in doing so we will address such questions as, is it feasible for a system to have full employment, and what are the consequences thereof?

One study concludes:

> But research shows extraordinarily high individual mobility in the market exchange economies, especially in the United States. That is, many people move into and out of poverty. More than three-quarters of all poverty spells are shorter than two years, and only 7 percent of the spells last seven years or more. (If discontinuous but repeated spells are considered, the percentage of spells lasting seven years or more rises to 20 percent, but the remainder of spells stay short-lived.) The same pattern is found among welfare recipients, where only about 30 percent of the cases are chronic. And, of course, there is mobility within the income distribution. Over a decade or more, 86–95 percent of all persons in the bottom quintile of

the U.S. income distribution move to a higher quintile, the majority becoming middle class."[22]

While Calvin certainly did not quantify his ideas in this fashion, his principles converged on these same truths. His theology led to sounder poverty relief than much statist welfare.

Faulty Assumptions of Modern Welfare: Calvin Knew Better

A proper discussion of charity must encompass a discussion of poverty. Moreover, no civic-minded businessman can ignore glaring poverty down the street. It has been estimated that approximately 10%–13% of the current national budget of the United States is supported by business taxes. In 2005, the federal budget as submitted by President Bush totaled $2.4 trillion, with $1.4 trillion of that spent in the form of transfer payments (Social Security, welfare, Medicaid, unemployment, etc.). These amounts are staggering. Besides indicating that welfare is very much a concern to business, the numbers suggest that we should solicit the advice of good business minds as we seek to provide effective and efficient assistance to the needy.[23]

22. Peter Gottschalk, Sara McLanahan, and Gary D. Sandefur, "The Dynamics and Intergenerational Transmission of Poverty and Welfare Participation" (1994) and John H. Hinderaker and Scott W. Johnson, "Inequality: Should We Worry?" (1996), cited in John E. Stapleford, *Bulls, Bears & Golden Calves: Applying Christian Ethics in Economics* (Downers Grove, IL: InterVarsity Press, 2002), 53.

23. In 2005 (the latest complete data available) $312 billion in tax revenue was reported from public and private U.S. corporations. Moreover, the United States spent $1.4 trillion that same year in transfer payments—$545 billion on Social Security and disability, $653 billion on Medicare and Medicaid, and $157 billion on welfare. Business taxes accounted for 21% of the 2005 federal transfer payments or 13% of the entire federal budget. In addition to this, many corporations are classified as "pass-through" entities (Subchapter S corporations, LLCs, LLPs, etc.) and are taxed on shareholders' personal income tax returns. Sources: Internal Revenue Service, *Statistics of Income, Final Corporation Income Tax Returns:*

While despiritualized approaches to wealth might consider this a topic of no concern, Calvin knew much more not only about poverty remediation but also about the macroeconomic connectivity between poverty and business. The Genevan Reformer also called his associates to be prudently charitable to those around them with true needs. In his century and ours, the same questions were and must be addressed. How does poverty occur? What is the poverty level? Who is to blame for poverty? And what is the best way to combat poverty? These are all underlying questions that each approach, including Calvin's, must answer before policies are applied. Not surprisingly, once the foundational assumptions about the poor and poverty have been clarified, the decisions on charity—how much, where, why, and who—are already settled and primarily require execution.

Therefore, the questions to be discussed are as follows:

- What are the foundational beliefs, that permeate society's approach to poverty?
- What does Scripture say about these beliefs, and are they congruent with biblically derived economic and business models?
- What is the economic history of these beliefs?
- How did these beliefs move from economics into the political and social arenas?
- What are the economic costs and results of these assumptions as they are manifested in various systems?

Over the past century of poverty relief in the United States, there have been five major foundational assumptions that have driven the effort and shaped the current governmental and institu-

2005 (Washington, DC: Internal Revenue Service, 2008); U.S. Census Bureau, *Statistical Abstract of the United States: 2008* (Washington, DC: Government Printing Office, 2007), table 522; and Office of Management and Budget, *Budget of the United States Government: Fiscal Year 2005* (Washington, DC: Government Printing Office, 2004).

tional system. First and foremost, modern welfare has been based on the concept that poverty can be eliminated. As we have noted above, however, the Bible is clear that the poor will always be with us. Furthermore, at no point in his ministry did Jesus advance an agenda of eliminating poverty. Many Christian socialists point to the Sermon on the Mount and the feeding of the five thousand as implicit endorsements of poverty relief. However, note that Christ's agenda was to teach his followers first and only afterwards to provide food, both as a means of providing temporary relief from hunger and as an instrument of further revealing his status as the Son of God. He did not enrich the poor as a whole; nor did he command that the poor should be enriched so that poverty would be eradicated.

Although through different means—for example, Karl Marx through the collective pooling of assets and labor and John Maynard Keynes through a market unhindered by short-term disruptions courtesy of fiscal and monetary policy—the underlying goal of eliminating poverty slowly seeped into the unconscious mind of twentieth-century social engineers and political leaders.

A second assumption underlying the modern approach to poverty relief is that money is the key to defeating poverty. Author Marvin Olasky captures this assumption brilliantly: "Materialistic thinking [in the Johnson administration] was dominant: one administration official put it, 'The way to eliminate poverty is to give the poor people enough money so that they won't be poor anymore.' Columnist Stewart Alsop wrote that for \$12 to \$15 billion a year (2 percent of the gross national product at that time) 'poverty could be abolished in the United States.'"[24] The effect has been a steady increase of transfer and relief payments with the thought that at some magic number of redistributed wealth the poor will cease to be poor. In light of the biblical axioms on this subject, the phrase "tilting at windmills" jumps to mind. Money

24. Marvin Olasky, *The Tragedy of American Compassion* (Wheaton, IL: Crossway Books, 2008), 174.

is not a panacea, and the continued increases in payments have probably done more harm than good on an individual level. At the macro level, the number of poor people (as defined by the Census Bureau) as a portion of the total population in the United States has remained consistently just at or slightly above 10%.

Year	Poverty Rate for Families
2006	9.8%
2005	9.9%
2004	10.2%
2003	10.0%
2002	9.6%
2001	9.2%
2000	8.7%
1990	10.7%
1980	10.3%
1970	10.1%

Source: U.S. Bureau of the Census, Current Population Survey, Annual Social and Economic Supplements. Poverty and Health Statistics Branch/HHES Division, U. S. Bureau of the Census.

The fact that the poor will always be present is not, however, a rationale to do nothing; rather, it is the realistic framework that contains a mosaic of effective strategies for poverty relief and charity.

Clear thinkers—Calvin earlier and many others more recently—have known this for some time. Comparing modern programs to earlier poverty-relief efforts, Amos G. Warner noted the effect of governmental charity in an 1894 study, observing:

> There is some tendency to claim public relief as a right, and for the indolent and incapable to throw themselves flat upon it. This feeling will always assert itself whenever it is given the opportunity to do so. . . . It is possible to do so much relief

> work that, while one set of persons is relieved, another will be taxed across the pauper line. . . . [T]he burden of supporting the State tends to diffuse itself along the lines of the least resistance; consequently, money raised for the relief of the poor may come out of pockets that can ill spare it.[25]

Since Calvin did not expect the civil government to provide charity, his practices (and those from earlier periods of history) may be all the more appealing to modern societies.

A third foundational assumption in the modern treatment and relief of poverty is that all men have a right to resources and freedom from want. One could speculate that this current belief is a mutation of two seemingly unrelated thoughts—the nature of man and the Marxist call to alleviate exploitation. In *The Communist Manifesto* Marx was clear that even in his utopian vision all men are required to work. He made no mention of relief for the poor. As earlier discussed, his motivation was the elimination of exploitation as he perceived it and the creation of an economy and society that would work collectively under the direction and for the benefit of the state. His enemies included capitalists, property owners, religion, and competition. His paradigm implicitly endorsed the concept of equal resources and benefits for all, at the expense of the wealthy.

Added to this presupposition was the belief that man is inherently good. The concept predates Calvin and, as set forth above, is in direct disagreement with his interpretation of Scripture and human nature. However, if an economist, governmental official, or relief worker believes that man is innately good, then it is natural for him to assume that all men have an innate right to have their basic needs met.

These thoughts form the foundation of the belief that man has a *right* to relief and resources. Under Marxism, a man in poverty is being oppressed and denied his right to the necessities of life. But

25. Quoted in ibid., 111.

Marx's emphasis upon the requirement of all to work means that pity should be given to the working poor (victims of exploitation)—not to the non-working poor. This hurdle was overcome when the belief of man's natural goodness was imported into this economic arena. The poor could now unashamedly claim their *right* to relief (which often is well beyond the basics of subsistence) and feel no compulsion to work or change their behavior. If man is naturally good or socially deserving, then the economically strong should rescue the poor—no one wants the good guy to perish or suffer in the movies; that is the final scene reserved for the evil villains. Therefore, one must only show up and demand his right to relief, irrespective of personal behavior or decisions. After all, by virtue of being human, he can expect that others will assume his intrinsic goodness. This second premise of modern poverty relief asserts a universality of deservingness and equal outcomes—two postulates that agree with neither Scripture nor Calvinism.

Since Christ himself taught the persistence (non-solubility) of poverty, we should factor into our norms the recognition that poverty cannot be totally or effectively eliminated in this life. This recognition affects both the levels of expectation and the goals of welfare reform. For example, if one targets full employment, universal health care, and the abolition of incomes below a certain annual figure, that will substantially alter the welfare reform if compared to an approach that stresses (as John Calvin did) personal responsibility, church involvement, and familial productivity.

John's gospel also includes this teaching as one of the last from our Lord's earthly ministry. In John 12:6 it is affirmed that Jesus was not insensitive to the poor. It was partially because Judas was a thief that Jesus responded as he did. Yet again, he reiterated, "Leave her alone. . . . You will always have the poor among you, but you will not always have me." Hence adherence to Jesus and his teachings is an even higher priority than poverty relief. It is an absolute goal. Jesus established neither relief shelters, nor

Union Missions, nor welfare vehicles. In terms of his activities, he seemed to be convinced that poverty would continue as part of the human condition, and he did not institute definite vehicles to alleviate it.

Also Jesus affirmed that our material sustenance is derived from providence. According to Matthew 6:25–34, he taught that the provender of life is given to birds, to flowers, and, by extension, to human beings by the providence of God. Whatever our lot in life, be it relative wealth or poverty, our condition is to be seen as flowing from the active providence of God in our lives. We are not to compare our wealth with that of others; nor should we worry about our apparent lacks. Instead, believers rightly related to their Creator-Provider should trust him and then act responsibly. This summary of biblical teaching underscores the fact that presuppositions will affect policy. The end expectation determines the means adopted.

William Willimon reiterates this, when he says:

> All philanthropy proceeds from a world view. The Nazis had an extensive system of social welfare. When Nazi doctors helped to exterminate those who were judged to be 'mentally defective,' they did so out of philanthropic motive. They saw themselves not as doing evil but as doing good to those who were 'less fortunate.' Likewise, the President who supported changes in the national welfare program because, 'Such changes will remove the poor from welfare rolls and make them taxpayers,' could also be said to be acting from philanthropic motives. *Christian* philanthropy arises from our claims about the nature of God. The parables that Jesus told were meant to depict a God who is by our standards, effusive, extravagant, and therefore odd. *Christian* philanthropy ought to proceed from this odd depiction of the way the world is.[26]

26. William H. Willimon, "The Effusiveness of Christian Charity," *Theology Today* 49, no. 1 (April 1992): 75–76.

Our attitude toward poverty, thus, is: (1) avoid it if you can; (2) seek to help others out of it; and (3) always provide assistance in a way that heeds biblical teachings. Successful businesses and caring churches have a role to play in poverty relief, but before launching a new crusade responsible leaders might wish to consult Calvin on this topic. A modern Calvinist summarizes it this way: "Those who gave material aid without requiring even the smallest return were considered as much a threat to true compassion as those who turned their backs on neighbors and brothers."[27] Calvin and his children do not find a universal right to relief in their authoritative scriptures.

A supporting corollary to man's right to relief and a fourth foundational assumption of modern poverty relief is that man is not responsible for his plight. As discussed earlier, Marx viewed much of man's want as a result of exploitation and competition, neither of which were under the control of the individual. In essence, exploitation and competition lessen personal responsibility. During the nineteenth and early twentieth centuries a different attitude predominated—namely, that man did have responsibility for his position and that his actions and decisions were factors in his current position or ingredients to his future ascent out of poverty. However, in the late 1960s social theorists began to preach a gospel based on the premise that the poor are victims. No longer were past behaviors, habits, and decisions examined; rather, "society" became the convenient scapegoat. Wed the belief that man is inherently good to the thought that man is not responsible for his predicament; then add the assertion that the only sources of evil are social distinctions of master and servant, rich and poor, and landlord and landless; and the final result is a case for distributing goods to all on moral grounds. In such a scenario everyone is weighed and measured except the central actor—the poor.

27. Olasky, *The Tragedy of American Compassion*, 21.

Under this model, in which society is viewed as being at fault, it is incumbent upon society to find solutions. Not only that, but if guilt is accepted and confessed, society has no right to ask the poor to modify their behavior. Like the ultimate enablers, relief workers smile approvingly at poor decisions and antisocial behavior. With no guilt, no shame, no pressure to work, and no compulsion to meet minimum standards of polite society (to say nothing of free food, shelter, medical care, and reading materials), who would want to change?

This is precisely the fourth assumption of modern macro views of poverty—that compassion does not require change or present accountability. The practice of awarding monetary transfers to the poor based on the belief that they were never responsible for their plights was recognized in the nineteenth century as a prime external cause of continued poverty. Each year from 1818 to 1824 the Society for the Prevention of Pauperism in the City of New York, a group whose goal was to attack destitution of all kinds, printed in its annual report a list of ten causes of pauperism. The first three causes were ignorance, idleness, and intemperance; then came "want of economy," imprudent and hasty marriages, and lotteries, followed by three institutional causes—pawnbrokers, brothels, and gambling houses. This list with its emphasis on personal failings and institutional lures typified most social thought of the time, but the Society also identified a new element: the tenth cause was "charities that gave away money too freely." There were not many of these, but in a growing economy any ease of subsidy was viewed as destructive both morally and materially.[28]

The Apostle's charge, "Those that do not work, shall not eat" (2 Thess. 3:10) was a sound principle of accountability that was understood in the early years of poverty relief in the United

28. John Griscom, *The First Annual Report of the Managers of the Society for the Prevention of Pauperism in the City of New York* (New York: J. Seymour, 1818), 12–22, cited in Olasky, *The Tragedy of American Compassion*, 17–18.

States. Indeed, by the mid-nineteenth century a new group, the New York Association for Improving the Condition of the Poor, was formed to tackle the concerns of unaccountability and free-flowing charity.

The Fifth Assumption: The Devolution of Charity by Delegating to the State

From Scripture the hierarchy of relief is clear: let the family provide for widows and orphans first (1 Tim. 5:1–8); if no family is present then the church shall maintain them; and external bureaucratic methods of relief should be made available only as the last resort. This model was promulgated by Calvin and appears throughout sermons in the American Colonies until the early nineteenth century. Moreover, as Marvin Olasky notes:

> The final pre-1800 poverty-fighting principle was an emphasis on family relationships. . . . This understanding was also reflected in the early laws of the Northwest Territory, which decreed that parents, grandparents, and children of "every poor, old, blind, lame and impotent, person, or other poor person not able to work" should "relieve and maintain every such poor person" unless they themselves were economically incapable. Those immediate relatives who would not offer such support were fined heavily.[29]

But for those individuals without family, the church and its various relief societies and efforts became a refuge. During the eighteenth, nineteenth, and the earlier part of the twentieth century much of charity was privately funded and organized, led by an army of volunteers who not only gave freely of their money, but also sacrificed their time and emotional energy to engage the poor, hold them accountable, meet their immediate needs, and prepare them for a life outside of poverty. However, as the needs

29. Olasky, *The Tragedy of American Compassion*, 13.

increased the call for governmental involvement grew louder. As the level of government increased, perhaps more than one volunteer felt a diminished personal sense of obligation and decided to allow the government even more control over the process. "The general sense was that many religious programs had effectively been secularized, and with it the excitement of sacrificing to keep them going was gone. There seemed to be no reason, except 'conservative stinginess,' to oppose the establishment of a new, massive governmental system. There seemed to be little reason to take seriously volunteer effort."[30]

Over time and with an expansionistic willingness, the conventional wisdom grew into an endorsement of government as the best entity to lead and coordinate the nationwide relief effort. That became the fifth assumption of modern poverty relief, or as Olasky has put it: "The trend was clear: Any time the charitable emphasis moved from the person to the mass and souls to stones, the government became the popular engine of progress."[31] Whether or not government is actually better positioned to lead the way in relief, the secondary effect was a move away from personal involvement and to a "transactional" view of relief. Why get involved with the local homeless when guilt can be assuaged by a monthly withdrawal tax that would eventually reach those "less fortunate"? As the role of government increased, the belief that government is best equipped to deal with poverty became cemented into the national consciousness. "The problems of supply (of private welfare agencies) were also a result of a long-term trend toward impersonal contribution. Philanthropy had become 'as cold as the payment of taxes,' with journalist Alan Herrick noting: 'Indeed the objectives of the two are often the same.'"[32]

Whereas Calvin entreated all believers to love thy neighbor as thyself, the recent institutionalization of poverty relief has made

30. Ibid., 149.
31. Ibid., 129.
32. Ibid., 150.

it more convenient merely to pay taxes to thy government and let someone else deal with the neighbors.

These five fundamental assumptions about poverty do not encompass the totality of relief efforts in the United States; nor do they completely handicap the work of charity. However, the concepts below are directly opposed to the theology and spirit of Calvinism:

1. Poverty can be eliminated.
2. Man has a right to sustenance.
3. Man is not responsible for his economic plight.
4. Compassion does not require accountability and change.
5. Government is the institution best suited to lead poverty-relief efforts.

Furthermore, this is not a sterile experiment; costs and effects have resulted from these suppositions.

These five premises are highlighted here as a demonstration of an impoverished underlying ideology and of the expense that is incurred by all parties involved in the equation—the poor, the relief worker, the government, and the non-poor. A complete analysis of the negative consequences of these five premises is beyond the scope of this book, but a quick listing of their ill effects is an argument with self-evidentiary logic. Among these ill effects are: (1) corruption, (2) inefficiency, (3) the entrenchment of "professional" relief workers and governmental agencies, (4) the skewing of taxation, and (5) the "politicization" of poverty relief.

Even in the eighteenth and nineteenth centuries, workers were constantly aware of and working against those who would "game the system" and appear at various centers in order to receive redundant aid. These miscreants were so adept at making the "rounds" that the colloquialism "rounders" entered the lexicon of many charities specifically to describe them. In the case of one town, some seventy recipients of government-sponsored relief owned more property (in terms of houses and cars) than the average non-poor resident of the community.[33] The lack of accountability, along with a sentimental, guilt-laden conscience, creates a powerful incentive for individuals who would prefer to take from others than to change their lifestyle.

Putting aside arguments relating to the progressive taxation system in the United States, there are multiple negatives embedded in the raising of funds by the state in order to provide for the poor and those in need. Take, for example, the HOPE Scholarship in Georgia, the supposed goal of which is to provide tuition relief to students in the state. According to the sponsor's website, the HOPE Scholarship is an "educational program to reward students who have earned good grades by helping with the expense of continuing their education after they graduate from high school. HOPE may be used at public technical colleges and eligible public or private colleges and universities in Georgia."[34] For most, it is a merit-based tuition program that combines state residency and continuing grade-point-average requirements. However, there is also a HOPE Grant program that offers complete tuition for any student who wishes to graduate from a Georgia technical college regardless of grade point average. At first glance, this is an ideal program to assist the poor who wish to gain further education. However, HOPE is financed through the Georgia Lottery for Education. Numerous studies of state lotteries indicate that on an absolute basis, lotteries are played consistently throughout all income ranges. Yet, when viewed on a relative basis, the participants in lower income tiers dedicate a higher portion of their income to lotteries. Those with potentially the least amount of disposable income are spending a larger percentage of their dollars.

33. "In Johnson, Rhode Island, it meant that seventy-three parents of children in a poverty program owned more property—fifty-eight homes and 113 cars—than the typical non-poor residents." Merritt Ierley, *With Charity for All* (New York: Praeger, 1984), 174, cited in Olasky, *The Tragedy of American Compassion*, 179.

34. See www.gacollege411.org.

This is a vicious circle that has the potential to bring more earners with marginal incomes under the state's umbrella of aid.[35]

Other stealth taxes on all citizens, including the poor and marginally poor, include property taxes, taxes on tobacco, and the general sales tax. Therefore, although one group is receiving help in one area (be it education, food, shelter, or medical services), another group—or even the very group receiving help—is being taxed through some other means. To quote once more from Amos Warner's 1894 study: "The burden of supporting the State tends to diffuse itself along the lines of the least resistance; consequently, money raised for the relief of the poor may come out of pockets that can ill spare it."[36]

As such, the one who controls the purse can control the people. Nathaniel Ware, after summarizing in 1845 his interpretation of Rome's fall, sadly predicted that an American governmental welfare system *would* develop, sooner or later, because officeholders liked to appeal to poor voters, who could give them not only the power to distribute large amounts of money, but also the patronage that accompanied expenditure. Ware noted that officers with more power would become more important and better paid.[37]

In the final analysis, some of the poor are here to stay. In God's providence, they are to rejoice in their calling and accept their lot, which for some may be vastly "richer" than that of Wall Street investment bankers. Those who are rich are called to be rich in "good deeds" and to care for widows and orphans.

35. See, for example, Texas Lottery Commission, "Demographic Study of Texas Lottery Players" (report prepared from data compiled by the Earl Survey Research Laboratory, Texas Tech University, 2005). This study shows those earning less than $20,000 per year spending 4.59% of their income annually. The group earning between $20,000 and $29,000 spent 4.38% of their income annually. For the top two income levels ($76,000 to $100,000 and more than $100,000) the amount spent playing the lottery was less than 1% of annual income. Perhaps this reveals that all men are equally tempted by the lure of easy money, but that the "poor" experience a larger impact to their earned income on a *relative* basis.

36. Quoted in Olasky, *The Tragedy of American Compassion*, 111.

37. Ibid., 48.

None of the costs or inadequacies should serve as motivation to disengage from the poor and the work of charity. Rather, an economic outlook worthy of the spirit of Calvin needs to weigh carefully the decisions to be made and to determine if they are more in line with biblical thought on the nature of man and his plight or with the erroneous assumptions typical of modern poverty-relief programs.

Large outlays of governmental relief do not necessarily confirm the extent of suffering that needs to be relieved; however, they may point to laxity or corruption on the part of officers and to a willingness on the part of able-bodied idlers to be fed at the public expense.[38] One antidote to such structural weaknesses is the approach that calls on the private sector, emphasizing the charitable work of free individuals over subsidy from an impersonal government, to put its hand to poverty relief.

Calvin's frequent expositions on love for one's neighbor led him and his followers to broaden the circle of philanthropy. Riding piggyback on growing profits and asset bases, the charitable spirit of Calvinism led to a new era for philanthropy, which was designed to flow from individuals and families to places of true need in order to stimulate fruitful development. However, over time the approach to poverty relief was transformed by grander thoughts of social equality and "justice." Calvin's thoroughgoing business ethic will best comport with systems or practices that work to eliminate the faulty assumptions on poverty that have emerged over the past fifty to sixty years.

38. Ibid., 64.

5

Sanctification and Service

Philanthropy, or love of one's fellow man, is both a theme and a by-product of Calvin's economic thinking. He consistently stressed that the goal for a person was not mere consumption or collection of economic assets. Instead, Calvin believed that those who have been given much bear a corresponding responsibility to care for and charitably give to those who have little.

Of course, this is nothing like a modern redistribution system. For Calvin, giving to others was a private or ecclesiastical activity, not a governmental prerogative. Even today, his various warnings about accumulating too much wealth can provide much-needed balance to Christians in business. With a calling to philanthropy—which may be understood as the strategic use of wealth provided by God to help others, contextualized by one's prior responsibility to provide for one's own family and church—Calvinists began to establish educational, artistic, and business institutions that would last for many generations. Such long-term giving, or using wealth to multiply good consequences into future generations, would become a hallmark of Calvinistic generosity.

Is Classlessness a Goal?

At this point, we may raise a legitimate question: Did Calvin or does Scripture advocate a classless society? While believers in many centuries have used a variety of verses from Scripture to reinforce the truth that no person is intrinsically better than another (some speak of the sinlessness of heaven, others speak of equality in the church, and still others speak of Christ's intention to make the first last and vice versa), still the teaching of Scripture is not that the family, the church, or society will strictly be without distinctions of some sort—at least not until the curse of the fall is fully redeemed. Some biblical texts are drawn upon more often than others in addressing this matter.

Commenting on Acts 2:44, Calvin clearly repudiated those who denied the ownership of private property, associating this view with the "drivellings of the Anabaptists and fanatics," who thought that private property ownership was wrong. Calvin noted that the author of the text, if rightly understood, did not "prescribe a law for all which everyone must of necessity follow, in relating the actions of people in whom the Spirit of God was manifest in a singular expression."[1]

The reality of different economic classes is woven throughout the biblical narratives and there is never any call to bring about a classless society. Nor is there an expectation that believers should act as if the rich among them were not rich or the poor among them were not poor. The expectation that the distinctions between rich and poor will disappear on earth is not one derived from Scripture.

1. Cited in André Biéler, *Calvin's Economic and Social Thought* (1959; repr., Geneva: World Alliance of Reformed Churches, 2005), 334.

On the other hand, the doctrine of providence helps account for poverty and wealth. Some people are given—by God's own assignment—more than others; and that is not a measurement of either merit or divine approval of righteousness. The sovereign Lord may dispense the amounts and assets he wishes to give in accordance with his plan; and the outcomes are not necessarily equal. By his providence, he may rightly give little to those who obey him and much to those who do not. All pious rationales aside, it may be little more than human coveting to expect all people to have the same level of assets. God seems quite comfortable in providing differing assets, to be used by each person for God's glory.

Correspondingly, biblical religion, especially the Protestantism of Calvin, identifies the responsibilities that are implicit in the fact that God has providentially arranged for different classes on earth. Rather than seeking to overthrow all classes, John Calvin called on people to accept God's providence, to give charitably to one's neighbor, and to find contentment in what God gives.

Liberality is also commended repeatedly in Calvin's commentaries. While disavowing giving as minimally as possible, he warned: "For what makes us more close-handed than we ought to be is—when we look too carefully, and too far forward, in contemplating the dangers that may occur—when we are excessively cautious and careful—when we calculate too narrowly what we will require during our whole life, or, in fine, how much we lose when the smallest portion is taken away."[2] Similarly, in comments on 2 Corinthians 8:13, he noted that it is "our part to stir ourselves up from time to time to liberality, because we must not be so much afraid of going to excess in this department. The danger is on the side of excessive [stinginess]."[3] Calvin seized on that occasion to denounce again (as he had in

2. John Calvin, *Commentary on the Epistles of Paul the Apostle to the Corinthians* (Grand Rapids: Baker Book House, 1979), 2:294.

3. Ibid.

his comments on Acts 2) the view of "fanatics" who believed that men should strip themselves "of everything so as to make everything common."[4]

Continuing his interpretation of 2 Corinthians 8, Calvin next launched into an important discussion of the meaning of equality (in Greek, *isotēs*). Calvin agreed with Aristotle on the essential meaning of that term as referring to "equality of proportional right" or opportunity "according to the stations of individuals and other circumstances."[5] Alluding also to Colossians 4:1, Calvin clarified that biblical equality does not entail a strict sameness of condition or station but calls for "humanity and clemency" in our treatment of all people, including servants: "Thus the Lord recommends to us a proportion of this nature, that we may, insofar as everyone's resources admit, afford help to the indigent."[6] Calvin believed that within the church this mutuality would produce a semblance of "befitting symmetry, though some have more and some less."[7]

Regardless of the class to which we belong, we are all called to face life without bitterness, envy, pride, or gluttony. An equality of intrinsic worth is given, but unequal levels of wealth are part of the providence of God, which is not to be despised or resisted.

One possible hope to affect classlessness is for the state to enforce full employment. Intensive research is not required, however, to learn that full employment is, in fact, structurally unstable and suboptimal. Basic economic theory identifies four types of unemployment: cyclical, frictional, classical, and structural. *Cyclical* unemployment occurs any time full hypothetical output is not attained. Cyclical unemployment can often be a result of underconsumption and decreasing demand. Accordingly, it is considered a part of the business cycle, and as such it cannot

4. Ibid.
5. Ibid.
6. Ibid., 2:295.
7. Ibid., 2:296.

feasibly be eliminated. *Frictional* unemployment is unemployment between jobs. In most cases frictional unemployment is voluntary and to an extent desirable as the employee searches for better labor. *Structural* unemployment is a direct result of changes in the economy. Often this type of unemployment results from technological advances or from drastic changes in demand. This type of unemployment is natural (and is typically a side effect of progress) and cannot feasibly be eliminated. Finally, *classical* unemployment occurs when the supply of workers exceeds the demand. This type of unemployment is often inhibited by wage laws and affirmative action.

By looking at the types of unemployment it becomes evident that full employment is neither feasible nor optimal. Furthermore, the undesirability of full employment can be summed up by three reasons—the first two of which relate to frictional unemployment. First, there are employees who will choose to invest in themselves through means such as education or additional training. Second, employees will seek to maximize their earning potential or job satisfaction through career changes. Third, labor specialization is absolutely necessary in a successful economic system. If an economic system mandates or otherwise calls for full employment, the results will prove chaotic due to the need for labor specialization. Full employment might employ a previously unemployed lawyer as a plumber. The plumber might have to take up lawn care as his profession, and gardeners might have to take up custodial work. There would be increasing frustration with the sacrifices required to meet this mandate.

Like the dream of classlessness, then, the goal of full employment is a plank in a utopian platform that agrees neither with Calvinism nor with long-term economic reality. While few theologies have ever emphasized the nobility of work and employment more than Calvinism has, nevertheless a Calvinistic perspective sees clearly that providence is a guiding force and that there will inevitably be periods with less than full employment.

Providence

…ertainly treated providence prominently. References to this … truth are laced throughout nearly every chapter of the *Institutes*. This notion is so much a part of the heart of Calvin that we cannot fully understand him if we ignore it.

From the outset of his great work, Calvin sought to clarify that providence is not to be confused with blind fate. Calvin viewed providence as "God's governance extended to all his works," which is "not the empty idle sort . . . but a watchful, effective, active sort, engaged in ceaseless activity" (*Institutes*, 1.16.3). He denied that God idly observes from heaven, and he viewed providence as "that by which, as keeper of the keys, he governs all events. Therefore we must prove [that] God so attends to the regulation of individual events, and they all so proceed from his set plan, that nothing takes place by chance" (1.16.4). Later Calvin asserted that "nothing happens except from [God's] command or permission" (1.16.8), and applying this assertion to an example of a merchant's death, he explained: "His death was not only foreseen by God's eye, but also determined by his decree. For it is not said that he foresaw how long the life of each man would extend, but that he determined and fixed the bounds that men cannot pass [Job 14:5]" (1.16.9). Thus, the Christian should view "a death of this sort [as] God's providence exercised . . . over fortune in directing its end" (1.16.9). For Calvin, providence is the determinative principle of all things (1.17.1), and indeed "the principal purpose of Biblical history is to teach that the Lord watches over the ways of the saints with such great diligence that they do not even stumble over a stone" (1.17.6). In sum, Calvin considered a proper understanding of providence to be both essential and practical, insofar as "ignorance of providence is the ultimate of all miseries; [whereas] the highest blessedness lies in the knowledge of it" (1.17.11).

Calvin noted the comfort of this doctrine: "Faith ought to penetrate more deeply, namely, having found [God] Creator of all . . .

to conclude he is also everlasting Governor and Preserver—not only in that he drives the celestial frame . . . but also in that he sustains, nourishes, and cares for everything he has made, even to the least sparrow" (1.16.1).

Calvin viewed the doctrine of God's providence as a very practical "benefit" (1.18.1; 1.17.11). Since God's providence is determinative of all things (1.17.2, 4, 7, 9), Calvin felt that it provided believers with security and confidence in the immutable decree of God (1.18.6). The final chapter of book 1 of the *Institutes* illustrates how Calvin saw the doctrine of providence as bearing immense comfort and application. He anticipated practical discrepancies and addressed them succinctly in that chapter (1:18.3–5). He further spoke of the gratitude of mind, patience in adversity, and incredible freedom from worry that "all necessarily flow from the knowledge" of God's providence (1:18.7).

Calvin was the preacher, not the rationalist, when he punctuated his discussion of providence with the rhetorical refrain, "if Joseph had stopped to dwell on his brothers' treachery . . . if Job had turned his attention to the Chaldeans . . . if David had fixed his eye upon Shimei" (1.17.8). Calvin argued that the absence of God's providence would leave us in an unbearable situation—hopeless in the face of innumerable evils (1.17.10). Furthermore, he expected "relief" and "solace" to flow from learning to trust God's providence (1.17.11).

Calvin extolled God's providence in these words:

> Let those for whom this seems harsh consider for a little while how bearable their squeamishness is in refusing a thing attested by clear Scriptural proofs because it exceeds their mental capacity, and find fault that things are put forth publicly, which if God had not judged useful for men to know, he would never have bidden his prophets and apostles to teach. For our wisdom ought to be nothing else than to embrace with humble teachableness, and at least without finding fault, whatever is

> taught in Sacred Scripture. Those who too insolently scoff, even though it is clear enough that they are prating against God, are not worthy of a longer refutation (1.18.4).

About a century after Calvin, the *Westminster Confession of Faith* (1646) perpetuated Calvin's view, describing providence in these words: "God, the great Creator of all things, doth uphold, direct, dispose, and govern all creatures, actions, and things from the greatest to the least by his most wise and holy providence." This view of providence is entirely consistent with the words of Paul who, in his discussion of spiritual gifts in 1 Corinthians 12:11, emphasizes that each person should be content with the gifts that God has apportioned according to his will. In turn, we should share our gifts with the body, or as Calvin put it in commenting on Paul's words: "Gifts are not distributed thus variously among believers, in order that they may be used apart, but that in the division there is a unity, inasmuch as one Spirit is the source of all those gifts."[8]

God's providence is present in all events. We need to learn to see his "invisible hand" working in all things. He is truly sovereign over all of history. To doubt that is to reject God's lordship. Such repudiation is not merely based on an absence of information; it is also a rebellion of the heart against one's Creator. Happy is the person who learns to see God's hand in all of life. Calvin had that perspective, and he well understood that to "avoid a senseless natural philosophy we must always start with this principle: that everything in nature depends upon the will of God, and that the whole course of nature is only the prompt carrying into effect of his orders."[9]

Providence Is Frequently Taught in the Bible

Early on in the Gospels, providence is seen in the life of Jesus' mother. Mary, who wanted to donate value and riches to the world,

8. Ibid., 1:398.
9. R. C. Sproul, *Chosen by God* (Wheaton, IL: Tyndale House, 1994), 46.

was poor. Yet, God used her to bless the world.
by an angel to go to Egypt, but she did not h
and Joseph did not even have enough to pay f
But God in his providence brought wise men
the East, and with these gifts Mary and Jos
obey God and go to Egypt. The Savior of the
safe by God's providence.

Jesus' dealing with Judas even displays the providence of God. As people read the passages in the Gospels that relate to Judas, they cannot help but ask, how could God allow something like that to happen? Jesus had an answer: God had raised Judas up for a specific purpose. To be sure he would betray Jesus, but that too was part of God's plan. It was not outside his providence that Judas would betray Jesus. Yet, the outcome would not be a pleasant one for Judas. It would have been better for him had he not been born.

In fact, the entire life of Jesus is a demonstration of God's providence. Jesus was never captured prior to the time that God wanted him to be arrested; nor was he taken a split second later. All of Jesus' life exactly matched the providence of God.

The same can be said of the leading Christian of the first century, the apostle Paul. He was converted exactly as God's providence planned. It was no accident that he went up to Damascus to persecute Christians. God met him on the way and provided not only salvation for Paul, but also a great missionary for the early church.

Later Paul was shipwrecked. In Acts 27 we see how God's providence extends to care for his people. Not only was Paul spared, but the lives of all the other shipmates were spared as well. Paul was kept safe by the providence of God, and he arrived at Rome just as God had earlier promised.

God's sustaining activity is taught in both testaments. God's providence is exercised in the sustaining of the entire universe (Col. 1:17). And Isaiah teaches that God's providence covers even

…rs: "Lift your eyes and look to the heavens: Who created all …se? He who brings out the starry host one by one, and calls them each by name. Because of his great power and mighty strength, not one of them is missing" (Is. 40:26). Furthermore, we read in Hebrews 1:2 that "the whole universe is made through the Son," and Job 12:10 notes, "In his hand is the life of every creature and the breath of all mankind."

Psalm 145:15–16 affirms: "The eyes of all look to you and you give [provide] them their food at the proper time. You open your hand and satisfy the desires of every living thing." In similar fashion, Psalm 147:8–9 states: "God covers the sky with clouds; he supplies the earth with rain and makes grass grow on the hills. He provides food for the cattle and for the young ravens when they call." Acts 17:25 teaches that "[God] is not served by human hands, as if he needed anything, because he himself gives all men life and breath and everything else," while Job 34:14–15 reminds us: "If [God] withdrew his spirit and breath, all mankind would perish together and man would return to dust."

If the providence of God were subtracted from God's character, one of two idols would be spawned: either a God who, not being provident, is also not the Creator; or a God who created but cannot sustain. Neither of those idols will nourish human existence; nor are they taught in the Scriptures.

Such an essentially Calvinistic idea extended so far in time as to be echoed in the words of George Washington, who lived two centuries after Calvin. "Providence," Washington once said, "has at all times been my only dependence, for all other resources seem to have failed us."[10] Similarly, the Declaration of Independence affirms: "With a firm reliance on the protection of Divine Providence, we mutually pledge to each other our lives, our fortunes, and our sacred honor." Earlier Christians were not afraid to confess

10. Cited in Sproul, *Chosen by God*, 12.

that providence was essential to God and to their living. It would do most Christians well to return to this view of God's providence as a mainstay in our daily lives.

God's providence extends to all people, all events, all ages, and all regions. The seventeenth-century Calvinist Thomas Watson said, "The diocese where Providence visits is very large; it reaches to heaven, earth, and sea."[11] It also reaches to the smallest of things, to sparrows that fall and to the hairs on our head (Mt. 10:29–30). Watson concluded, "Surely if providence reaches to our hairs, much more to our souls."[12]

Calvin's teaching on providence has many ramifications. One of these applies to the institution of free markets. For if God has sovereign government over economies, then the free market might easily be an instrument of his will. He might have had a hint that in larger economies, management of highly complex markets might not be possible. One modern work summarizes the point this way.

> The free market is consistent with the Biblical view of human nature in another way. It recognizes the weaknesses of human nature and the limitations of human knowledge. No one can possibly know enough to manage a complex economy. No one should ever be trusted with this power. This statement applies with equal force to people who control large corporations, to politicians who control a nation and to the small group of appointed individuals who control the Federal Reserve System. In order for socialism to work, it requires a class of omniscient planners to forecast the future, to set prices and to control production. In the free market system, decisions are not made by an omniscient bureaucratic elite, but made across the entire economic system by countless economic agents.[13]

11. Thomas Watson, *A Body of Divinity* (Edinburgh: Banner of Truth, 1984), 120.

12. Ibid., 121.

13. James P. Gills and Ronald H. Nash, *A Biblical Economics Manifesto: Economics and the Christian Worldview* (Lake Mary, FL: Creation House, 2002), 25–26.

Given the discussion of divine providence, we now turn our focus to its implications for business. In particular, we shall explore how providence lays the groundwork for what we call "economic sanctification." Before we treat the theme of sanctification, however, it might be helpful to say a few words about the doctrine of election. Often spoken of in spiritual terms, election is the natural complement to God's sovereignty and is relevant to the calling of men, their position in life, their wealth, their talents, and their resources. However, to confine election to the spiritual realm is theologically insufficient and sets the stage for a myriad of faulty worldviews and beliefs that affect business theory and practice.

At one end of the spectrum is the concept of Reformed, biblical economic election. As discussed previously, a major truth is that both the poor and the rich are always present. Furthermore, the Reformed view holds that each man is elected or called to the economic status and occupational role in which he finds himself. There are no cosmic accidents of wealth or poverty. Although man plans and makes choices, it is God who decides the ultimate outcome. However, man is not free to do nothing and wait upon God's grace for sustenance. Man has both general responsibilities and specific responsibilities both to God and to others as God reveals his economic election and calling. First and foremost among these responsibilities is the requirement to work. Second, man is required to act within the confines of the legal and governmental system under which he finds himself. Third, if under a master or employer, he is required to obey and serve with a gracious heart, as working unto the Lord. Now, if a man is elected to be wealthy in this world, he is required to be "rich in good works," generous, and forgiving. The poor also have responsibilities—e.g., not to succumb to jealously or theft. Both have the responsibility to be content and to give thanksgiving to God in all their circumstances. Under biblical economics some are elected to wealth, some are elected to poverty, and some are elected to the middle class. Members of each group are given certain responsibilities. Applicable to all classes, the model is also dynamic; in other words, this economic election is not permanent—movement between classes is possible and probable. At the other end of the conceptual spectrum is the classless and non-dynamic system made famous by Marx. Trading the Reformed perspective for the utopian stability and strawberry fields of equalized sustenance for the rich and the poor may appear tempting at first glance. However, a comparison of the two extremes—including an analysis of their foundational assumptions, their prerequisites, and a few of their practical results—exposes the folly of the classless ideal.

Sanctification

A proper question to ask when discussing any system is, what behavior does the system motivate or encourage? Under Marx, the goal was equality, often obscured under the rubric of justice. However, a Marxist system creates by-products that need to be examined before they are embraced. For example, the classless system reduces the incentive to excel above the norm. Correspondingly, it also persuades some individuals either not to work or simply to rely on others. This system yields some workers who are not reaching their full potential and some who are simply not working at all. For example, assume an employer has three employees, all of whom he chooses to pay on an equal annual basis in order to achieve economic justice. Each of the three employees performs different tasks within the organization. If one of the three employees finds out that his salary increase, year after year, is identical to that of the other two employees, regardless of performance, he will seldom be motivated to excel. The employee is trapped. In a worst-case scenario the employee will, in fact, do nothing, and he will rely on the employer's previously displayed desire for economic justice.

A classless system eliminates the vital concepts of personal accountability and consequences; it also reduces the incentive of personal reward. When human nature is presented with those by-products, it responds in a way that has a decidedly negative impact on business efficiency and productivity.

Several prerequisites are required in order to achieve a classless system. Karl Marx mentions three. The first is the abolition of private property, which was discussed earlier. The second prerequisite is equal education for all. A 1996 article in the *New Internationalist* describes the Marxist view:

> Free education of equal quality for all is fundamental to the classless society. It can then begin to serve its real function, to bring out the natural talents of everyone. Education on class-based societies is wasteful of talent and teaches most children to devalue themselves so that they will fit in. It is hard to imagine anything more pernicious than this. In a classless society the education of privilege will be an acronym.[14]

What is interesting about these words is the assertion that classless education frees all individuals to pursue their different talents and to do the things that match their distinctive gifts. Therefore, a classless society is also a conflict-free society. However, those two characteristics are mutually exclusive. First of all, a classless education will eventually teach to a lowest common denominator, because individuals with superior talents in various fields will be trapped. They will not be motivated to pursue their talents. Eventually, there will be no one pursuing certain talents, no one with enhanced talents, and thus no teachers or schools for many disciplines within education. Additionally, this theory is predicated on man acting in a perfectly rational and sinless manner. It assumes that money or the reallocation of resources is the

14. Editorial board, "Manifesto for the Millenium," *New Internationalist* 281 (July 1996).

only variable in the equation. The assumption that an increase in money and resources automatically brings an increase in education needs far more empirical support than most Marxist analyses provide. However, this view simply assumes that all men have the same ambition, the same motivation, the same diligence toward education, and that their education provides them each with the same level of marginal utility. Furthermore, it assumes that all opportunity costs are equalized.

Classical economic theory is often ridiculed for its assumption that all men are acting rationally. However, considering the list of underlying assumptions required to sustain the Marxist version of equal education for all, it appears that the ridicule is misplaced. Furthermore, one could contend that education for all is currently available, particularly in Western society. For better or worse, there are multitudinous educational opportunities available (mechanical school, collegiate education, medical school, law school, etc.) to any individual who is willing to apply himself. Therefore, education is already an option for everyone, even without a classless society.

The third explicit prerequisite for a classless society, as envisioned by Marx, is the elimination of money for commercial exchange. Marx postulated that money dehumanizes us and creates a transaction-based society. In his perfect society, a baker will bake and distribute his product appropriately; he will also pick up his clothing from the tailor who picked up a basket of bread yesterday. However, this quaint arrangement is shattered by the problem of scarce resources, not to mention the reality that some work is harder than others.

For example, assume one is called to be a distiller of fine scotch whisky. Good scotch, by its nature, is scarce. With respect to this career path, therefore, several inconsistencies appear in a classless society that has eliminated money. First, scotch takes time. Second, it is produced in limited quantities. Third, assume that the individual distilling the scotch is passionate about his work and wants to produce the very best scotch possible (an attitude that Marx assumes of all workers in his classless society). If that is the goal, then the distiller will want the malt to sit longer in the cask, because the longer it sits, the better it becomes. But this creates an implicit conflict between him and the classless secretariat of distilling, which wants the scotch immediately. The distiller wants it later, because he knows it will be better—and that leads to an unavoidable conflict of interests. Last, once he delivers the scotch, it will be difficult to distribute on an equal basis, for it is a scarce commodity. Everyone will not be content to have a mere dram of fine scotch once a year. The use of money eliminates these conflicts and allows him to produce his scotch to the best of his ability and to command a higher price within the market so that he may properly pursue his calling.

The practical result of these three prerequisites and the incentives involved is that eventually a group of elite leaders must come together. This group will have to make allocation and production decisions. In order for this situation to be justified, humans, particularly those who are leading, must have sinless natures that prevent them from abusing their position. Historical evidence confirms the opposite.

On the other hand, the system that accepts the reality of different economic classes (but simultaneously affirms the equality of value and dignity of each human being) incentivizes individuals to pursue their callings and to move forward within the economy. The characteristics of such a system, as put forth by Adam Smith, are as follows: it produces opportunities; it enforces property rights; and it regards risks and labor. In producing opportunities, the system entails a codicil—namely, that the more rationally an individual acts, the better. Furthermore, information is a key lubricant to this process, as demonstrated by the emergence of the Internet, which has rapidly created multiple opportunities for individuals. In regard to property rights, the best system is the one in which there is a quick appeal to these rights. Speed of response for claiming, asserting, and protecting property rights makes the system more robust. Moreover, with respect to rewards for risks and labor, the implication is that the system will also allow for consequences and/or punishments for those who choose not to work or make bad decisions.

Practically, the majority of the systems within the world today exist in the middle of these two extremes. When looking at the more open of the systems there are still multitudes of inefficiencies and distortions worthy of comment. Under opportunities, for example, there are distortions to the entrepreneur and the capitalist whenever regulation and taxation hinder the ability to start an enterprise and do business.

In a recent issue of *Forbes* magazine, Steve Forbes writes about a book entitled *Doing Business*, which is issued annually by the World Bank. The book "surveys 178 economies—from Afghanistan to Zimbabwe—in regard to their regulations that affect how businesses are started and conducted." According to Forbes:

> Countries are judged in ten categories that span the life of an enterprise, from its launching, to coping with licenses, obtaining credit, paying taxes, enforcing contracts and dealing with bankruptcy or dissolution of the entity. It comes as no surprise that the most prosperous countries are those that rank well in these indexes. Property rights and the rule of law are essential for businesses to be created *and* to expand. Poor countries don't lack for entrepreneurial energy. What they lack are the structures and institutions that enable this energy to be channeled and rewarded in ways that lead to sustained economic growth.[15]

Forbes goes on to quote directly from the book as it discusses Egypt, which is awarded top honors as a reformer in the 2008 edition of *Doing Business*. "Its reforms went deep," the book says

15. Steve Forbes, "Mighty Book," *Forbes*, June 30, 2008, 17.

of Egypt, noting that the country "made starting a business easier, slashing [by 98%] the minimum capital requirement and halving startup time and cost. Fees for registering property were reduced from 3% of the property value to a low fixed fee. New one-stop shops were launched for traders at the ports, cutting the time to import by seven days and the time to export by five. The first private credit bureau was established. And builders now face less bureaucracy in getting construction permits."[16]

At the industry level, and subsequently the consumer level, opportunities are distorted whenever countries decide to implement quotas, tariffs, and government subsidies. Examples of this include the textile industry and the sugar industry. For years, the United States has limited the amount of textiles coming into the country from places such as Africa, India, and China. The "benefit" of this is "economic justice" for workers in America, who are ostensibly supported in their ability to earn a living wage making shirts and pants. The distortion is that American labor is misallocated into jobs that can be performed at the same level or better by individuals worldwide who are willing to be paid less. This goes beyond the problems of sweatshops, child labor, and forced labor. The fallout is that industries among Africans (who are in dire need of demand in order to increase employment and raise a standard of living that is grossly below ours) are hobbled in order to insure that a factory worker in Indiana can buy the DVD player that he wants. Such a protectionist approach implies that justice only applies to the citizens of the United States. Therefore, these shortsighted and utopian policies attempt to protect one group of individuals at the expense of others, to whose votes American politicians are not beholden.

The discussion of economic election leads to an important application of the concept of sanctification that Calvin emphasized. Sanctification within the life of a believer is marked by the

16. Ibid.

enduring presence of the Holy Spirit working to eliminate sin and to conform the believer to the image of Christ. It is a process of lifelong improvement and sometimes resembles a cycle of ups and downs as a believer sins, persists in sin, is convicted, repents, and makes changes in his lifestyle. However, the overall trend is an upward trajectory of character with conformity to the life of Christ as the goal. Calvin taught that God is faithful and forgiving and that perfect moral actions are not prerequisites for salvation.

In many ways the business cycle is symbolic of this act of sanctification. There are excesses (sin) and poor allocations that cause a down cycle. During a down cycle, capital is reallocated, thinking and behavior are changed, new focus is brought, discipline is strengthened, scarce capital is recognized, structural changes may be made (new laws), and core incompetence is identified and focused upon anew. The Bible speaks of cycles and makes no moral judgment on them. Joseph is instructed to prepare for the down cycle with regard to wheat. Interestingly, the abundance during the seven years prior to the famine was integral to his preparations. Farmers were not chastised for growing record crops, and undoubtedly many were enriched as Joseph filled the storehouses and bought grain at above-market prices. Regardless, cycles are a fact of reality, and their ill effects can be soothed partially by proper planning.

However, both Marx and Keynes maintained a radically different view on the role of business cycles, and both of them aimed to stop the cycle. They envisioned a noncyclical utopia in which pain avoidance in the short-term was the primary driver. Marx wanted to achieve this utopia through strict state control of resources and profits. Keynes wanted to achieve it by allowing government to tweak monetary and fiscal policy. When Keynes first announced these concepts, they were rapidly welcomed by many economists because they offered a palatable solution that contained most of the benefits of Marxist ideology with very little of the baggage of socialism. However, the cycle should not be eliminated since it represents a type of sanctification within the marketplace. In order for "economic sanctification" to occur there must be a freedom to fail, a freedom to succeed, and a freedom to change.

The first true prerequisite for sanctification is failure. If the world were free of failure and sin, there would be no need for a savior, and in turn no need for sanctification. When applying this to markets, the natural tendency is to speak about market freedom or laissez-faire markets. Most discussions about market freedoms tend toward debates about success, government involvement, the positive and negative aspects of unregulated wealth, etc. Therefore, it may seem odd to be speaking about failure as a needed element for economic systems. The key, however, is that both men and economic institutions need room to fail and to experience the full pain and consequences (economic and otherwise) of the trough.

In Calvin's teaching on personal sanctification, he focused much of his attention on the law, and he did not suggest that the standards of the law be lessened. However, that is the temptation man faces when addressing his own corrupt nature. Man tends to lessen the scrutiny of the law in an attempt to justify his own sinfulness. Thus, man is constantly seeking to decrease the gap between what should be and what is. Likewise, when speaking of economic sanctification, the same temptations are present. Speaking economically, the standard is a business entity that is maximizing profit, maximizing utility, allocating resources, making rational decisions within governmental and legal frameworks, and benefiting both itself and others within the marketplace. However, our worldly yen for security often finds ways to mitigate the corrections of the free market.

On May 28, 1987 a German pilot by the name of Mathias Rust landed his plane next to Moscow's Red Square. Flying from Finland he eluded Soviet air defenses several times. Upon landing he was greeted by Soviet citizens and onlookers. He was eventually taken away by the KGB. Within days the Soviet defense chief was fired. Weeks later, hundreds within the Soviet military lost their jobs. It was the biggest turnover in the Soviet military command since Stalin's bloody purges in the 1930s. This was two years prior to *glasnost* and at what some would consider the height of the cold war. This story exemplifies the concept of consequences within the workforce. Ironically, the consequences were on full display in a country that was, at the time, Communist. Frequently, decisions are made to avoid layoffs and consequences at any cost. Sanctification, however, often begins with failure. To proceed in grace begins by recognizing sin as sin, accepting it, and rebuilding with conviction and resolve. Unfortunately, for many economic accountability is muted, and the accountability shown by the illustration above seldom occurs.

The ideal economic system will be one that permits the full repercussions of the trough to be felt. Ours will remain a fallen universe. A key element to maintaining the sanctifying lessons of the trough is the continual presence of competition in both labor and capital markets. Adam Smith adamantly asserted that competition is vital to keep self-interest in check. Thus, a series of checks and balances is necessary. Biblically, the checks and balances in the believer's life involve a combination of internal and external sources. Internally, the Spirit of God works by giving man the desire to love and obey God, as this is his true calling and self-interest. Without the work of God, man's self-interests are centered only upon the flesh and can lead to ruin if unabated. Externally, the man is limited and guided by the church through such means as accountability (Mt. 18:15), training (Heb. 12:11), encouragement (1 Thess. 4:18), and reproof (2 Tim. 3:16). As it is with man, so it is within the efficient market—self-interest (the internal control) is tempered by competition (the external control). From Adam Smith's *Wealth of Nations*, one may learn:

> But man has almost constant occasion for the help of his brethren, and it is in vain for him to expect it from their benevolence

> only. He will be more likely to prevail if he can interest their self-love in his favour, and shew them that it is for their own advantage to do for him what he requires of them. Whoever offers to another a bargain of any kind, proposes to do this. Give me that which I want, and you shall have this which you want, is the meaning of every such offer; and it is in this manner that we obtain from one another the far greater part of those good offices which we stand in need of. *It is not from the benevolence of the butcher, the brewer, or the baker that we expect our dinner, but from their regard to their own interest. We address ourselves, not to their humanity, but to their self-love, and never talk to them of our own necessities, but of their advantages* (emphasis added).[17]

Implicit to Smith's statement is the assumption of the inherent balance of the marketplace. Competition ensures that an individual's self-interest will not rage uncontrollably, but will rather be checked by the equally strong self-interest of others. If an individual relies upon "benevolence only" from others or seeks to gain at the loss of others, the painfulness of failure dealt by the efficient hand of competition awaits him.

In the course of economic cycles, there are times when business entities fail and fall short of bringing accountability. When that happens, they fall below the standard. The temptation is the same here as it is with personal sanctification—i.e., to reduce artificially the gap between what should be and what is.

As a result of succumbing to this temptation, we have allowed many of the underlying themes and assumptions found in Marx and Keynes to work their way into our current economic systems. For example, individuals who are experiencing personal economic downturns (or troughs) often seek relief through institutional programs such as welfare and food stamps. Such programs, if

17. Adam Smith, *An Inquiry into the Nature and Causes of the Wealth of Nations* (New York: Modern Library, 1937), 14.

used without limits and accountability, often serve to heighten man's fallen condition and selfishness, producing relief that can be analogous to an individual living on a credit card with increasing limits but no practical method of future payment in sight. They can encourage individuals to live outside of their means, and as such they reduce the lessons that the trough of the business cycle is intended to provide. Thus, motivation to improve is lost, and reliance on others is increased.

Through governmental transfer programs, one man's trough is subsidized by another man's peak. Aside from the obvious reduction in the motivation of one party, other consequences of this invisible transaction include a dislocation of family responsibilities and a lowering of incentives for future generations. For many in the United States today, it is easier to go to Uncle Sam for a handout than it is to ask a family member for assistance and/or advice.

On the corporate side, the attempt to eliminate economic troughs has led to a variety of distortions in the form of price controls, government subsidies, tariffs, and quotas. At the extreme, there are even examples of government bailouts of entire industries (e.g., the bailout of Chrysler in the early 1980s and current discussions involving the home-mortgage industry). The result of these distortions and inefficiencies for both individuals and corporations is an artificial narrowing of the gap between what should be and what is. But closing that gap delays economic sanctification by postponing decision-making, accommodating a poor work ethic, decreasing urgency, reducing consequences, and retarding the sense of purpose to which everyone within the marketplace is entitled.

Economic children of Calvin should support systems that enforce legal and structural standards, allow for failure within the marketplace, and resist the kind of delaying mechanisms that merely avoid the hard lessons taught by the trough of the business cycle. A key consequence of behaving otherwise is that final prices for consumers and participants within the marketplace are increased. These higher prices reduce the amount of resources that individuals have to save and to give. So in many ways, not only is the individual experiencing the trough robbed of motivation, but also the successful individual is deprived of the highest peaks of his potential earnings.

According to conventional wisdom, the alcoholic must hit rock bottom before true change can begin. Similarly, fiscally irresponsible individuals and corporations that are not sound must experience failure in order to mature and advance economically. An economic system that is built without accountability and consequences will inevitably become one-sided and full of individuals who are content merely to rely on the wealth of others to meet their needs.

Failure is actually healthy for the marketplace because it promotes competition, provides opportunity, and keeps the risk-reward equation in balance. On the other hand, the marketplace must also give businesses the freedom to succeed to their fullest potential. Individuals and corporations alike need to maximize wealth and profits for the purpose of optimizing their giving and future investments. Successful entities evaluate and embrace their calling, allocate their resources with wisdom, and are motivated to achieve their goals through hard work and sacrifice.

Unfortunately, in many systems today there are inefficiencies and distortions that skew success and attempt to limit gross success. The distortions that are incongruent with sanctification are in many ways similar to the distortions that retard the lessons associated with failure. Currently, the U.S. Congress is discussing allowing additional profit taxes on oil companies. Although this is politically popular, the ramifications include a potential reduction of funds available for future energy research. Energy research, however, has the potential to reduce the cost of energy beyond the ability of any degree of taxation. Similarly, the progressive tax system of the United States imposes marginal tax increases on individuals as their income grows. In many ways this places a governor on success.

At a basic level these practices reduce the pool of investable wealth and property that can be used for charity and for reinvestment in the future. In today's marketplace, success is most commonly measured by profits. Both Marx and Keynes viewed profit as a morally negative, temporary surplus due to exploitation. Implicit in these claims is the idea that profit is nothing more than a short-term inducement to attract the capitalist. Underlying all of these ideas is the concept that there is no continual place within the economy for profit. But as Joseph Schumpeter (1883–1950) demonstrated in the early twentieth century, continuing profit should be embraced as a necessary outcome that sustains subsequent input in the form of reinvestment.[18] His analysis correctly recognized capitalism as a system that is always changing through dynamic equilibriums. In fact, the key to such an ever-changing economy is innovation.

The profits that come from innovation and its successful operations are needed to continue to hire labor and build more capital. Profit is not evil; rather, it is a sign of innovation and a moral imperative for further production and labor. Therefore, profit fulfills a very essential economic function and practically serves as an input.

In the concept of sanctification as discussed by Calvin, there are times of both reaping and sowing when the believer experiences the joy and the peace that come with obedience to God and embracing a calling. This, in turn, moves the believer to greater faith as grace and forgiveness are applied. Likewise, the economic entity that reinvests wisely will normally experience great economic growth and economic sanctification. Such a process requires

18. Peter Drucker, "Modern Prophets: Schumpeter and Keynes?" *Forbes*, May 23, 1983.

engagement in creative destruction but also a plan to store up for future downturns that are sure to come.

Therefore, systems need to embrace profit without governmental disruptions for three main reasons:

1. An increase in profit means an increase in potential wealth that can be used to serve others.
2. Profit is a moral imperative to continued enterprise, fair pricing, and innovation.
3. The storehouse of success can be used by entities to survive future downturns.

In many ways excessive taxation, regulation, quotas, and tariffs reduce the storehouse, thus inadvertently creating a weaker aggregate entity. Therefore, when downturns occur, the entity is forced to rely on the same governmental crutches that have previously prevented the entity from achieving maximum profit. Those who propose governmental reallocation of resources often do so under the claim of offering protection to the struggling. However, the profit-reducing actions that are taken at the peak of the cycle are often ignored.

For a system to embrace both failure and success, it must also allow for economic change. Sanctification, by its definition, is all about change. The Scriptures are full of examples of men who experience radical change in their lives (e.g., Paul and Matthew). Within strictly planned economies freedom to change is very limited. The individual is tasked to do whatever the state assigns to him. However, even in the United States many prevailing practices and concepts relieve individuals of the responsibility to make hard decisions. For example, the concept of easy credit is designed to promote one's economic standard of living without great effort. This encourages persons and businesses to live beyond their means. There are also agencies that provide relief to individuals without requiring them to make hard changes in their lifestyles. Calvin would advise greater reliance on divine providence, hard work, and contentment.

In the midst of creative destruction, adaptation without long-term government aid or intervention is a key to survival. However, another aspect of change could be better termed "creative construction." This is the freedom of individuals to go into completely different areas and venture forth to new callings completely outside of their current occupational realms. Creative destruction occurs when the profits enjoyed by a service or good are reduced to the minimal amount, and the provider/entrepreneur is forced to "destroy" some or all of an existing production process, product, or benefit, in order to create some new efficiency, use, or attractiveness that will restore a healthy profit level. Typically, the term is used in the context of economic entities, companies, and industries. On the other hand, creative construction involves an individual or company that is required to abandon one calling or product line and either to create something completely new or to enter into a new area of employment. Often the destruction that is required for such an activity has already occurred, not voluntarily as an act of self-preservation but involuntarily as a result of factors in the marketplace. Hence, the individuals or entities are frequently "treading water" as their service or product suddenly is marginalized to the final degree. The challenge for survival then lies in their ability to radically adjust and move into completely new or different arenas while still maintaining their core skill sets. On a micro level, an example may be a minister who has suddenly found himself unemployed and unable to reenter the ministry. Rather than pursue ministry-related or parachurch opportunities, he may engage in "creative construction" by repositioning himself in marketing, human resources, sales, education, or healthcare.

On the corporate level, the recent history of Corning hints at creative construction on a larger scale. In 2000 Corning was enjoying record revenues of $7.2 billion and profits of $410 million. Moreover, as the source for fiber-optic cable throughout the world, the company's stock traded as high as $113 per share. However, in 2000 and 2001 the telecommunications industry stalled out due to overcapacity. The demand for fiber dropped precipitously. By 2003 Corning's revenues were less than half their record levels, $3.03 billion, and profits were nonexistent. The stock value dropped to a low of $1.10 per share in October 2002. Creative destruction implies that Corning should have made their fiber production more efficient (which they did), with more bandwidth capacity per line (which they achieved), and greater flexibility in the fiber to accommodate more difficult and broader applications (which they accomplished). However, all these changes were to no avail. Creative construction brought Corning to the point of pursuing an entirely new application of their skill set—the production of flat-screen monitors for computers and televisions. Today Corning is one of the world's leaders in flat-screen innovation and production. Revenues for 2007 were $5.8 billion, with record profits of $2.1 billion; meanwhile, the value of Corning's stock has risen well above $20 per share.[19] This illustrates how market systems need to be open and flexible to allow individuals and entities the opportunity to change to any degree—either through creative destruction or through creative construction. Furthermore, it suggests that any system that impedes or retards flexibility stunts economic sanctification and possibly exposes companies and workers to economic disaster at some later time.

Change, flexibility, adaptation, and growth are all needed. There is a place for each of these; and the fact that they also yield profit is a virtue, certainly not a vice. Furthermore, within this pro-profit grid there is also room for charity.

Sanctification, or improvement toward virtue, is a concept that should be included in the business sector. It is not impossible for growth and improvement to occur; on the contrary, those are

19. Financial data on Corning (GLW) courtesy of Thomson Reuters Baseline Database, http://www.thomsonreuters.com/products_services/financial/financial_products/investment_management/research_analysis/baseline.

normal expectations within a good business culture. Calvinism is helpful at this point also, for it reminds us that often improvement only comes after a trough. Failure, sin, mistakes, miscalculations, and error all occur. Economic sanctification does not seek an environment in which these never occur; rather, it requires the opportunity and the freedom to learn from our mistakes—first, of course, by admitting them and then by changing course so that our activities are brought more into line with God's ways.

It is worth reiterating in this context that neither the firmest reliance on God's providence, nor a complete openness to God's continual correction, permits individuals or businesses to be lethargic in terms of improving profit or caring for real needs around us.

Does Providence Condone Inconsiderateness toward Poverty?

In light of the above insights and teachings from Calvin, what should our attitudes be toward the poor? As with many other things, a fine balance is needed, and those blessed with wealth should pose this question often. It is certainly possible to become too callous or wasteful. Calvin and his followers digested much of the OT wisdom in the book of Proverbs.

Proverbs 11:24 illustrates that poverty can result from not sharing as God wants. Proverbs 13:23 also exhibits the vulnerability of the poor, whose work produces an abundance only to be blown away by injustices. Proverbs 13:18 identifies one cause of poverty—not learning from mistakes. The failure to heed correction, like the ignoring of discipline, brings poverty and shame. While the rich may accumulate friends as well as wealth, the poor seldom amass a multitude of friends (Prov. 14:20; 19:4, 7). Similarly, the person who is kind to the needy is blessed (Prov. 14:21).

Two proverbs (14:31 and 17:5) contain the same warning: "He who oppresses the poor shows contempt for their Maker, but whoever is kind to the needy honors God" (see also Prov. 29:13). Proverbs 19:17 further comments that persons who are kind to the poor lend to the Lord and will be rewarded for their kindness. Material poverty, however, is not the worst of conditions; it is better to be poor and blameless than to be a fool with perverse lips (Prov. 19:1). Moreover, it is better to be poor than to be a liar (Prov. 19:22) or a rich man who is perverse (Prov. 28:6).

Callousness to the plight of the poor is condemned by the wisdom of the OT (Prov. 21:13), which reminds us that both the wealthy and the impoverished have a common Maker (Prov. 22:2). Proverbs 22:22–23 warns that exploiting the poor, like crushing the needy in court, will lead the Lord to "plunder those who plunder them." A truly generous man is blessed and "shares his food with the poor" (Prov. 22:9), showing the kind of philanthropy that should overflow from a godly work ethic. Proverbs 22:16 warns that the person (in Proverbs 28:3, the ruler) who oppresses the poor to increase his wealth will come to poverty. According to Proverbs 28:8, if one increases his wealth by exorbitant interest, he may only amass it for another, who will be kind to the poor. Similarly, Proverbs 28:27 notes that he "who gives to the poor will lack nothing, but he who closes his eyes to them receives many curses."

Several conclusions about poverty may be reached from this short study:

1. Providence is one cause of poverty; that is to say, the Lord does not prescribe wealth or the same level of wealth for all.
2. Often poverty is due to sloth (see also Prov. 10:4).
3. We are not to take advantage of the poor, and God disapproves of those who do.
4. We are not to take the possessions of the poor (see also 2 Sam. 12:5).

5. We have a positive obligation to take care of the poor (see also Prov. 31:9).
6. There are blessings for those who care for the poor.
7. There is a distinction between the materially poor and the spiritually poor.
8. There are worse things than being impoverished (see also Prov. 19:4; 19:7; 21:17; 22:7; and 28:11), which may suggest that poverty—since it is not the worst of states—should not become the dominating point of welfare reform.
9. Poverty is here to stay.

Poverty also has numerous causes according to Scripture. In the list above, we note that providence and sloth can both be causes of poverty. With respect to sloth, George Grant has commented: "The teaching on sluggards is clear and precise. The Bible says that sluggards waste opportunities (Prov. 10:4), are victims of self-inflicted bondage (Prov. 12:24), and are unable to accomplish anything in life (Prov. 15:19). A sluggard is boastful (Prov. 10:26), lustful (Prov. 13:4), wasteful (Prov. 12:27), improvident (Prov. 20:4), and lazy (Prov. 24:30–34). He is self-deceived (Prov. 26:16), neglectful (Eccl. 10:18), unproductive (Mt. 25:26), and impatient (Heb. 6:12)."[20] Other causes of poverty mentioned in the Bible include poor planning or lack of saving for emergency and God's curse on a land. Responses to these various conditions and causes call for different paths. If the cause is rooted in providence, then acceptance of God's will is warranted. However, if poverty is rooted in human behavior (e.g., slothfulness), then we may seek to change problematic attitudes and behaviors.

NT principles are entirely compatible with the foregoing OT standards, reflecting a unity between the Testaments. However, contrary to the predominant modern liberal perception of Jesus—which views him as a glorified social worker or as a political activist

20. George Grant, *Bringing in the Sheaves: Transforming Poverty into Productivity* (Powder Springs, GA: American Vision, 1995), 161.

and advocate for the oppressed, who constantly prattled about the poor and economic empowerment—relatively few teachings of Jesus normatively address the treatment of the economically poor. In fact, only about ten separate and distinct teachings of Christ, out of the entire volume of his sayings, directly use the word "poor" in an economic sense. When this is recalled, it is perhaps more than anything else a sign of the pervasive ideology of social liberalism that the common image of Jesus attributes to him an almost obsessive concern with the materially disadvantaged. It may be the case that, rather than culture being judged by the standards of Christ, Jesus has instead been conformed to the norms of the statist "Great Society," with the corresponding gospel accounts read through that filter. A more balanced handling of the totality of Scripture was provided by Calvin, who avoided the excesses in interpretation often found in the socialistically slanted eisegesis of some modern thinkers.

The Initial Calvinistic Business Spirit

Within days of Calvin's death in 1564, his mantle of leadership passed to Theodore Beza (1519–1605). Geneva found itself on the world's stage as various groups, such as Catholics and Anabaptists, hoped to overturn the newly founded Calvinist establishment. The crucial forty-year period between the death of Calvin and the death of Beza would establish Calvinism as a lasting force in Geneva and elsewhere. Arthur Ainsworth attributes much of Geneva's growth and stability during this period to the intellectual magnetism of Calvinism.[21]

In addition, support for Calvinism in Geneva was in part dependent on the city's prosperity. Prior to Calvin's time, Geneva had experienced economic hard times. The neighboring Duke of Savoy extorted "free gifts" of massive amounts—taxation by

21. Arthur David Ainsworth, *The Relations between Church and State in the City and Canton of Geneva* (Atlanta: The Stein Printing Company, 1965), 30–45.

another name—from the 1450s until 1526.[22] In the early sixteenth century Geneva also owed her Bernese benefactors large debts. Moreover, taxation on wine and rising property taxes in the late fifteenth century only served royalty while robbing the citizens. With Calvin, however, the patterns of taxation and income were altered. The prosperity ethic that followed his time in Geneva is one of the wide-ranging effects of his thought and practice.

At least four large sources of income fueled Geneva's new economic engine during this period. First, revenue for Geneva increased dramatically from 1550 to 1570 primarily due to the large number of new citizens (refugees).[23] In two years (1555–1556), Calvinist refugees who were flocking to Geneva contributed approximately 20% of the total revenue to the city coffers.[24] The popularity of Calvin's Academy further boosted revenues in periods of need, and the influx of wealth continued for decades.[25] By the 1580s many of the donors in times of crisis were people who had been refugees of the previous generation.[26] Growth in the population enhanced prosperity.

Second, after Calvin's arrival in 1536 Geneva retained many of the revenues formerly raised by the Catholic diocese. Parish tithes

22. E. William Monter, *Studies in Genevan Government, 1536–1605* (Geneva: Librairie Droz, 1964), 11.

23. The total population of France at the time was approximately twenty million. Some scholars estimate that the number of French Huguenot sympathizers in the period ranged from 10% to 25% of that population. Doug Kelly sets the range at 5% to 25%. Douglas Kelly, *The Emergence of Liberty in the Modern World: The Influence of Calvin on Five Governments from the 16th through the 18th Centuries* (Phillipsburg, NJ: Presbyterian and Reformed Publishing, 1992), 38.

24. Monter, *Studies in Genevan Government*, 25. William Naphy charts the revenue to Geneva from bourgeois admissions for the period running from 1536 to 1556. William G. Naphy, *Calvin and the Consolidation of the Genevan Reformation* (Manchester, UK: Manchester University Press, 1994), 24, 216.

25. Monter notes that the cost of the Academy was borne by selling off the estates of exiled enemies. Monter, *Studies in Genevan Government*, 25.

26. Ibid., 40. Monter thinks it "an interesting commentary on the Calvinist conscience" to note that Beza, Calvin's nephew, and theology professor Antoine de la Faye were also able to contribute during times of need (ibid., 43).

were still contributed and, as one historian has wryly noted, "The last thing which a Reformed state wished to do was to abolish any Papist tax; and Messieurs knew that a preacher, even Calvin, was less expensive to maintain than a well-bred cathedral canon. . . . All in all, the Republic took in perceptibly more revenue from traditional ecclesiastical sources than it spent on Reformed ecclesiastical institutions."[27] Thus, the conversion and redeployment of preexisting assets helped the local economy.

Third, Geneva surged ahead in the development of new information industries. The printing businesses of Protestant immigrants made significant fiscal contributions to the local economy. Calvin's thought and action impelled this to new heights.

Fourth, Geneva was successful in soliciting funds from other sympathetic Calvinist countries. During one very difficult period (1593), thanks largely to solicitations by Beza, Calvinist sympathizers in Germany and elsewhere accounted for as much as 25% of Geneva's total budget.[28] Historian Alain Dufour summarized the situation this way: "Geneva survived principally on loans from her citizens in 1589, on foreign loans in 1590, and on collections from foreign churches in 1591."[29]

Beza also continued the political model of his mentor, favoring close interaction between the separate jurisdictions of church and state. The types and frequency of interactions between Beza and the various councils testify to the strength and longevity of Calvin's impact. Examples from the late sixteenth century[30] illustrate how this cooperative Reformation worked.[31] As early as 1580 Beza

27. Ibid., 20.

28. Ibid., 48.

29. Quoted in ibid., 42.

30. Beza's role was viewed as so important by Jesuits from Germany and France that they called for his assassination in October of 1597.

31. Lest these Calvinists be seen as overly ascetic, consider the following note from June 5, 1598: "M. de Bèze having received from l'Hôpital a barrel of light red wine that was too young, Syndic Favre is asked to deliver to him a half-barrel of older wine." Calvinists were not easily cheated out of good wine.

spoke out against a 10% interest rate as usurious.[32] In 1581 city fathers consulted him about an appropriate sentence for a notorious criminal.[33] In 1588 Beza and other pastors went before Geneva's Small Council again to protest excessive usury.[34] In January 1596 Beza and the pastors urged the council to compensate the teachers of the Academy.[35] Beza and the pastors were frequent consultants of the council. Moreover, the types of discussions also indicate that the city governors wished to support the Reformation while not usurping the role of the ministers. Throughout 1596 the council minutes indicate close consultation between pastors and council members on the appointment of clergy, disciplinary measures, the regulation of printing, and the search for Beza's eventual successor. On April 7, 1596 the council heard a complaint by Beza about poor church attendance, and the council agreed to encourage citizens to attend. Specific pastors were approved for transfer or ordered to remain in their pulpits by the council. Geneva's separation of jurisdictions by no means erected an iron curtain separating church and state. None of this limited her growth and prosperity.

Rather, the historical record is clear: where Calvinism became thoroughly rooted, citizens saw economic growth. With the delicate combination of enhanced freedom and opening economies, Calvin's prosperity ethic would outlive him. The new work ethic fueled by the spirit of Calvinism changed the world.

Work Is Sanctifying

Labor, the act of work, was not created by God simply because he needed chores done around the celestial home. Neither was

32. Monter, *Studies in Genevan Government*, 37.

33. Ibid.

34. Ibid., 109.

35. References to the 1596 Register of the Company of Pastors are taken from Kim McMahan's translation originally published at http://capo.org/premise/98/FEB/p980209.html.

work established as punishment, although the painfulness stemming from it certainly was a consequence of man's sin. Labor is multifaceted in God's economy; however, at its core it is a redeeming activity, a sanctifying endeavor—an aspect of life that will continue in heaven for eternity. The very acts of washing windows, cooking food, vacuuming floors, analyzing stocks, preparing a lecture, arguing a case, and building a house contain an element of sanctification for the believer. As such, work is valuable and directly related both to our sinful nature and to our future glory. Were there no sin in the world, there would be no unpleasant work—only enjoyable hobbies would exist. Were there no heaven, there would be no incentive for future development.

The abiding obligation of man to work leads to a host of benefits all waiting behind the door of sanctification. Work is man's first and primary exercise of stewardship. It is also a path out of temporary poverty, and it can break the bondage of long-term structural welfare. Finally, it provides the fuel for enterprise. From the first summer job to the apex of an executive career, individuals exercise stewardship when they decide to work. Various costs and benefits are internally weighed against an inventory of known talents, abilities, and inclinations. Whether working for themselves or to support a family, workers engage in stewardship by balancing time, needs, wants, and resources. Frequently the workplace becomes that first class in the school of hard knocks that matures a young person. Whether we know it or not, our decision to work and the execution of our work constitute a tremendous training ground of stewardship and responsibility. As one recent author puts it, "Human beings have an obligation to work and their societies must afford them many opportunities to do so, since work is the principal means for exercising stewardship."[36]

An integral part of the stewardship equation is monetary benefit. Work is the primary means to alleviate temporary poverty

36. Victor V. Claar and Robin J. Klay, *Economics in Christian Perspective: Theory, Policy, and Life Choices* (Downers Grove, IL: InterVarsity Press, 2007), 22.

as well as the foundational element in breaking the bonds of a welfare lifestyle. Calvinist Marvin Olasky argues in *The Tragedy of American Compassion* that much of the damage done by the welfare system in the late twentieth century occurred when work was removed from the list of prerequisites for relief.[37] Labor is so important, so God-designed, that if removed from a social equation, the outcome is devastating. In earlier times, charities and relief agencies went to considerable efforts to discern between the "deserving" and the "undeserving" poor. Many relief organizations prudently instituted work "tests" in which a potential recipient of aid would have to demonstrate a requisite industry, e.g., by chopping wood or sewing clothes. The Society for the Relief of Poor Widows with Small Children (founded in 1797) urged those under their care to "find work, because society would accept only those clients who 'would rather eat their own bread, hardly earned, than that of others with idleness.'" Those who refused to work were spurned with a fundamental goal in mind—their own good. This charity's refusal to give subsidy for indolence was not rooted in a mean-spirited disdain of the poor; rather, it reflected a sound understanding of the nature of man, the design of God's creation, and the principles of productive philanthropy. It also worked. Calvin's poor relief had instituted such aspects centuries before. Commenting on 2 Thessalonians 3:10 he wrote that "indolence and idleness are accursed of God," for "we know that man was created with this view, that he might do something." [38] Moreover, Calvin believed that this verse prohibited the giving of food to those who could work but refused to do so.

The long-term remedy for individual poverty is not a function of increased payments or more programs to entice the homeless into shelters—it is work. As Olasky has observed,

37. Marvin Olasky, *The Tragedy of American Compassion* (Washington, DC: Regnery Gateway, 1992).

38. John Calvin, *Commentaries on the Epistles to the Philippians, Colossians, and Thessalonians* (Grand Rapids: Baker Book House, 1979), 3:355.

"Those who adopted the traditional work-hard-and-rise pattern by staying out of the welfare system usually succeeded in rising—but ... Americans who took advantage of the preferred liberality stayed put."[39]

Beyond the individual benefits of work, the engine of market societies relies upon the fuel of workers to move forward not only in terms of productivity, but also in terms of efficiencies, advancements, and utility. The abject failure of the Soviet Union and other economies based on the Marxist model served to keep these societies decades behind their market-based counterparts in living standards, luxuries, and freedoms. This failure was due not to unemployment or the lack of workers, but rather to the lack of freedom for citizens to engage in the work that best suited them. Individuals who have the opportunity for education, freedom of career choices, and mobility of resources and family customarily bring a higher level of enthusiasm to their occupation. However, the Soviet system, with its five-year plans and centralized decision-making, gave little thought to such niceties. "Communism," observes one recent work, "is incapable of providing high living standards using top-down directives. Citizens paid dearly for a system that failed to utilize the tremendous energy and knowledge that are embedded in ordinary people everywhere, and can be released only if people freely make their own choices about buying, selling and working."[40]

Work is a sanctifying act that not only betters the souls of men, but also enhances a person as an economic participant and student, helps him to rise above the dark waters of permanent welfare, and unleashes energy for the advancement of enterprise. It yields these virtues only to the extent that the prevailing economic system allows opportunity and freedom to work where one is most capable. Systems that plan a man's career, that

39. Olasky, *The Tragedy of American Compassion*, 185.
40. Claar and Klay, *Economics in Christian Perspective*, 35.

retard his choices under the auspices of central planning, that reduce his opportunity under weighty bureaucracies and taxes, or that discourage him to labor through a cornucopia of relief and transfer payments—these systems are ultimately inefficient and incongruent with the economics of the Reformation. Calvin condoned no such ideas and viewed hard work as a noble and God-commanded activity.

Although he professes no Calvinist sympathies, Thomas Sowell sounds as though he was fed early and large doses of Calvin's ideas when he concludes:

> Unemployment rates tend to be chronically higher, and the periods of unemployment chronically longer, in countries like France or Germany, where minimum wage laws and government policies requiring employers to provide benefits to their employees are more generous than in the United States—and the rate at which these countries create new jobs tends to be far lower than the rate at which new jobs are created in the American economy.[41]

Sowell also astutely observes:

> Government spending is often said to be beneficial to the economy, as the money disbursed is spent and re-spent, creating jobs, raising incomes, and generating tax revenues in the process. But usually if that same government money had remained in the hands of the taxpayers from whom it came, they too would have spent it, and it would still have been re-spent, creating jobs, raising incomes, and generating tax revenues in the process.[42]

Calvin knew that work was a part of sanctification after Eden.

41. Thomas Sowell, *Economic Facts and Fallacies* (New York: Basic Books, 2008), 5.

42. Ibid., 8.

A Dignity to Man's Work

Under the economic concepts found within the Bible, there is a certain dignity to human work. A person's work is something that not only brings personal gratification, but also requires a certain level of respect. It is also valued by God. All work, secular or sacred, is a part of God's divine providential calling and as such is dignified and worthy of honor. Furthermore, the dignity in a man's work is enhanced not only by the fact that it is an act of worship, but also by the fact that his work is a blessing to his fellow man. Lee Hardy, writing in the tradition of Calvin, explains that "we have to use our talents and abilities for our neighbor's sake. Therefore, we are obligated to find a station in life where our gifts can indeed be employed for the sake of our neighbor's good."[43]

In the macro sense, the dignity of a man's work is allowed to flourish in those systems that allow him to choose and develop his career without constraints or inefficiencies. Yet, even in most market systems that allow for the freedom of labor there are corruptions that reduce the dignity due him. Admittedly, dignity is a subjective measurement. Furthermore, no one receives a paycheck that exhibits units of dignity as the method of payment; the terms the market assigns to dignity are almost universally presented as currency. Thus, a common measure for dignity (or respect) is the wage a laborer receives for his efforts. The argument for diminished dignity addresses the distortions within the labor markets that implicitly and explicitly reduce a worker's wage due to some force outside the area where the supply and demand for labor intersect.

For example, take the reduction of dignity implied by the implementation of minimum-wage laws. Apart from the inefficiencies they bring to the labor market in terms of greater unem-

43. Lee Hardy, *The Fabric of This World: Inquiries into Calling, Career Choice, and the Design of Human Work* (Grand Rapids: Eerdmans, 1990), 66.

ployment, minimum-wage laws have the effect of insulting certain members of the workforce, particularly those who work in a field where they are paid just above the minimum wage. For instance, consider on the one hand a group of men who work in lettuce fields picking lettuce, at a required minimum wage of $8.50 per hour. Now consider another group of men who work in another part of the town as house painters, at a prevailing market rate of $9.50 per hour. In this example, the minimum wage is in fact subsidizing the dignity of the lettuce pickers. However, it takes substantially greater skill to be a fine house painter. So we must ask ourselves the rational question, is the lettuce picker (who has virtually no training and is doing something that requires little skill) worth 90%–95% of the wage being paid to the house painter? If not, there is a subsidization of his dignity, and consequently there is an insult to the dignity of the house painter. This twists the concept of dignity.

On the other extreme is the concept of wage ceilings, particularly artificial ones. The best example of this is the present political hot button—executive pay on Wall Street. There are howls currently for some kind of formulaic mathematical way to limit the wages paid to these executives. However, one has to weigh the value CEOs add to their organization. What benefits do they bring to the economy? One must also factor in the concept of scarcity. How many other people are qualified to do that job? If answering these kinds of questions indicates the rare value of top executives—and there are certainly CEOs who have historically shown that their individual efforts have created tremendous amounts of wealth and benefit to their organizations, shareholders, and employees—then why should there be artificial restrictions on their compensation? Artificial wage restrictions—whether set by a government, an industry group, a union, or a culture—are insulting. They reduce the level of dignity due to an individual for the efforts he puts forth. They also minimize the proper role of financial incentives.

These are extreme, non-systematic examples. When looking at national economies, there are systematic examples in which the dignity due to a man for his labor is reduced across all levels to some degree. The best example may be the progressive tax system of the United States. In this system the benefits that should be due to a laborer are taxed at a progressively higher rate for each marginal unit of compensation that he receives. For the following example, assume that the market is setting compensation rates. Consider a bankruptcy lawyer who has gone to college, graduate school, and law school; who has invested forty to eighty hours a year in continuing education; and who has made various investments socially, economically, and intellectually. Take the last unit of his annual production compared to that of a truck driver with a high school education. The truck driver is taxed at a rate of 22% while the lawyer is taxed at 40%. At these marginal levels there is a high degree of disregard toward the efforts of the lawyer. Workers in the upper tax brackets have little incentive to output that additional unit. This is a fault and inefficiency that pervades any system with a progressive payroll and employment tax.

The Calvinistic spirit of business can be welcomed as a draught that refreshes workers who thirst for true dignity and advancement without governmental interference. Often in the past five centuries it has been. Calvin even presciently alluded to intellectual capital when he spoke of pastors, whose teaching efforts deserve the price of labor. "For that which is due in the way of right, is not a thing that is gratuitous, and the price of the labour which teachers lay out in behalf of the church is much greater than the food which they receive from it."[44] He continued to affirm that there are many different ways of laboring and claimed that "whoever aids the society of men by his industry, either by ruling his family, or by administering public or private affairs, or by counseling,

44. Calvin, *Commentaries on the Epistles to the Philippians, Colossians, and Thessalonians*, 3:353.

or by teaching, or in any other way, is not to be reckoned among the idle."[45] By contrast, he condemned "lazy drones" who live "by the sweat of others while they contribute no service in common for aiding the human race."[46] Among these drones he counted monks, priests, and other ministers who do little but "chant in the temples for the sake of preventing weariness," which he calls "living musically" but not productively.[47] Calvin also noted that the biblical use of the term "wages," as in Romans 6:23, was suitable for spiritual comparisons—and not an economic reality that needed denunciation. Moreover, Christ's own promise (Mt. 13:8; Lk. 8:7) that thirty, sixty, or hundredfold increases could come is never contradicted. Both market wages (Mt. 20:15) and the repaying of debt (Mt. 18:27) are alluded to, without correction, in various gospel passages.

Economic sanctification, or the increase in virtue through business, is actually a helpful concept that is hardly supported by other religions or philosophies. There is little room within Marxism, for example, for the improvement that comes through economic sanctification, since a flattening equalization is assumed as normative from the outset. To excel above one's fellow workers is not encouraged and has little place in that business culture. The notion of excellence itself is more supported by the spirit of Calvinism than by Marxism and other economic systems.

Even though Calvinism acknowledges that perfection will not be reached in this life—and correspondingly that failure must occur and be repented of—it is not wrong to strive for improvement, success, and profit, as long as our attitudes comport with biblical teachings.

Not only is the act of charity an appropriate response of a thankful heart, but it is also an act of sanctification as the believer sacrifices some of his individual blessings for the good of others.

45. Ibid., 3:355.
46. Ibid.
47. Ibid.

However, a system that forces this giving through government intervention diminishes the impact of charity. Calvin asserted that Scripture does not command giving as a means to achieve identical equality; classlessness is not the goal. Rather, men are called to live contentedly in the economic station that providence has provided, while giving to others as the Spirit leads and engaging in their occupational callings with dignity and growth in their spiritual life. Just as Calvin asserted that individual callings would not be identical, so also he understood that equality in the marketplace would not result in identical outcomes for all. Indeed, the assumptions required for Marx's utopia are not only unachievable—they are irrational. By contrast, an open market system allows for the unhindered effects of both the peaks and the troughs of the economic cycle. This serves as a means of deploying profit as a needed input in the creative cycle and of using the forces of competition to sharpen, develop, or retire suboptimal ventures. The historical example of Calvin's ministry in Geneva bears witness to the truth that he did not call Christians to heartlessness or apathy. His was, on the contrary, a call to a living and vibrant exercise of obedience and mercy.

Calvin also taught that one day our sanctification will find its fulfillment in glorification, or perfection, the hunger that God so deeply implanted in the human heart.

6

Eschatology

John Maynard Keynes (1883–1946) once said, "Long run is a misleading guide to current affairs. In the long run we are all dead."[1] Though often misquoted and misapplied, the statement still hints at a shadow that darkens all economics that lack an eternal view of God. Absent a belief in something greater than this life, what incentive is there to promote charity, calling, thrift, investment, and profit except for the animal spirits of man's pride and desire for power? Perhaps what has troubled so many socialists is the concept of self-interest devoid of both the presence of God and the hope of a glorified eternity in which all men will be judged. Even in the midst of explanations and rationales that try to make capitalism and markets operate around an "enlightened self-interest," socialists—who would

1. John Maynard Keynes, *A Tract on Monetary Reform* (London: Macmillan, 1923), 80.

like to profess an altruism that denies the fall of Adam—may struggle with the thought of man acting with any consideration of his neighbor. Although relegating religion to the status of an "opiate of the masses," they are undoubtedly aware of the sinfulness of man and even of their own sinfulness. Without an eternal God to constrain man's selfishness and to move men to behavior beyond the immediately and economically profitable, socialists may be justified in promoting a system that strives for cookie-cutter equality in this life. This goal differs markedly from that of Calvin, who offered a radically different vision for the future and the human race.

Eternal security, coupled with the confidence that a sovereign and good God controls the future and all its contingencies, gives humans freedom and boldness to invest, take risks, store, invent, and produce. Calvin, as much as any other Reformer, noted that the Christian is liberated from the paralysis that so often prevents one from building a better future. On one occasion he warned against a crippling anxiety that could imagine thousands of fears. Elsewhere he summoned disciples to keep the long-term horizon of the future in mind for daily living (*Institutes*, 3.9–10).

Calvin repeatedly compared generous giving to sowing.[2] He cautioned that charity should not fear diminishing itself, but he expected that "the season of harvest will come, when the fruit will be gathered. For as the Lord reckons everything that is laid out upon the poor as given to himself, so he afterwards requites it with large interest."[3] Long-term investing was not to be discouraged by "fear of loss," and charitable investment was to be given with "large and bountiful liberality," knowing that "God requites the beneficence of believers not only in heaven but also in this world."[4]

2. John Calvin, *Commentary on the Epistles of Paul the Apostle to the Corinthians* (Grand Rapids: Baker Book House, 1979), 2:308.

3. Ibid., 2:309.

4. Ibid.

Calvin's view of the future—his eschatology—and his firm reliance on the providence of God propelled many of his followers to think multigenerationally. As he and his colleagues founded lasting social and ecclesiastical institutions—such as the Academy, the *Bourse française,* publishing ventures, and the Company of Pastors (which still exists to lead church life in Geneva)—Calvinism became a lasting garden in the landscape of human culture. Had his beliefs been monogenerational or shortsighted, lasting influence would not have occurred. One of the key ideological components that fueled his views of the future was the belief that faithfulness is required in one generation and that such faithfulness should include planning and provision for future generations.[5]

Calvin the biblical scholar knew well the teaching of Proverbs that wise parents and grandparents should prepare for future generations. Certainly this was a correlate of covenant theology, but Scripture explicitly assigned this duty. In Proverbs 10:7 parents are called to leave a lasting memory that will be a blessing (see also Prov. 17:6), and it is a part of virtue to "leave an inheritance for [one's] children's children" (Prov. 13:22). In addition, it is perfectly lawful and blessed for houses and wealth to be inherited from parents (Prov. 19:14); thus, no encumbrance or taxation of estates is required by the Creator. Calvin could not ignore the multigenerational calling to expand one's providentially supplied assets. Proverbs 14:26 speaks of the "secure fortress" that wise believers provide as a "refuge" for their descendants. This view of both families and the transference of wealth from generation to generation exhibits the long-term horizon of Calvinism.

At least four other aspects of Calvinism must be noted to comprehend his view of the future. Each of these is treated below.

5. While few treatises address Calvin's eschatology formally, Heinrich Quistorp, *Calvin's Doctrine of the Last Things* (Richmond, VA: John Knox Press, 1955) serves as the best overview on this topic.

The Present Is Better Defined by Eternity Than by Itself

Of course, many folks enjoy the mocking motto that "some Christians are so heavenly-minded that they are no earthly good." John Calvin did not merely vehemently oppose the Roman Catholicism on his right; he equally loathed the Anabaptist and utopian tendencies of the libertines and "Enthusiasts" on his left.[6] Few Reformers realized and opposed to a greater degree the inchoate Gnostic fiber of movements that pursued heaven to the exclusion of earthly realities. In fact, friend and foe alike recognize in Calvinism a world-affirming streak that contributed to its pervasive spread. Thus, Calvin certainly cannot be convicted of inspiring a movement that led to such heavenly-mindedness as to nullify its here-and-now witness and benefit.

Notwithstanding this fact, Calvin was not looking for the realization of heaven on earth that some progressive liberals have anticipated. Fundamental to his eschatology was the sturdy belief that we must live today in view of eternity and not become fixated on the idol of the present tense. The view that regards the long-term future of the church, society, and humanity is vastly different from, and a good corrective for, liberal views that immanentize the *eschaton* (to borrow Eric Voegelin's phrase). Calvin wrote that a correct understanding of the future leads to practical, present-tense moral codes and to actions that inspire long-term investing.

Calvin seemed to be clear that the long range is always more important than the short range. Disruptions occur, and all is not perfect in the short run; still he advocated continuing to trust God with all human affairs. That calls for self-denial, and it begins to view life as having very few accidents. If we know that all of life

6. See John Calvin, *Treatises against the Anabaptists and against the Libertines*, trans. and ed. Benjamin W. Farley (Grand Rapids: Baker Academic, 2001).

is ordered by an omniscient God, then we will "receive it with a placid and grateful mind, and will not . . . resist the government of him" who rules over all (*Institutes*, 3.7.10). This perspective of the eternal was critical for Calvin's actions in so many areas.

In fact, Calvin recommended that whatever the present challenge before us, it should "train us to despise the present and thereby be stimulated to aspire to the future life" (3.9.1). This aspiration certainly did not dampen the involvement of either Calvin or his disciples in many fields of human endeavor. Rather, it gave them a better perspective.

In one of his superb summaries, he put it this way: "If heaven is our country, what can the earth be but a place of exile? If departure from the world is entrance into life, what is the world but a sepulcher, and what is residence in it but immersion in death?" (3.9.4). Rather than thinking that all is sown and reaped in one short lifetime, it would be better to view oneself as passing through, having been assigned a post or calling until the Lord transfers us, with prospects of improving the future.

Accordingly, the first part of Calvin's eschatology involved his realization that this world is *not* all there is (contra Wittgenstein). There is, in fact, more to human life than the present tense; and a God-centered view of eternity calls us to build for the future, executing plans for culture-shaping, multigenerational endeavors that will outlast our own lifespan. Such ideas led to enormous practical outcomes, providing an exponential expansion of Calvin's thought.

Long-term Investment and Biblical Faithfulness

When considering Calvin's eschatology, we must also look at his attitude toward long-term investment. Calvin was quite critical of those who hoarded or who feared to act on the propositions of belief due to fear or distrust of God's sovereignty and power. He realized that both "reaping and sowing" were needed. And he was realistic enough to comprehend that sowing could take decades or generations. His comments on Jesus' parable in Matthew 25 remind readers that large harvests might take a long time.

For Calvinists, the alternative to hoarding (whether for personal greed, familial control, or because of unbelief) was reinvestment. The concept of taking profits and then using them for even greater multiplication is one that was implemented by few cultures prior to Calvin's time. To be sure, people in agrarian societies often handed on large tracts of land, but multigenerational businesses or corporations are largely post-Reformation phenomena.[7] With an enduring ideological propensity to use the cycle of *invest, take profits, invest, multiply profits, and invest,* Calvin's children led modernity toward massive capital formation; and this never would have occurred absent some eschatology.

Calvin was emphatic that investment for future growth was not the same as hoarding. In fact, he clearly understood the words of Jesus, who taught that a seed must be immersed in soil, giving itself before it can yield crops (John 12:24). Hoarding is problematic in the following respects.

First, it stems from fear—specifically, the fear of taking risks. In the classic parable of the talents (Mt. 25), the placing of the owner's asset in the ground, with the failure even to garner simple interest, was strongly rebuked by Christ. Calvin seemed to interpret this as meaning that Christ's followers have received a mandate to invest. Moreover, he perceived that this mandate is a part of our calling and stewardship in service to the Master, not so much in service to ourselves. Whether one personally gains or not does not contradict the imperative to invest and sow. Reaping might come later, but sowing is a perennial calling, both for

7. This is not so much a claim of strict causality as it is a historical observation. It is doubtlessly true that macro variables such as the creation of modern states, the Industrial Revolution, the liquidity of currencies, and other massive technological changes have altered the ecology of business models.

ministry and for financial assets. Mere risks or doubts cannot be allowed to mitigate this mandate. Calvin also recognized that the underlying psychology of hoarding frequently stems from excessive greed or from distrust.[8]

Second, hoarding takes assets out of the market that might otherwise be used for productivity; thus hoarding decreases total potential assets. Calvin and his avant-garde followers rapidly grasped the fact that capitalism could multiply. Consistent with the Reformer's commentary on Genesis 1–2, namely, that man was placed in the garden to be fruitful and multiply, Calvinists went beyond the ersatz static models. Whether they intuitively grasped the power of capitalism or were simply following the implications of the Protestant business ethic, Calvinists supported relatively novel measures and ideas, such as lawful interest (as opposed to the traditionally static non-use of capital under usury restrictions), international trade, fairs and free markets, expansion of intellectual capital, and the role of education—all in the service of increasing wealth. With this new goal of wealth creation or multiplication, Calvinism no longer feared profit; nor did it support the control of business in the hands of an oligarchy (as monastic models did). Rather than restricting assets, the new Calvinistic anti-hoarding economics fully supported the use of all assets not only in free markets but also for leverage and collateral for future expansion under sound business plans. A newly discovered rational exuberance marched westward across Europe and to the new world as Calvinists embraced not only a correct theology but also an economic system reformed to superior principles.

Third, hoarding became more and more unpopular because it did not increase estates. With the views outlined above, one can see how Calvinists hoped, not to provide only for themselves in a self-centered way, but to improve the lives of their children, their churches, their communities, and their

8. Calvin, *Commentary on the Epistles to the Corinthians*, 2:297.

distant neighbors. Assets and wealth could be used beneficently for all these things; thus, increase—rather than mere static retention—became the norm.

Thus, Calvin's thought provided the motivation to build, invest, increase capital, and expand—all in a period of world history when his followers were also given (in the providence of God) natural resources, liberty, opportunity, and entire colonies in which they could experiment and succeed with these essentially covenantal ideas that sought improvement beyond the spheres of one's own family or generation.

Calvin's eschatology, when coupled with his doctrine of calling and the biblical teaching on stewardship, led to a massive expansion of business capacities. His worldview was, as suggested in our introduction, an integrated nexus of thought. The whole was more than merely the sum of its individual parts. Such organic consistency added potency to the Calvinistic view of economics and business; and it certainly aided in the successful transmission of this view to other cultures and generations.

Preparation and Asset Gathering

While God's providence has supplied what believers need, there is also a calling—lamentably ignored by many in the modern West—to save and prepare for coming days. The hysteria over the never-realized Y2K meltdown was exhibit A in the case. It showed that most modern citizens are ill prepared for troughs, depressions, scarcity, or emergencies. The technological delusion has led many to think that they are beyond or immune to shortages of any kind. As a result, many fail to prepare for the immediate future, much less for the long-term future. Personal savings and retirement provisions have steadily declined over the past half century as many people expect some government agency, someone else somewhere, or (in an almost postmodernist reprise of *Mad* magazine's Alfred E. Neuman's "What, me worry?") their own reckless indifference to take care of the future. Accordingly, the kind of planning that prepares for the future is virtually a dying art form.

Calvin and his disciples believed in saving; often it was a prerequisite for broader investing. Bolstered by the long-term views described above and freed from the expectation that the world would catastrophically dissolve at any moment (as the chiliasts of his day believed), Calvinists inculcated a tradition of saving. This differed from hoarding in two key respects: (1) it was not motivated by pessimism or fear; and (2) it was viewed as a utility to increase assets to be used later for the glory of God, instead of merely for the enhancement of self or family. Calvin believed that one is to aspire to "honor the Lord with your wealth" (Prov. 3:9), a goal that transforms business.

The book of Proverbs is full of summons to make plans, either "by seeking advice" (Prov. 20:18) or by avoiding nonproductive fantasy schemes. Proverbs 21:5 advises that "the plans of the diligent lead to profit as surely as haste leads to poverty." Thus, Calvinists construed that poor planning could lead to material decrease in the future, while they saw God's promise attached to diligent, rational, and thoughtful planning. Investing on whims or with insufficient research is not a signature of Calvin's teachings. The final chapter of Proverbs also features a godly female commended for her investments in real estate, her industry, her business sense, and her planning (Prov. 31:10–31).[9]

Proverbs 6 offers an illustration from nature that commends a small insect—the ant. Although miniscule and sometimes pestiferous, ants are discussed because they transport tiny grains of dirt and build what is, to them, a mountain. These small creatures line up, follow the leader, and get the job done on a large scale.

9. Grudem notes that the Hebrew term used for "merchandise" in Proverbs 31:18 "refers to profit-producing commercial transactions." Wayne Grudem, *Business for the Glory of God: The Bible's Teaching on the Moral Goodness of Business* (Wheaton, IL: Crossway Books, 2003), 43.

In Proverbs 6 God provides a parable that encourages humans to study the efficiency and work ethic of ants. He evidently wants other creatures to learn from them. We will summarize this entrepreneurial wisdom by highlighting five principles from this passage:

1. We are made in the image of God so as to be able to learn from nature. "Go to the ant." Ants do certain things that can provide lessons for us. God believes that we can consider their ways and be wise. We can learn from the things around us because God made the universe to be comprehensible to his creatures. Rational solutions, thus, are good.
2. Ants can be very productive, even without domineering leadership. Ants, apparently, are not very hierarchical. They each do their own job and do not rely on the whip of leaders to make them efficient. This is a verse with wide ramifications for organizational, political, and corporate cultures. It seems to encourage a decentralized approach instead of a pyramid structure. Ants get the job done as each individual ant does its work. Humans might be well instructed by this principle when they consider the best structure for government and corporations.
3. In order for this to work, self-discipline and industry must be present. We must not think that prosperity happens all by itself. There is work to do, and those who do it without a strong centralized authority are the ones who have learned from this parable.
4. Planning for the future is commanded. Future planning is needed in many areas, and our plans must include provisions even for bad times. One of the first steps toward maturity is to learn to defer gratification. We may not, in other words, be able to have everything as early as we might wish. It is sometimes necessary to deny ourselves now in order to save for the future. Whereas instant gratification

may be the natural tendency, any athlete will sacrifice and endure long hours of training for the prize. All that anguish, grunting, pain, and strain is not fun; but good athletes defer their celebration until after the game. That takes discipline. The same is true in many other areas. The ant exhibits discipline, around the clock.

5. Laziness and love of sleep are surefire ways to bring on poverty. It doesn't take much. A little sleep, a little slumber, a little folding of the hands to rest, and poverty will come on you like a bandit.

A Calvinistic business ethic is derived from Scripture. Among its axioms are the following. Ill-gotten gain is denounced, along with those who pursue it (Prov. 1:19; 10:2). Honesty in business transactions and all of life is, thus, enshrined (Prov. 11:1). Calvinists also realize that virtue, a good reputation, and wisdom are more important than material profit (Prov. 3:13–14); thus, gain is good but put in its place. Treatment of employees is to be characterized by generosity (Prov. 3:27–28). Proverbs 16:11 also calls for honest and reliable currency markets and exchange rates (see also Prov. 20:10, 23). A fortune made by deceit will dissipate (Prov. 21:6). Proverbs 22:16 warns business owners not to oppress the poor in the pursuit of wealth—and Calvin clarified in his commentary on the eighth commandment that investors and entrepreneurs also carry an obligation to assist in the wealth enhancement of their neighbors, whether they be poor or wealthy. These themes began to construct the Calvinistic spirit of business.

On the subject of debt, Calvin had much to teach. He knew that "the borrower is servant to the lender" (Prov. 22:7). Calvin understood the enslaving tendency of personal debt and also warned against putting up security for debts that might not be repaid (Prov. 22:26). A form of indentured servitude could result from being overextended. Instead, Calvin persistently called for people to live within their means. Better to moderate one's desires than to feed those desires by a debt that cannot be repaid. One of the unintended consequences of Calvin's unleashing effect on capital markets was that undisciplined consumers could assume too much debt and, as a result, be forced to mortgage either their morality or their opportunity.

Risk Taking and Reward Gathering Are Allowed and Encouraged

Private property is allowed and meant to be multigenerational. It may also be used to take risks and invest in untried business ventures. Those who invest their own assets may yield the fruit of their investment. Risk taking also has a good effect on wealth acquisition; it actually has a tendency to decrease selfish individualism. One recent study observes:

> Such social reciprocity promotes virtuous conduct, curbing what many feared would be the amoral individualism of a commercial society. This constraint, according to Smith, is reinforced by competition and by the jurisprudence system, which Smith was writing about at the time of his death. When the system of natural liberty and free markets prevails, Smith believed, the sovereign must attend to only three duties: protection of society from foreign invasion, the erection and maintenance of certain public works, and "duty of protecting as far as possible, every member of society from the injustice of oppression of every other member of it, or the duty of establishing an exact administration of justice."[10]

The same work adds that while communal property rights may take away the risk-taking incentives that go with investing, "private property rights encourage property to be treated as a long-term

10. John E. Stapleford, *Bulls, Bears & Golden Calves: Applying Christian Ethics in Economics* (Downers Grove, IL: InterVarsity Press, 2002), 34–35.

asset and provide a direct link between individual effort and economic return."[11] Calvin sensed this connection early on, particularly as he applied the OT to business concerns of his day. Under the strong providence of God, investors—since wealth was not all that mattered—were liberated to take risks and seek higher returns.

Proverbs 12:11 promises that the person who works his land (or his factory or home office, for that matter) will have abundant food. In contrast, one who chases fantasies lacks judgment. Such teaching calls not only for hard work but also for wise planning and preparations for business models. A subsequent reiteration of the same theme (Proverbs 28:19–20 indicates that fantasy planning leads to poverty) reinforces this necessity while also tying it to the rich blessing that is given to faithfulness. But like 1 Timothy 6:10 in the NT, Proverbs 28:20 warns against covetousness and denounces an eagerness to get rich. Elsewhere the Hebrew book of wisdom makes this observation about incentives, so fraught with economic impact: "The laborer's appetite works for him; his hunger drives him on" (Prov. 16:26). This passage seems to codify the reality that workers in this fallen world often work only for necessity.

According to Calvin, assuming risks also must be matched by a return on investment. Calvinism's long-term vision affects decisions en route to the *eschaton*. The unfolding of the future impacts the present. Calvinism is not unique in this way; Marxism and Keynesianism also have an eschatology. One of the more potent theories of the last century, Keynesianism offers a vision of the future that drives the present actions of its practitioners, too. A recent work describes it this way:

> Keynes's model of aggregate demand management changed the dismal science to the optimists' club: man could be the master of his economic destiny after all. His claim that government could expand or contract aggregate demand as conditions required seemed to eliminate the cycle inherent in

11. Ibid., 58.

> capitalism without eliminating capitalism itself. Meanwhile, a laissez-faire policy of economic freedom could be pursued on a microeconomic level.[12]

Furthermore, to a society craving antidotes to the Great Depression, "his theoretical heresies also created a postwar environment favorable toward ubiquitous state interventionism, the welfare state, and boundless faith in big government. His theories encouraged excess consumption, debt financing, and progressive taxation over saving, balanced budgets, and low taxes."[13] All of these features were driven by utopian assumptions looking for the golden age of an economically enlightened future.

Keynes's followers readily endorsed savings as a virtue during periods of full employment, but one Keynesian, Paul Samuelson, was convinced it seldom happened. "Full employment and inflationary conditions have occurred only occasionally in our recent history," he wrote. "Much of the time there is some wastage of resources, some unemployment, some insufficiency of demand, investment, and purchasing power."[14]

The Keynesian model leads to the odd conclusion that consumption is more productive than saving. In other words, an increase in the "propensity to consume" (a lower saving rate) leads to full employment. Keynes applauded "all sorts of policies for increasing the propensity to consume," including confiscatory inheritance taxes and redistribution of wealth in favor of lower-income groups, who consume a higher percentage of their income than the wealthy.[15]

This static equilibrium model represents Samuelson's (and Keynes's) view that capitalism is inherently unstable and can be stuck indefinitely at less than full employment. No "automatic mechanism" guarantees full employment in the capitalist econo-

12. Mark Skousen, *The Big Three in Economics: Adam Smith, Karl Marx, and John Maynard Keynes* (Armonk, NY: M. E. Sharpe, 2007), 136.

13. Ibid., 137.

14. Quoted in ibid., 174.

15. Ibid., 175.

my.[16] Samuelson compared capitalism to a car without a steering wheel; it frequently runs off the road and crashes. "The private economy is not unlike a machine without an effective steering wheel or governor," he wrote. "Compensatory fiscal policy tries to introduce such a governor or thermostatic control device."[17] While many might find flaws with Keynesian theory, what we primarily hope to have shown is that it, too, even though thoroughly secular, has an eschatology and seeks to tie its economics of today to the hopes of tomorrow.

More consistent with Calvin's ideas is the classical model, which was developed by Adam Smith and endorsed by his disciples. This model consists of four general principles:

1. Thrift, hard work, enlightened self-interest, and benevolence toward fellow citizens are virtues and should be encouraged.
2. Government should limit its activities to administer justice, enforce private property rights, engage in certain public works, and defend the nation against aggression.
3. The state should adopt a general policy of laissez-faire non-interventionism in economic affairs (embracing free trade, low taxes, minimal bureaucracy, etc).
4. The classical gold/silver standard restrains the state from depreciating the currency and provides a stable monetary environment in which the economy may flourish.[18]

Calvin and Education

If Calvin's commentaries vibrantly brought the hues of scriptural teaching to life and if his eschatology excited the heart of man

16. Paul A. Samuelson and William D. Nordhaus, *Economics*, 12th ed. (New York: McGraw-Hill, 1985), 139.
17. Quoted in Skousen, *The Big Three in Economics*,171–72.
18. Ibid., 36–37.

to think beyond himself and his own time, then Calvin's belief in the priesthood of the believer enticed men to educate themselves and future generations so that all could read the Bible for themselves and partake in the blessings of God's written word. Even in Calvin's day, the Academy of Geneva was established in order to provide public education to all so that men could read the word of God themselves. Further, Rodney Stark argues in *The Victory of Reason* that religion played a primary role in the establishment of education, particularly in the new colonies:

> One doctrine most widely shared among the various dissenting Protestant movements was that everyone must consult scripture for themselves. So when the pilgrims arrived in 1620, one of the very first things they did was to concern themselves with educating their children. In 1647 the Massachusetts Colony enacted a law asserting that all children must attend school. . . . Other states soon followed suit, and free public schools became a fixture of American life. . . . By the end of the eighteenth century North America had by far the "most literate population in the world."[19]

Within twenty years of the pilgrims' arrival, Harvard University was founded. By the time of the Revolutionary War the American colonies had ten institutions of higher learning as opposed to only two in England. Nine of these ten were affiliated with a major denomination. Major economic studies have shown that one of the most important factors in economic development is education.[20] Often ideas can lead to unexpected consequences. By enflaming the hearts of men to think beyond the temporal, Calvin and his disciples (among others) laid fresh kindling on the fire of education. Within two centuries of Calvin's death, education of the common man had become an attainable reality. The

19. Rodney Stark, *The Victory of Reason: How Christianity Led to Freedom, Capitalism, and Western Success* (New York: Random House, 2005), 226–27.
20. Ibid., 229.

unanticipated effect was the introduction of educated, well-trained workers and future entrepreneurs into a society that would help shape much of the market system known today.

Calvin's emphasis on education was based on the platform that advancement was possible and good. Seeking to improve future generations, especially in a continuing tradition, was an outworking of Calvin's eschatology.

Calvin and Thrift

In his work *The General Theory of Employment, Interest, and Money,* John Keynes stated that "the more virtuous we are, the more determined by thrift, the more obstinately orthodox in our national and personal finance, the more our incomes will fall."[21] Oddly enough this was not an atypical statement for Keynes. During the 1930s he lashed out at savers for keeping down "effective demand." In a radio broadcast in January 1931, for example, Keynes asserted that thriftiness could cause a "vicious circle" of poverty, and that if "you save five shillings, you put a man out of work for a day."[22] Keynes's antagonism toward thrift reached its zenith in *The General Theory,* where he referred to traditional views on savings as "absurd."

By contrast, Calvin elevated the biblical tenet of thrift and preparation for the future. As stated earlier, the parable of the ant that labors and builds its storehouse is designed to encourage all persons to save for the future and provide for their families. Saving and thrift are not only monetarily wise; they are also means of providing for future generations. Saving is forward-looking and multigenerational—it extends beyond the immediate.

Calvin advocated savings for stewardship reasons, although some of his sayings, if isolated from the context of Calvin's corpus,

21. Quoted in Skousen, *The Big Three in Economics,* 157.
22. Quoted in ibid., 156–57.

may look ascetic—as Weber interprets. Regardless of interpretation, Calvin advocated savings, and such seed assets soon gave his Reformed children the capital bases to invest in manufacturing or other commercial ventures. The crucial building block of thrift was later summarized by American industrialist Andrew Carnegie in these words:

> Saving is the first most important duty. Parsimony is a necessary precondition of every progress. Without saving we would not have railways, channels, boats, telegraph, churches, newspapers, in short—anything that is great and expensive. . . . Man's first duty is to build him a sufficient fortune and become independent, but that does not at all end his duties. His further responsibility is to do something about his neighbors in need; his duty is to do something good for the society he belongs to. . . . Aspiring to leave the world better than it was found means pursuing a noble life objective.[23]

Unfortunately, although Keynes's theories of savings and thrift have been discredited by other economists, an underlying remnant of his thought persistently holds sway in policy circles. Policymakers are often lured into a trap, because consumption—whether by the consumer, industry, or government—can provide a positive, immediate jolt to a weak economy. Therefore, short-term needs encourage consumption even at the expense of savings and long-term fiscal responsibility. In the spring of 2008, the United States government mailed out "stimulus checks" to the majority of taxpayers for up to $600 per individual. Implicit in the name "stimulus check" was the desire that most recipients would use the money not to invest or pay down debt, but to engage in the time-honored tradition of shopping. An economist for Merrill Lynch, David Rosenberg, even noted with some disappointment

23. Quoted in Sergey N. Bulgakov, "The National Economy and the Religious Personality," *Journal of Markets and Morality* 11, no. 1 (Spring 2008): 173. (Orig. pub. 1909.).

that (according to figures provided by various retail organizations) the consumer was not spending his stimulus check but was rather deploying it elsewhere.

Keynes's belief that the increase of consumption (a lower saving rate) leads to full(er) employment is a foundational brick in all sorts of policies, including inheritance taxes and the redistribution of wealth in favor of lower-income groups, who are more likely to consume than the established wealthy.[24]

Without an eschatology, what benefit is there for delaying anything? The temptation of immediate gratification encourages consumption and action today without regard for the future. Calvin's writings persuade men to delay the immediate, to save for the future, and to make multigenerational preparations. The Reformed businessman needs to be wary of programs and policies that see nothing beyond the short term and lead citizens to mortgage the future in exchange for the present.

Calvin's eschatology may have helped lay the foundation that enabled godly men to discern and communicate a system of markets and economics that is measured by a divine judge and controlled by a sovereign God. Adam Smith, raised in traditionally Calvinist Scotland, spoke of an "invisible hand" that guides men to act and interact with each other without coercion and toward an outcome that is mutually beneficial.

> As every individual, therefore, endeavors as much he can both to employ his capital in the support of domestic industry, and so to direct that industry that its produce may be of the greatest value; every individual necessarily labors to render the annual revenue of the society as great as he can. He generally, indeed, neither intends to promote the public interest, nor knows how much he is promoting it. By preferring the support of domestic to that of foreign industry, he intends only his

24. Skousen, *The Big Three in Economics*, 175.

> own security; and by directing that industry in such a manner as its produce may be of the greatest value, he intends only his own gain, and he is in this, as in many other cases, led by an *invisible hand* [emphasis added] to promote an end which was no part of his intention. Nor is it always the worse for the society that it was not part of it. By pursuing his own interest he frequently promotes that of the society more effectually than when he really intends to promote it. I have never known much good done by those who affected to trade for the public good. It is an affectation, indeed, not very common among merchants, and very few words need be employed in dissuading them from it.[25]

To Marx, the "invisible hand" was an iron hand that crushed the worker; and it may well be such if the "invisible hand" does not entail the providence of God.

Even the economic truths taught throughout Scripture devolve into mere rules and guidelines without a final conclusion that holds all men accountable and provides opportunity to look into eternity and see behavior today as acts of worship for now and forevermore. Without mentioning a single monetary or economic thought, Calvin's vivid vision of the end of days and the eternity to come may have done more to embolden capitalists than many of his other insights and commentaries.

The Five Points of Economic Calvinism

Above, we have discussed many concepts that John Calvin articulated; and we have sought to update many of them. Since Calvinist theology is often associated with a five-point scheme, we offer below a summary that places these concepts in just such a scheme. Irreducible economic Calvinism for us is seen in the following five points:

25. Adam Smith, *An Inquiry into the Nature and Causes of the Wealth of Nations* (New York: Modern Library, 1937), 423.

1. The inequality of wealth is an enduring dynamic and must be accepted. In other words, classlessness will not be reached in this life; nor did God intend for it to be reached. Differences in income and status will persist. In whatever station of life we find ourselves, a spirit of contentment, diligence, and thankfulness should prevail.
2. God made us to be creators, developers, and entrepreneurs. In the opening chapters of Scripture, Calvin and others have seen both the abundance of creation and the call to shape, tame, and order it. Man, made in God's image, is designed to work and create.
3. Because of sin, accountability and incentives will always be needed. Selfishness will counteract good if we are not properly motivated. One way to motivate is to offer wages and incentives, and human beings are not above needing such a stimulus. Conversely, accountability, including the withholding of benefits if counterproductive behavior occurs, must be designed and expected.
4. Personal freedom (or non-interference from outside hierarchies) is necessary for business to thrive. If overlords must be satisfied, then feudalism will occur. The freer the markets, the more personal freedom fuels development. The sovereign God may be trusted to use such markets as means for his providence.
5. Profit is commended in order to provide more for others. A charity ethic, which seeks to use profits philanthropically, derives from the best Calvinism.

Conclusion

Calvin often emphasized the theme of contentment with the measure (sometimes more, sometimes less) that God has ordained for us. He explained that this is what the term "sufficiency" means—"not that everyone may keep to himself what he has received, but that there may be a mutual participation among us, according as necessity may require."[26] Christians are not born merely for themselves; nor should they use their estates only for themselves. In the end, "true riches" rely "on the providence of God," and "nothing is more famished and starved than the distrustful, who are tormented with an anxious desire of having."[27]

Commenting on 1 Timothy 6, Calvin spoke to our motivational level, applying excellent psychology. He warned against covetousness, which could become "an insatiable gulf, if it be not restrained."[28] Moreover, "the reason why we transgress the bounds," he explained, is "that our anxiety extends to a thousand lives which we falsely imagine" (158). In this observation and elsewhere, Calvin alerted readers to the fact that prosperity has its dangers, since it can lead to more lust. He recommended that instead we should be "satisfied with a sufficiency" and desire "nothing but what is necessary for supporting life" (158). Furthermore, the individual who avariciously lusts to be rich must be on guard not to "give himself up as a captive to the devil" (159). In reference to 1 Timothy 6:10, Calvin indicated that, as a root of evil, the love of money has often "copiously produced . . . innumerable frauds, falsehoods, perjury, cheating, robbery, cruelty, corruption in judicature, quarrels, hatred, poisonings, murders; and, in short, almost every sort of crime" (159).

Calvin knew the allure of riches and, while admitting that there were wealthy people within the church ("warn those who are rich," 1 Tim. 6:17), he cautioned that great wealth often bore pride, pretension, or presumptiveness instead of reliance on God's

26. Calvin, *Commentary on the Epistles to the Corinthians*, 2:311.

27. Ibid., 2:314.

28. John Calvin, *Commentary on First Timothy* (Grand Rapids: Baker Book House, 1979), 158. In the following paragraphs page numbers in parentheses refer to this volume.

providence. He advised against placing trust in material riches "not only because they belong to the use of mortal life, but likewise because they are nothing but smoke" (171). In this passage Calvin also referred to the "lawful use of riches," according to which the wealthier a person is, "the more abundant are his means of doing good to others" (172). He then reminded readers of Paul's admonition that those with wealth should lay a good foundation for themselves by their charitable giving—although not, of course, as an attempted means of meriting salvation, for "if God should call us to a strict account, there is not one of us who would not be a bankrupt" (172).

To our knowledge, Calvin never wrote an economic treatise; nor did he ever present a market theory or financial equation. What he did was expound on biblical truth and shape a tradition of theology. In doing so, he touched on all of the foundational questions of religion: What is the nature of man? What is man's purpose? Who is God? What does he require of us? What will happen to man after death? In the process of answering these questions, Calvin often commented on biblical economic truth as it reveals itself in Scripture. Although there is no complete system of economics and markets in Scripture, there is clear economic truth that can be observed and directly overlaid on some areas of commerce today.

One of the primary premises in this book is that business and economic theories are not value-neutral. Of course, many would agree, and economics can be highly political. However, the thesis presented here is that every theory, equation, system, and fact holds within it a wealth of information bearing on the same questions that John Calvin addressed in the 1500s. Like an archaeologist, the reader is encouraged to dig deeper, pushing aside the dirt and noise in order to find the foundations of each theory. Follow the inherent assumptions to their final end and suddenly concepts like progressive taxation, import quotas, the minimum wage, monopolies, and the theory of labor pull back their curtains to expose a theology and worldview much larger than the intersection of supply and demand curves.

For example, by increasing taxes, men are made poorer, and if a person's willingness to give increases with total income, then his willingness to give will be lower as a result of higher taxes. Progressive taxation flows from a presupposition, and we must ask in the first place, is it the right or best one? We will also want to inquire, what system allows for the maximization of profit?

It is as crucial to realize that wealth development is a creational activity as it is to understand that it is a cognitive activity, one that involves many interrelated variables. Neither wealth development nor the real world of business operates in a value-free zone. Instead, business culture coincides with values, and every economic model is built on premises that lead to related outcomes. One's choice is to identify and implement the best business foundations.

Ideally, the writings of John Calvin can be directly placed within the evolution of current economic practice. Again, the "impact" of his work does not require that he pointedly pontificate about labor and wages. Arguably, his commentary on the eighth commandment and theft may have shaped the assumptions used by others to reinforce new theories of labor and commerce, and thus may have carried a tremendous impact. Absent a "smoking gun" of correspondence or journal entries, the proof of causality can be overwhelmingly difficult to establish. However, it is hard to imagine that Calvin's commentaries and sermons did not somehow find their way into the minds, pulpits, and libraries of the intelligentsia of the next several centuries.

The practical goal of this work has been to compare and contrast Calvin's implied economics with the buffet of business worldviews presented today. This discussion has sought not only to identify those perspectives that are contrary to Calvin and the Bible, but also to examine the café choices and see what ingredients simmer within each dish. Some of these economic worldviews are immediately toxic to those who wish to follow Scripture carefully (as Calvin did), and others may seem appetizing only to contain noxious elements that will slowly poison correct biblical thinking. Before tasting, one needs to understand what each theory, each belief, and each program implies about the nature of man, government, and markets. After identifying some of the culture-shaping ideas of John Calvin, this work has invited readers to measure all other economic paradigms against them. This exercise is simple at the macro level (i.e., when we look at communism, socialism, capitalism, and state-directed economies as comprehensive systems), but it can be most overlooked at the margin where regulations and policies can slip into large, healthy systems and sow the seeds of humanism, unaccountability, or even government-sponsored theft.

The most efficient way to boil a frog is to do it slowly. Economic practice is ingrained in much of life, and its rising temperature is often underestimated. Let the reader beware of the implications of mundane decisions and lend support to them (either in thought or practice) only after testing them against biblical economic truth. In that process, we believe that Calvin will inevitably be a helpful assistant toward achieving the goal of biblically consistent financial behavior.

We also trust that this review of Calvin will serve to spur a revival of philanthropy. We hope readers hear Calvin's voice clearly as he calls those with profit and wealth to use all their assets charitably, compassionately, and with purpose.

In a parable that has almost the tone of realpolitik, Jesus taught in Luke 16 that business transactions could also be used to make friends on earth. In considering this parable, Calvin heard the Lord teaching that a "seasonable and well-judged liberality may have the effect of restraining and moderating unnecessary expenses."[29] Of course, he was also quick to condemn making "donations out of

29. John Calvin, *Commentary on a Harmony of the Evangelists, Matthew, Mark, and Luke* (Grand Rapids: Baker Book House, 1979), 2:177.

what belongs to another man" as theft. However, he drew several helpful lessons from the parable. One was stated this way:

> It is certain that no man is so frugal, as not sometimes to waste the property which has been entrusted to him; and that even those who practice the most rigid economy are not entirely free from the charge of unfaithful stewardship. Add to this, that there are so many ways of abusing the gifts of God, that some incur guilt in one way, and some in another. I do not even deny that the very consciousness of our own faulty stewardship ought to be felt by us as an additional excitement to kind actions.[30]

Calvin also perceived that Jesus' parable in Luke 16 cautions against a "highly criminal indifference," which does not provide for "the future, with at least as much earnestness as ungodly men display by attending to their own interests in this world." He continued to note: "How disgraceful is it that the children of light whom God enlightens by his Spirit and word should slumber . . . while worldly men are so eagerly bent on their own accommodations, and so provident and sagacious."[31] Calvin also wisely advised:

> One who possesses extensive influence or wealth, if he procure friends during his prosperity, has persons who will support him when he is visited by adversity. In like manner, our kindness to the poor will be a seasonable relief to us; for whatever any man may have generously bestowed on his neighbors the Lord acknowledges as if it had been done to himself.[32]

Honoring his Lord who said, "To whom much is given, much is expected," Calvin also commented that Christ wants all his

30. Ibid., 2:176.
31. Ibid., 2:178.
32. Ibid., 2:179.

disciples "to act faithfully in small matters, in order to prepare themselves for the exercise of fidelity in matters of the highest importance."[33] Calvin taught this. And the much that was given to him has certainly been multiplied hundreds of times.

The nineteenth-century Baptist preacher Charles H. Spurgeon showed his Calvinistic roots when he summarized things this way: "God's intent in endowing any person with more substance than he needs is that he may have the pleasurable office, or rather the delightful privilege, of relieving want and woe."[34] In his commentary on Luke 19:13, Calvin stated: "But whatever gifts the Lord bestows on us, let us realize that they are like money deposited with us, for us to make some gain and profit out of it (1 Corinthians 12:7). For there is nothing worse than keeping God's graces buried and not making good use of them, since their force consists in their fruit."[35] The Calvinistic business ethic became a force that still bears fruit.

33. Ibid., 2:180.

34. Charles Spurgeon, "The Good Samaritan," sermon delivered at the Metropolitan Tabernacle Pulpit, June 17, 1877.

35. Cited in Biéler, *Calvin's Economic and Social Thought*, 389.

Index of Subjects and Names